THE HEART IN THE GLASS JAR

THE MEXICAN EXPERIENCE

William H. Beezley, series editor

The Heart in the Glass Jar

LOVE LETTERS, BODIES, AND THE LAW IN MEXICO

William E. French

University of Nebraska Press | Lincoln and London

A small portion of "The Lettered Countryside" was
originally published as "'Cartas y cartas, compadre . . .':
Love and Other Letters from Río Frío," by William
E. French, in *Latin American Popular Culture since
Independence: An Introduction*, 2nd edition, ed.
William H. Beezley and Linda A. Curcio-Nagy,
68–84 (Lanham MD: Rowman & Littlefield, 2012).
© 2012 by Rowman and Littlefield Publishers, Inc.

Publication of this volume was assisted by
the Virginia Faulkner Fund, established in
memory of Virginia Faulkner, editor in chief
of the University of Nebraska Press.

Library of Congress Cataloging-in-Publication Data
French, William E., 1956– author.
The heart in the glass jar: love letters, bodies,
and the law in Mexico / William E. French.
pages cm—(The Mexican experience)
Includes bibliographical references and index
Summary: A history of love and courtship in Mexico
from the 1860s through the 1930s based on love
letters preserved in legal cases involving courtship.
ISBN 978-0-8032-6678-0 (cloth: alk. paper)—
ISBN 978-0-8032-8416-6 (epub)—ISBN 978-0-8032-
8417-3 (mobi)—ISBN 978-0-8032-8418-0 (pdf)
1. Love-letters—Mexico—History—19th century.
2. Love-letters—Mexico—History—20th century.
3. Courtship—Mexico—History—19th century.
4. Courtship—Mexico—History—20th century.
5. Letter writing—Mexico—History—19th century.
6. Letter writing—Mexico—History—20th
century. I. Title. II. Series: Mexican experience.
PQ7211.F74 2015
306.73'40972—dc23   2015001007

Set in Garamond Premier by M. Scheer.
Designed by N. Putens.

To my son, Evan, from whom I am learning so much.

CONTENTS

HEADING

The first part of a personal letter, commonly referred to as a "heading," is often used to situate its writer in time and in a particular place. Adherence to such a convention, although not completely absent in the love letters that, taken together, compose the main primary source upon which this book is based, does not characterize the majority of letters I encountered in the archive. Being initial engagements with the written word that accomplish that act of writing tentatively, as part of a group process and often with great difficulty, love letters written in northern Mexico during the late nineteenth and early twentieth centuries were low on formalities—not only those of form but also such things as grammar and punctuation—and high on emotion, on the give-and-take that, as you will see, often characterized courtship, and on the symbolic meanings attached both to the letter form and to the written word. If letter writers or their amanuenses at that time either did not know about or found it unnecessary to tether their written messages so tightly to such conventions, perhaps it is not too much to ask of the reader to allow me the same degree of flexibility. Following in the spirit of their writing I offer these acknowledgements in the form of a heading, that of a very long letter in book form, and one that, rather than stressing the current date and place of writing as one would in a personal letter, situates the work within a long process of research and writing that led to its completion, one characterized by many kindnesses, much support, extensive discussion, and the opportunity to present in written and oral form earlier versions of what you now have before you.

A more conventional heading might read, "Parral, Chihuahua, Mexico," as it was there—while conducting research for what would turn out to be a book on the struggle over the time and work discipline in industrial mining—where I first encountered love letters in the judicial archives. Many of the people who helped with access to the archives and with logistics in Chihuahua, and who offered their friendship and sympathetic ears for that first project, continued to do so as I returned numerous times to Parral to carry out further research on love, courtship, and the law. Most trips there began with a stopover in El Paso, Texas, where Richard Baquera and his family made me very welcome, offering a place to stay, home cooking, and family stories. Once in Parral, I was fortunate to meet Carolyn Sexton Roy, who provided not only knowledge about the archives, accommodation, and friendship but also an introduction to many in the community. Long involved in the rescue and preservation of archives there, Robert McCaa helped me realize the importance of contributing to those endeavors, even if in a small way, as part of the responsibility of carrying out research. Rosa María Arroyo Duarte always welcomed me to the archives and facilitated my research, participating, at one point, in a microfilming project involving some of the judicial archives. Some of my favorite memories are of singing *corridos* with Jesús Vargas Valdez, then of the Centro de Investigación y Documentación del Estado de Chihuahua (CIDECH), as we drove around the state to participate in the process of cleaning, sorting, and storing various collections of documents.

This all seems like a very long time ago and, indeed, it was. In many ways, it feels as if I have been working on this book most of my academic career, and perhaps I have. Other projects intervened, the subject I thought I was writing about changed in subtle and not-so-subtle ways, and it was not until I found my own voice, one that seemed appropriate to the subject matter of love and personal letter writing, that it became possible to finish. I am very grateful for the feedback I received along the way on papers I presented on various aspects of love letters and related topics at such gatherings as the *reuniones* of the Historiadores de México, at the annual meetings of the American Historical Association, and at various yearly meetings of the Rocky Mountain Council for Latin American Studies (RMCLAS). I was very fortunate to participate in a session on love letters and personal correspondence in Chicago in 2007 at the Social Science History Association (SSHA) meeting, chaired by David Gerber, who has written extensively on personal correspondence and the challenges posed by such sources to historians, and commented on by Laura Ahearn, whose book on love and literacy in Nepal was pioneering in many ways, including taking love and letters seriously. The care they both took in offering incredibly useful comments, criticisms, and suggestions is greatly appreciated. In addition to offering formal comments, a few colleagues, especially Ann Blum, William Beezley, Rob Buffington, Pablo Piccato, and Eddie Wright Rios, have allowed me to impose upon them, offering me suggestions, critical readings, and support, along with a willingness to listen carefully, helping me to formulate my ideas as I strove to express them. Although we weren't singing corridos, William Beezley listened patiently as we drove back from a RMCLAS meeting to Tucson as I set out the entire outline of the three parts that would eventually become this book.

Writing short papers to present at conferences and annual meetings is one thing; forming these into the chapters, or in this case sections, that eventually would result in a book, was another. As part of a sabbatical leave I took almost ten years ago I decided to relocate to Whistler, British Columbia, for one month with the intention of fulfilling two of my greatest aspirations—those of writing this book and of becoming a better-than-ordinary snowboarder. My goal was to write in the mornings and snowboard as much as possible in the afternoons. I thank Geoff Horner and his family for renting me their condo there so that I might be able to do so. Unfortunately, it turned out to be the coldest and iciest January in memory, providing little incentive to venture up to the slopes. I wrote most of the first section of this book in that condo, wrapped in a blanket, drinking hot tea, wondering why the fireplace wasn't putting out more heat (my lack of know-how, not the fault of the fireplace), and hoping that the water lines at the condo would not freeze and burst. It turned into a very productive month of writing. I never have learned to carve that perfect turn.

An incredibly lively and motivated group of graduate and other students at UBC helped me think through the next two sections of the book. At

one point, I had intended to include as part of it an appendix composed
of love letters in the original Spanish along with their English translations.
As part of accomplishing that goal, I was able to obtain some funding to
offer to graduate students. I thank Miguel Angel Avilés Galán and Ruth
Mandujano López, doctoral students who subsequently finished their
own dissertations on Mexican history with me at UBC, for their work of
translating or, better, interpreting these letters. It was not an easy task.
Miguel Angel and I spent most of one afternoon at a coffee shop going
over possible interpretations of one sentence in one letter. It was he who
suggested I look more carefully at *coplas*, a verse form discussed in section
2, as a way to think about the letters. Although the letters presented serious interpretive challenges, attempting to overcome them led to one of my
fondest teaching experiences. One summer in Oaxaca a group composed
of Gabriela Aceves Sepúlveda, a doctoral student at that time; Paulina
Rodríguez, Heather Escobar (née Russell), and Sara Buczynski, under-
graduate students who had participated in a UBC term abroad in Mexico
and then in the graduate program in Oaxaca; and me gathered daily at
Gaia, a coffee shop, to drink homemade yogurt smoothies and to discuss
interpretations of key words in the love letters and possible ways to express
them in English. Doing so meant contextualizing such expressions within
the legal, social, and cultural contexts of their time—in short, doing what
it is that historians do, exploring possible interpretations and generating
alternative understandings of the documents with which we were working. Although in the end I decided against providing such an appendix
(many of the letters are quoted extensively in certain sections of the book,
especially the third), the discussions were extremely valuable, and I thank
those who took part in them and helped in the process of interpretation.

Section 2 took shape not in a single physical space but as an engagement
with a metaphorical one, the lettered city. Perhaps it was team teaching
with Rita De Grandis, my colleague in Spanish literature, whose concern
with foundational fictions and the lettered city informs much of her work
in the classroom, that prompted me to explore some of the *rincones* of that
neighborhood. I thank her for her ongoing encouragement and for allowing
me to present some of my work to her graduate class. Jon Beasley-Murray,

another colleague in Spanish literature, arranged for me to present my ideas at the weekly colloquium organized by the French, Hispanic and Italian Studies Department. Doing so led to a discussion of a number of novels, some of them utilized here, as well as to pointed questions about my work that I have attempted, to a greater or lesser extent, to answer. Marv Cohodas, as well, has always encouraged me to finish and insisted that I include my own work on love letters as part of the course material in classes we co-taught. At a critical point in the writing of that section, Eva-Lynn Jagoe and Ken Mills kindly invited me to present some of my work based on the love letters exchanged between Pedro and Enriqueta, whom you will meet shortly, to the Latin American Studies group at the University of Toronto. The questions and the discussion that followed, as well as the opportunity to exchange ideas with Peter Blanchard, Valentina Napolitano, and other faculty in the Toronto area, were extremely valuable, and I thank Eva-Lynn and Ken for the opportunity. At times, this second section seemed as though it had taken on a life of its own. Parts of it appear as chapter 4, "'Cartas y cartas, compadre . . .': Love and Other Letters from Río Frío," in *Popular Culture in Latin America since Independence: An Introduction*, second edition, edited by William H. Beezley and Linda A. Curcio-Nagy. Other parts, especially those dealing with the verse form known as the copla, are introduced here and then developed more fully in a chapter, "I'm going to write you a letter: Coplas, Love Letters, and Courtship Literacy," in a book entitled *Mexico in Verse*, edited by Stephen Neufeld and Michael Matthews. I thank all the editors and various readers for their comments on these versions of my work.

Section 3 was the final section to be written. It took shape partly in response to comments by my colleagues in Vancouver, especially Alejandra Bronfman, Alec Dawson, Paul Krause, and Danny Vickers, and by graduate students, especially Stephen Hay, who kindly provided me with written comments on a presentation I gave in a departmental colloquium. Anne Gorsuch, friend, co-teacher, and longtime colleague, read and offered comments on not only this section but the entire manuscript despite taking on the added responsibilities of departmental head. I appreciated her encouragement throughout the long process of writing this book, and although I missed the final deadline for having the book finished as stipulated in an informal contract we drew up on a sheet of paper and tacked to my office wall, my hope is that I will still be able to collect on the reward promised for finishing: one gin and tonic. In colloquia and in everyday interactions, the Department of History at UBC has offered a particularly stimulating and collegial environment. It was my colleague Alejandra Bronfman who encouraged me to build this final section of the book around the "organs" of the sentimental anatomy and who read the introduction and postscript with care. Joy Dixon has always made time to listen to what I have had to say; her comments and suggestions for further reading, pertaining both to my own work and as part of discussions with graduate students in conjunction with preparing for field examinations, have been thoughtful and well worth heeding. Allen Sinel, recognizing the importance of expressing verbally what one is working on and thinking about, has been willing to listen and to offer critiques along with encouragement. He is greatly missed. Paul Krause has offered humor along with suggestions for reading. Written in Vancouver, this section, along with the introduction and postscript, benefited from a number of trips to the Vancouver Art Gallery, a place where ideas often seem to suggest themselves.

Colleagues in Mexico, in addition to arranging for me to speak about love letters on numerous occasions, have also been kind, gracious, patient, helpful, and extremely generous with their time and ideas. I thank Dale-Jane Lloyd for the opportunity to give a talk and teach a weeklong workshop on the history of emotion at the Universidad Iberoamericana, which I enjoyed tremendously. Her comments, along with those of Ilan Semo, were useful in pushing me in new directions; the students in the seminar, supportive critics of my work and highly articulate in presenting their own ideas on emotion in history, renewed my energy, enthusiasm, and commitment to the book and about the field more generally. To them, I am very grateful; I wish I could participate in more exchanges of this sort. Other individuals, as well, merit special thanks. Carmen Nava y Nava never lets me leave Mexico City without insisting that I take one or more of her own books; I still have her two-volume set of *Bandidos de Río Frío* (thank you, Carmen). Guillermo Palacios y Olivares has always welcomed me and, at times, wandering members of my family, offering good humor, great company, much encouragement, and introductions to many in the academic community in Mexico City. He provided support for a Canada–Latin America–Caribbean Research Exchange Grant that enabled me to research and write one summer. Ricardo Pérez Montfort has always been both helpful—offering suggestions for additional things I might want to read—and encouraging, helping to draft a *demanda* one memorable evening in Oaxaca, signed by all present, requesting that I finish my book. I was also fortunate to be able to present some of what has turned into this book at the law school in Oaxaca City; while all the questions the talk generated were useful, the impromptu commentary by the dean of the school was incredibly so. Other colleagues in Oaxaca drew my attention to works I did not know about. This book, in my opinion and whatever its faults, would not be what it is without their generosity and spirit of sharing and intellectual exchange. I am only half joking when I say that I am, nevertheless, relieved that this book is about northern Mexico and not Oaxaca—no book presentation there need be forthcoming!

The physical and scholarly pathways taken in the research and writing of this book have led to and through many places. Along the way, some things have changed; a few have remained constant. These paths seldom take me to Chihuahua any longer; they always seem to pass through Oaxaca, with the Oaxaca Summer Institute serving as a consistent point of arrival and departure. My home for parts of June and July over the last fourteen years, the institute has provided an intellectual and social space for exchange with scholars and graduate students from Mexico, the United States, and Canada. It has been a pleasure to regularly cohost a week of the monthlong seminar there with Ann Blum; her questions and interventions have prompted me to think about gender and family in ways I hadn't previously considered. I have also enjoyed working with Monica Rankin, who has brought family members, many students, and a well-needed dose of fiscal responsibility to the institute. Co-directors Gabriela Soto Laveaga and María L. O. Muñoz have helped breathe new life into the seminar with their own work and by inviting many of their colleagues to participate in the weeks they have organized. A lively group of scholars in Oaxaca, including Lucero Topete,

Francisco José Ruiz Cervantes, Daniela Traffano, and Carlos Sánchez Silva, along with others who have made Oaxaca their home at various points, including Francie Chassen-López, Martha Rees, and Mary Kay Vaughan, have welcomed us each year, giving presentations on their work, introductions to the history of the state, and access to archives and people as well as offering comments on my work. It has been my privilege to have met and worked with the many graduate students whose own paths have led them there as well. After having left, many of them have often returned as faculty members to present their work; I especially acknowledge and thank those among them who continue to send me material and references they think will be of interest. In this, as in many endeavors, my biggest debt is to William Beezley, the force behind the Oaxaca Summer Institute, whose work has done so much to advance and promote the study of cultural history in Mexico and whose students have traveled from the summer institute into faculty positions in universities throughout North America. Although "gender" isn't like gravity, his insistence that it is will likely lead us to continue our conversations and arguments until his goal of Oaxaca xx (that is, "Oaxaca dos equis") becomes a reality.

One of my paths now leads to Pennsylvania. Perhaps it is no wonder, given the topic I chose to research and write on, that love would come to shape my personal life as well as my professional life. For that, and to María, I am thankful every single day of my life.

THE HEART IN THE GLASS JAR

Introduction

Though the heart in the glass jar no longer beats, it continues to invigorate life at the very center of the "lettered city," a phrase that Angel Rama coined to capture the relationship between power, the written word, and the urban center in Latin America from the colonial period to the present.[1] Today, the heart stands in a display case, preserved in formaldehyde, in a small museum recently established within the facilities of the Colegio Primitivo y Nacional de San Nicolás de Hidalgo, a high school within an institution of higher learning in the city of Morelia in the state of Michoacán. San Nicolás, or "Prepa 1," as it is now known, was originally founded in Pátzcuaro in 1540 and then moved to Valladolid (now Morelia) in 1580. As an institution, it boasts a long history of educational accomplishments within the state and the nation and claims such distinguished alumni as Miguel Hidalgo y Costilla, José María Morelos, and Ignacio López Rayón, figures prominent in the movement for independence. Before the recent creation of the museum, that is, for approximately the previous 140 years, the heart occupied a place of honor in the library of the colegio.

As living tissue, from 1814 until 1861, the heart sustained the life of Melchor Ocampo, a statesman prominent in mid-nineteenth-century public life. Ocampo, captured by a conservative army as part of the conflict over the Reform Laws, had barely had time to write out his will, donating all his books and papers to the colegio, before meeting his end in front of a firing squad in 1861. His body, recovered from the tree in which it had been left hanging, was taken to Mexico City, where his heart was removed during autopsy and sent to one of Ocampo's daughters, who subsequently donated it to his beloved San Nicolás.[2] In recognition of his contributions to these midcentury struggles and of his ultimate sacrifice, his body lies in repose in Mexico City at the Rotonda de las Personas Ilustres (formerly Rotonda de los Hombres Ilustres), where it now serves the country as one of its sacred dead, a symbol to be honored and venerated by a grateful nation.

A greatly admired and much-honored figure of the Liberal Reform era, Ocampo was, in addition to being a lawmaker, politician, and lawyer, a passionate advocate of secular and lay education.[3] One of the measures most identified with the Reform was the Law of Civil Matrimony that came into effect in 1859. This law limited the power of corporations, especially the church, by establishing a civil registry; abolishing special corporate privileges, mandatory tithes, and parochial subventions; and forcing the sale of property held by corporations. In addition to withholding state recognition of religious marriage and establishing marriage as a civil contract, this law incorporated into its articles an epistle, or letter, written by Melchor Ocampo, and appended as article 15. The epistle sets out the supposedly inherent qualities of both men and women and their respective responsibilities and obligations within marriage. According to the epistle, the man, whose attributes are described as those of valor and strength, owed the woman protection, nourishment, and direction and the kind of magnanimous and generous treatment that "the strong owe to the weak." For her part, the woman, whose principal characteristics were said to include abnegation, beauty, compassion, understanding, and tenderness, was required to give her husband obedience, kindness, assistance, comfort, counsel, and "the veneration owed to the person who supports and defends us." The epistle further mandated that the wife treat her husband with the care or tact of someone "who does not wish to exasperate the brusque, irritable and harsh part" of him, qualities deemed appropriate to his character. Since the time of its writing, the epistle of Melchor Ocampo has been read out loud as a kind of secular sermon at many civil marriage ceremonies, a practice that has only very recently come to an end.[4]

Just as his words in the form of the marriage epistle, his body, resting in the pantheon of national heroes, and his heart, preserved in the museum in San Nicolás, have continued to resonate with many down to the present, so too has Ocampo's name. The relationship between name and place that would later be made official grew out of more personal connections that he himself forged while still alive. When in Michoacán, Ocampo called the modest estate where he lived Pomoca, an anagram of his own name, attempting perhaps to link person and place, endowing the land with his own personality and qualities while signaling his desire to embody the physical characteristics of the land itself in his own being.[5] Upon his death, Ocampo was declared a hero and Michoacán, the state, was officially renamed Michoacán de Ocampo, another manner of bringing together individual and place, this time as part of a process of national or regional imagining. Incorporating Ocampo's name into the state simultaneously established both a heroic past that could be remembered and a set of patriotic values that citizens, present and future, could aspire to emulate. When it comes to the availability and malleability of serving as symbol and metaphor, few seem equal to Ocampo, who has given heart, body, a letter, his name, and perhaps even his soul to doing so.

But this book is not about Melchor Ocampo. Nor is it concerned with the struggles of the Reform era or even with specific historical events in the state of Michoacán. It does, however, take as its subject matter hearts, bodies, letters, and the law, matters crucial to Ocampo in life and in death. And although its focus may be on different aspects of these subjects, an emphasis on their properties as symbols and metaphors remains central. Rather than Ocampo's world of the lettered city—a venue composed through literature, history, the law, politics, and higher education—this book attempts to chart some of the territory that I refer to as the lettered countryside, a place that, despite being removed from urban centers of power, was nonetheless characterized by varied and complicated engagements with the written word. Rather than a heart preserved for posterity in formaldehyde at the center of a museum, the hearts in this book are (mostly) figurative, belonging to those young lovers who pledged them to each other as part of the promises and prevarications of a courting relationship. Later finding themselves enmeshed in legal processes that followed from their behavior, their correspondence, just as Ocampo's heart, was preserved, but this time in a historical archive. Finally, rather than being examples of the epistle, a formal or didactic form of written correspondence, even if in the service of matrimony, the letters that compose the sources for and main preoccupation of this book are of a different genre: that of the love letter. The authors are men and women of mostly humble circumstances who found themselves, at least for a time, in the mining districts and rural communities of the Mexican state of Chihuahua during the lead-silver boom of the late nineteenth and early twentieth centuries. Writing, especially in the hands of men like Ocampo, was certainly a technology of power, a means of shaping visions of the past and future in the service of national projects and in the interests of a powerful few. Writing was also something that many, I have found—including mine workers, rural laborers, and women concerned with domestic labor—could not imagine engaging in courtship without, even if the letters they exchanged were composed collectively, by a group or by other people, and not always by themselves individually.

Love letters written by everyday people circulate through this book, their prose inspiring almost every page. The book's central intellectual conceit is that these letters can yield a history. Convincing them to do so has meant situating love letters within a number of particular and historically specific social settings and practices, each informed by contested assumptions and understandings concerning such things as age, gender, authority, the meaning of the written word, and agency. The genre of the letter was shaped by these contexts while it helped shape both official forms of documentation and new forms of mass-mediated writing, including the novel, the newspaper, and the writing manual. As a material object, the love letter could also serve as a powerful symbol, of a courting relationship, of the body, and as a means of calling forth the absent writer, actual or presumed. As a form of inscription, the love letter brought into being a particular kind of space, one marked by the effusive expression of desire and into which the world of the ideal couple, as it was imagined, could be inscribed and within which an epistolary body took shape. If this was a textual world in which selves and bodies could be configured through writing, it was also one in which the equality presumed by the epistolary pact, that act of corresponding with another, foundered in the face of unmet expectations and the violent enforcement of male prerogatives in the world outside that composed in epistolary space. As much as it is about love, at least of the type expressed in letters exchanged as part of courting relationships, this book is also, unfortunately, about violence, at least of the type that could characterize intergenerational struggles over women's choices of partners and the behavior of some male suitors, often expressed and, at times, excused as a form of passion out of control.

The properties and purposes of love letters exceeded those arising from the needs of the couple in a courting relationship to express desire and elicit commitment to their relationship. Under certain circumstances, love letters could also serve as evidence in various legal proceedings, a fact that now makes it possible for historians to consult them and for you to read about them. Given that the law formed one of the major pillars upon which the lettered city was built, designed not only to adjudicate disputes but also to teach and enforce the values and categories upon which rule was based, locating love letters within such a setting requires taking great care to determine what purposes they could serve and how the fact that they could potentially serve as evidence might have shaped their writing and, in fact, their existence. It also means coming to terms with the ways in which those in the judicial system wielded power, often less by means of passing judgments (although certainly in that manner as well) and more through giving priority to certain qualities and characteristics distinguishing those appearing before them over others, separating bodies according to those criteria and inscribing the law, at times directly onto them.

To write a history of love letters I have organized the book into three separate yet interrelated sections, each focusing on a site or location within which these letters circulated and took on meanings as they, simultaneously, imparted them. "The Letter of the Law," section 1 of the book, is concerned with the circumstances that led to the lodging of love letters within the judicial archive as well as with situating the written word, including love letters, no matter how humble their authors might be, within or as part of an apparatus of power that privileged some and penalized others and that was designed to accomplish certain ends. Even the period covered in this book, the 1870s until the late 1920s, has been determined in large part by

the formal requirements as to the type of evidence required by the law—
that in writing. The book begins with the drawing up of legal codes shortly
after the death of Melchor Ocampo, in the late 1860s and early 1870s, by
those who followed in his ideological footsteps. It ends when new legal
codes in 1929 and 1931 removed the stipulations in the previous code that
had resulted in the submission of love letters to judicial officials under
certain circumstances in certain kinds of cases having to do with what
lawmakers referred to as the good order of families. The book begins, then,
by exploring the broader context within which the formation of couples
took place as well as that within which writing and the written word were
adjudicated. Much like money or passports, love letters, as written documents, could serve as important scrip that enabled one to gain access to
the lettered city, at least in theory.

Encountering love letters in the archives of the state, especially its judicial branch, was initially something of a surprise. Examples of what might
be called vernacular or everyday literacy, they appear as anomalies not
only when contrasted with the massive amount of official documentation
lodged along with them in those archives but also within a historiography
that has, at times, seemed premised upon the existence of a great divide
between oral and literate cultures. Whenever I have made presentations at
conferences about the love letters exchanged between men and women who
described themselves as workers, artisans, campesinos, and those engaged
in domestic labor, the most common question I have been asked has been
"But what percentage of people during the late nineteenth century was
literate?"—often prompted by the (unstated) assumption that such a question could only have one answer and that everyone present shared the same
definition of "literate," a word that, as a result, did not really need to be
discussed or defined.

Even Angel Rama, whose exceptional book *The Lettered City* continues to inspire the imagination of scholars in history, literature, and other
disciplines long after its publication and to whom anyone working on the
subject of literacy in Latin America is indebted, seems to premise his work
upon the acceptance of a binary that pits "literate" against "oral." For Rama,
whereas oral culture is traditional, literate culture is modern; whereas change

is slow in oral cultures, it is much more rapid in those characterized by "literacy" (and much more amenable to individualization, which leads to literature); whereas oral culture might be seen as a continuum, the written is susceptible to rapid change. In short, the rural becomes constructed as the opposite of the urban, the characteristics of which Rama is interested in identifying.[6] Published posthumously in 1984 and then translated into English in 1996, *The Lettered City* defines this locale as the site of extensive production of texts through which the independent countries of Latin America were brought into being and ruled, and through which that rule, along with the hierarchies and values essential to it, was justified. Rama, pointing to the impact of what he refers to as the "ever-expanding circuits of the written word," the spread of urban educational standards, and the accelerating arrival in the countryside of cultural substitutes originating in the city in the period after 1870, charts what he sees as the destruction in rural areas of living memory and oral traditions, premised precisely upon their dependence on oral communication. *Letrados*, those producers and consumers of the written word, men (mostly) like Ocampo, then attempted to "fix" or solidify these traditions in the service of the creation of national literatures and national histories.[7] It is important to note that Rama does not see the complete elimination of rural cultures under the impact of the city and its writerly ways. Rather, he sees a process of selection and adaptation at work in which rural cultures absorb and utilize what is deemed useful in responding to the changing circumstances being brought about by the modernizing city. As part of this process, new forms of rural culture, characterized by the mixture of orality and writing, emerge. As this is not Rama's main interest, he does not spend much time developing his ideas about these new, mixed forms that were both urban and rural, nor, perhaps, does acknowledging the existence of these forms solve the issues identified by those opposed to the "great divide" version of the orality/literacy debate.[8]

Debates over the relationship between oral and literate culture, ongoing at the time of Rama's book, received added impetus with the publication of Walter Ong's work *Orality and Literacy: The Technologizing of the Word*. Ong, in that book, made broad claims about literacy's supposed impact on such things as memory, understandings of and constructions of the self, senses of privacy and time, and the conceptualization of history, all characteristic of what he referred to as the "chirographic mentality." "More than any other single invention," he concluded, "writing has transformed human consciousness."[9] Others have been critical of what they have described as this "autonomous" model of literacy, that is, one that claims that the advent of literacy results in the same changes in every society. Such a model, they argue, leaves little room for actual historical analysis. These scholars find in the very term "literacy" a problem to be addressed rather than a simple fact signaling preordained conclusions. Writing about the relationship between love letters, literacy, and social change in Nepal, for example, Laura Ahearn draws from an extensive body of research stressing the importance of studying literacy as a social practice, paying close attention to the contexts in which literacy occurs and being specific about the changes that actually take place and under what circumstances.[10] Scholars adopting the "event-centered" approach to literacy, as it is referred to, often focus their analysis on one particular social setting or context to ask how such a literacy, in that particular instance, derives its meanings from the broader contexts in which it is practiced. The "event-centered" approach leads to a concern not with literacy in the singular but with literacies in the plural, each one associated with different domains of life, different social groups, different institutions, different genders, and each shaped by and helping to shape power in different ways.[11] Each literacy, as well, becomes a subject in need of investigation rather than the fulfilling of a trajectory already set out, as in the "autonomous" model, where the result is already seemingly known in advance.

Frank Salomon and Mercedes Niño-Murcia, authors of a recently published book on writing in a Peruvian village, have adopted the event-centered approach to literacy to great effect. Highlighting both their debt to Rama and their engagement with his ideas in their work aptly entitled *The Lettered Mountain*, they approach literacy as a social practice with a long history in non-elite societies, finding that, even before Peruvian independence in the early nineteenth century, villagers had "thoroughly internalized the graphic order despite having no schools of their own."[12] Focusing on Tupicocha, a recognized peasant community located in Huarochirí Province in the central Peruvian department of Lima,[13] they chart the development of an "internal graphic community" there premised upon the writing of manuscript books, in a highly legalistic idiom, composed mainly of administrative papers, particularly minutes of meetings, account books, receipts, memoranda, and some local histories. Such record-keeping, the authors insist, formed the linchpin of communal life, providing for villagers a defense against fraud and abuse and a means of acquiring dignity and social respect, serving, in short, as a weapon of the community. As for acquiring literacy sufficient to this task, people in Tupicocha, likening the learning of literacy to catechism, have had a near reverence for writing manuals like *El Mosaico*, a compendium of sample manuscripts first published in the mid-nineteenth century and then republished extensively since that time, from which they read and copy various genres of texts. While I have found much in *The Lettered Mountain* with which to engage, perhaps most significant for the present discussion has been its charting of what its authors refer to as the "democratization of the lettered city" in the second half of the nineteenth century, due, in large part, to the influence of such writing manuals, by which time, contrary to elite expectations, "peasants were becoming their own letrados."[14]

Nor were peasants in highland communities of South America unique in confounding expectations, whether of those writing about them or of elites in their own country, as to their supposed shortcomings when it came to the written word. Writing about working-class letter writing among migrant workers in early twentieth-century South Africa, Keith Breckenridge argues that the characterization of that region as suffering from supposedly widespread functional illiteracy masks the success of certain forms of letter-based communication within and between households and the emergence of what he refers to as a "lettered private sphere" among migrant workers. Breckenridge, finding overwhelming evidence that unschooled migrants wrote, points to the collaborative forms of literary intimacy that enabled the composition of letters, particularly love letters, and the importance of those letters in enabling migrant workers to address the problems in their lives, especially those of subsistence and desire, better than any other means of doing so.[15] Nor was writing on that continent limited to South Africa. In her introduction to a recently published collection of essays on the "hidden" histories of Africa, Karin Barber points to what she sees as a veritable "explosion" of writing in colonial Africa, in which individuals such as wage laborers, clerks, village headmasters, traders, artisans, and others wrote and archived many kinds of texts. Barber finds, in what she calls "tin-trunk literacy," not an isolated or sporadic phenomenon but a "remarkably consistent and widespread efflorescence" happening all over colonial Anglophone Africa, a process that enabled the imagining of "new kinds of personhood, new ways of being social, and new ways of relating to the world of officialdom," among other things.[16] Lynn Thomas, a contributor to Barber's edited collection, shows how the letters written by schoolgirls in central Kenya that ended up in pregnancy-compensation-case records constituted what she refers to as a form of "collective privacy," constituting particular kinds of publics while combining personal and instrumental ends.[17]

Just as peasants in Tupicocha and non-elites in Africa, South Asia, and, likely, elsewhere,[18] were acquiring particular and multiple forms of literacies, embedded within a multiplicity of social settings and practices, so too were some mine workers, campesinos, artisans, women carrying out domestic work, and others in northern Mexico in the late nineteenth and early twentieth centuries participating in various ways in specific kinds of literacies, especially those forms associated with the writing, reading, and exchange of love letters. In this book, I explore the particular "literacy event" associated with love letters.

After situating love letters within the context of the judicial system, section 2 of the book, entitled "The Lettered Countryside," explores some of the ways that love-letter literacy may have been acquired or accomplished in mining camps, rural communities, and small towns in the north, if not through the formal educational opportunities that were growing in number there in the late nineteenth century then through informal means or in cooperation with others. Focusing on novels, newspapers, advertising, letter manuals, and coplas (a popular non-narrative oral verse in which stanzas stand more or less independently of each other), this section also offers a broader discussion of the letter form in an attempt to delineate what I refer to as the emergence of a "passionate public sphere," one in which scandal and spectacle were deployed in an attempt to bring into being a passionate public that shared a common horror and fascination with crimes of violence, that is, with passion out of control. At the same time, the section seeks to measure the degree to which the letters helping to compose such a sphere might have served as models for those love letters actually exchanged between those in courting relationships in the lettered countryside.

As will become evident in the sections that follow, the sources consulted for this book offer only the briefest glimpses of the specific circumstances under which the writing, reading, and exchange of love letters was accomplished. Working mostly with hints and intimations, I have no way of being certain most of the time whether the letters I am drawing on and referring to were written by those exchanging them, by others—perhaps friends or family members, part of a group writing process—or by amanuenses, scribes paid to carry out such tasks. My experience, not only in the archives, suggests that the creative ways of accomplishing letter writing that exist in the present may have had, as well, their counterparts in the past. Stopped in the middle of the day in the street in Ciudad Chihuahua sometime in the late 1980s, I was asked by a person from there if I could read and write. As I assured the gentleman in norteño hat, belt, and boots that I could, he asked whether I would write a letter on his behalf, one not concerning love but informing his employer in Texas of the date he would be returning to work. In this instance, communication in letter form across two languages and three countries (if we count Canada, my home) was accomplished, although the utility of the final product may have been placed under some question when I refused payment for it, as if, for the person concerned, the quality of work was directly related to the amount it cost to carry it out.

In addition to revealing one of the many ways that letter-writing literacy might be achieved, this personal anecdote may also help illustrate some of the circumstances that might call forth the need or desire to acquire some form of literacy among certain groups of people. Although the mining regions and agricultural communities in the state of Chihuahua during the Porfiriato and the first few decades of the twentieth century are a far cry from the urban center that Ciudad Chihuahua became, both shared circumstances that made writing, especially of letters, useful, perhaps even essential, for those living and working there. Just as in the more recent past, mobility—especially that of workers who moved back and forth between jobs in the mines and worked as railway labor, not only in other parts of Mexico but also in the United States—characterized the mining regions of the state in the late nineteenth and early twentieth centuries. With the arrival of the railroad in southern Chihuahua in the late nineteenth century, the mining industry boomed there, drawing workers, for various periods of time, from other mining regions in Mexico. At the same time, the concentration of land ownership and the dispossession of corporation-held land, under the impact of those same Reform Laws to which Melchor Ocampo was so committed, compelled others to leave their communities to become wage laborers while still others combined periods of agricultural labor with work in the mines and other jobs that paid a wage, leaving their jobs once they had made earnings sufficient to get them through to the next harvest. All in all, the mining regions were characterized by cycles of boom and bust and a concomitant flow of people who experienced them in unique ways, not least of which being a growing dependence on the vagaries of the price and quality of the ore being mined and on the policies and investment decisions of foreign mining companies, among other factors. Thus, although the population in areas like Hidalgo District numbered only in the tens of thousands, even at the height of mining operations, it was home to a highly mobile and floating population, many itinerant, stopping as long as work might be available, searching for better opportunities that seemed, elusively, almost always to be just around the next bend.[19]

This was precisely the kind of population for whom writing, especially letter writing, might have been not a luxury or indulgence but rather an essential means of maintaining ties with family and others at home. In her fine study of literacy acquisition among a group of women in Mixquic, a town that, although near Mexico City, has only recently experienced a transition from being a rural town to becoming part of an urban area, Judy Kalman makes an observation that, although an aside and not directly concerned with the arguments she develops in her book, seems particularly revealing. Reflecting on the low incidence of letter exchange in the community as measured by the fact that only a small minority of women in the literacy group she worked with there in the late 1990s acknowledged that they had ever received or written letters, she reports that women in the group nevertheless told stories about receiving correspondence "at some point" in their lives from a "forbidden boyfriend." The women also acknowledged that letters had circulated in town in the 1940s, a time when the town's source of water dried up, making farming impossible and forcing many of the men to move elsewhere for work. As Kalman reports, the women "thought that many of the men who had left the town looking for work had to learn to read and write so that they could send news home; others hired public scribes to write for them."[20]

Just as the forced migration of community members in search of work created the need to establish and maintain long-distance communication in the Mixquic of the 1940s, the same circumstances prevailed in the mining regions of the north during a slightly earlier period. Likewise, the admission of the women in her literacy group, even if they were reluctant to go into detail, that they had received letters from men even in the absence of economic necessity, that is, as part of courtship rather than because of distance, is portentous. Their candid asides reveal not only the ongoing exchange of letters up to the end of the twentieth century among men and women who considered themselves unable to read and write but also the continued importance of letter writing to courtship there. I argue in this book that such was also the case a century earlier, in the late nineteenth century and the early decades of the twentieth, as letters and courtship, for many, went hand in hand, however such correspondence might have been accomplished.

If letters and courtship went hand in hand, this may have been due in large part to the representational and performative properties of letters themselves—that is, to their ability to compose the very things, including courtship, love, and the body, that they were writing into being. In section 3, entitled "The Body of the Letter," I draw on the metaphorical relationship between the body and text to establish the contours or physical attributes of the body in love, as those exchanging love letters composed and understood it, as well as to suggest its internal emotional or spiritual characteristics. Here I seek to give shape to what I refer to as the sentimental anatomy, those parts of the body implicated in love. If the sentimental anatomy includes such organs as the heart and the eyes, it is also characterized by such less tangible entities as the soul and will. The metaphors and the symbolic language of love employed in the composition of love letters, a language in which body and text each implicate or imply the other, have bled into my own manner of thinking and writing and are reflected in this book in ways I may not fully recognize.

Above all else, the sentimental anatomy that love letters brought into being was gendered, with one of its most inquired-after characteristics being the state of the woman's hymen. Moreover, it was men's passion that gave birth to the sentimental anatomy in the first place: passion was the emotion that compelled men to set pen to paper and initiate courtship, as it was the characteristic that served as one of the main qualities of the male form of that entity (that is, of the sentimental anatomy). As you will read, emphasis on the supposed legibility of women's bodies; the various fears, panics, and protestations that congealed around passion; and a reiterated concern with *voluntad* (will), of both women and men, are like the love letters themselves themes common to all three sections. Their existence illustrates that although the book has been organized in order to contextualize love letters in three separate locales—within the law, in the lettered countryside, and in the body of the letter—these venues were hardly isolated, an insight developed more fully in the postscript that ties the three sections together.

The flow of love letters through the institutions, locales, and spaces that their circulation helped bring into being determined the organization of this book. Only after I had finished writing it did it become apparent to me how closely the themes of the three sections I had chosen mirrored, only in reverse order, the focus on the new kinds of personhood, new ways of being social, and new ways of relating to the world of officialdom that Karin Barber identifies as some of the main consequences of the spread of tin-trunk literacy in colonial Anglophone Africa.[21] Various forms of writing in northern Mexico certainly generated much that was new. The legal system, the subject of section 1, privileged the written word, generating new and more numerous documents through which rule might be accomplished and categories of subject brought into being, all of which required new ways of dealing with officialdom. Yet notable consistencies are also apparent. Judicial procedures, as practiced, seemed to offer space to let old, existing ways of working things out continue to take place, especially once parents of couples in courting relationships got involved.

Likewise, section 2 provides much to support the view that a new sense of time, new commonly held sentiments, the privileging of emotion, and the creation of new publics were nurtured by the novel, newspapers, model letter-writing guides, and etiquette manuals. These forms of writing helped foster new ways of being social, acting as venues for the leveling of hierarchies of social class and gender. Yet they were often rooted in common and longstanding understandings of family, morality, and order. Rather than the supplanting of the oral by the written, these sources represent a profound engagement between the written and oral worlds.

Finally, as much as section 3 focuses on endowing the epistolary body with a sentimental anatomy, it is also concerned with the ways those attempting to form couples could use the pages of the love letter to conjure new senses of personhood. The epistolary space constituted in the love letter was the territory of an ideal self and an ideal couple, entities that emerged as writers tried out new roles and imagined futures that they themselves might mutually write into being. Those in courting relationships made claims as to their honesty and trustworthiness in matters of the heart; they often envisioned romantic love in radically egalitarian terms, that is, as the mutual or reciprocal exchange of will between equals.

It is precisely at this point, through their imaginings of alternative futures and their insistence on reciprocity, even equality, in love, where the love letters upon which this book is based contribute to a debate that has structured discussion in the field of the history of romantic love for the last twenty years—specifically, to the debate over the transformation of intimacy in modern societies. In his book of that name (*The Transformation of Intimacy*), published in 1992, Anthony Giddens explores the origins of what he refers to as the "pure relationship," characterized, as he sees it, by sexual and emotional equality and a democratizing of the interpersonal domain.[22] He associates its emergence with the rise of romantic love, which he dates to the late eighteenth century in Europe. Distinct from passionate love, romantic love, he argues, shares much with the novel, its contemporary, especially a form of emplotment, one in which self and other can be fit into a personal narrative with "no particular reference to wider social processes."[23] Equally important, in Giddens's opinion, is the manner in which this narrative form projects not only a mutual narrative biography for the couple but also a course of future development for them to follow.

Since its publication, Giddens's work has helped define the questions and analytical frameworks used by those researching romantic love during other time periods and in other geographical regions. In more recent studies, romantic love has become the measure of modernity, serving as a strategy for affective mobility and a "very individually oriented technique for framing oneself as a modern subject."[24] When applied to twentieth-century rural Mexico, Giddens's work has helped structure the terms of an inquiry into marriage that dates the arrival of romantic love there to very recently. According to Jennifer Hirsch, as late as the 1950s and 1960s marriage in rural Mexico remained an obligation, the mutual fulfillment of gender responsibilities, and love, "if it existed, was the result of living well together."[25]

Rather than a single narrative, however, it is the multiplicity of ways that the bonds leading to the formation of a couple could be described that is most striking in the love letters and legal testimony consulted in the writing of this book. For some, marriage was envisioned as a gesture of appreciation, undertaken to endow a woman with respectability and resources in exchange for the care she had provided, in one instance to a widower and the members of his household. For others, marriage was not even within the realm of the realistic. These men and women described their relationships as long-term common-law unions that were to last "as long as they both should want"; in explaining these arrangements to judicial officials and others, women and men alike repeatedly stressed the bonds of necessity that brought them together, with coupling premised upon the woman's agreement to carry out domestic duties in exchange for the man's provision of money to run the household, a sum known as the *diario*. Not only common-law unions but marriages as well could be characterized in material, rather than or as much as in emotional, terms.

Still others formed their relationships through the composition of mutual narrative biographies, often by means of love letters, that removed the couple from their present circumstances and propelled them into a relentlessly personal and self-absorbed future. It was under these circumstances where love most threatened social and gender hierarchies, given that it was imagined as the reciprocal or mutual exchange of will among equals. As you will see when you read the love letters of people like Refugio and Enriqueta, such imagining extended to women who described themselves as concerned with domestic duties and whose partners labored in the mines. At the very least, the multiple meanings of love set out in love letters from northern Mexico place very much in doubt the attempt to make generalizations about the relationship of romantic love to marriage in rural Mexico or to date the arrival of romantic love in the countryside to only the very recent past.[26]

No image seems to bring into a single frame the themes of the present book quite like that of Ocampo's heart at the very center of the lettered city, if only to point toward the existence of other possible venues, like the lettered countryside, and other possible bodily metaphors, those emerging from the demands of the judicial system or the sentimental anatomy that was being written into being in love letters. Rather than with Ocampo directly, the rest of the book concerns itself with those who, in many ways, might be considered his heirs—those who aspired to reside in the lettered city he had helped compose and those who resided outside it but insisted on some relationship to writing nonetheless; those who would go on to write the legal and criminal codes of the second half of the nineteenth century that can be regarded as an important legacy of the Reform era as well as a key component of the lettered city; those who wrote love letters, mostly outside its hallowed walls; those who heard or hoped to hear his words recited at civil marriage ceremonies throughout the country until very nearly the end of the twentieth century; and those who shared in understanding the body not only as flesh and blood but also as a powerful symbol, as metaphor, capable of shouldering sentimental or emotional anatomies that could help inspire and bring into being the very things they represented, including patriotic and romantic love.

Thus you, dear reader, might consider yourself the fictive addressee of a letter (a long one, I'll grant you that) in book form. Influenced by the letter genre, I have tried to express myself here in a manner that is engaging and that addresses you, at times, directly. If the endnotes betray that this is a work of historical research, my hope is that the manner of its writing does not. But only you can judge that.

While the subjects of this book and the evidence used to explore them have been drawn from the written traces left by a mobile population in a mining region in northern Mexico, its concern with love, letters, and the law addresses broader currents having to do with the meanings of literacies; access to and the uses of writing and the letter form; and the performative, symbolic, and metaphorical properties that link the body and the written page. As much as through the lettered city, these currents, like those writing the letters themselves, flowed through the mining camps, small towns, and agricultural communities of northern Mexico and beyond them. The book is also concerned with love, especially as those in courting relationships composed it in written form. Here, the epistolary power that such writing could give to women made of love something that might be understood as reciprocal and mutual rather than as hierarchical or unequal, despite all the assertions to the contrary in the marriage epistle penned by Melchor Ocampo. It is his heart, nonetheless, enveloped in a glass jar and serving as an open letter for all to read, that has had the final word. Until now, that is.

SECTION ONE

The Letter of the Law

Having yielded to their desires as well as to the strong arms of the brothers O., the Martínez sisters were spirited out of their parental home in Balleza, a relatively populous agricultural municipality within the Parral mining district in Chihuahua, one night during the dry season in 1901. Unlike many fathers who found themselves in similar situations, their father, having denied his permission for his underage daughters to marry, stubbornly refused to change his mind after their abduction. Rejecting the seeming fait accompli of their elopement, he recovered his daughters, deposited them in a respectable home for safekeeping, and then sought to recoup family honor by denouncing the brothers before judicial authorities. Much like his honor, however, the walls of their new house of detention were soon breached. Promising marriage, one brother again abducted a Martínez sister (although a different one than he had the previous time) with what she stated to be her full consent and cooperation and the complete absence of violence. Brought yet again before judicial authorities, he admitted that, while he had done something wrong, his actions were justified as they had been in aid of a worthwhile goal, that of marriage. How could these acts have constituted a crime, the Martínez woman added, when she herself had set the time and date for her abduction to take place?[1] By contrast, in an unrelated incident that had taken place a few years earlier, when another young woman, aged fifteen and from the same district, changed her mind shortly after leaving the parental home to accompany her suitor, things quickly turned violent. Rather than allowing her to return, she testified, her suitor had grabbed her by the arm and, threatening her with a knife, forced her to accompany him into an empty house where, fearful of being beaten or worse, she did not resist, she told the court, while he sexually assaulted her. No promise of marriage was formally offered and none took place.[2]

Despite the differences in intent, circumstances, and outcome, the men mentioned in the two above examples (with the exception of Señor Martínez, the father of the underage daughters) appeared before judicial officials to answer for the same crime, that of *rapto*. It is in the commission of this and related crimes that the love letters that form the basis of the present book came to be part of the archive of the judicial system in Chihuahua, Mexico. In crimes like that involving the Martínez family—those having to do with the unauthorized removal of a young woman from the household of her parents or guardians and, often, with the subsequent initiation of sexual relations, referred to, respectively, as the crimes of rapto and *estupro* (discussed further below)—love letters could serve as a form of legal proof and, thus, enter into the official record as evidence of a written promise of marriage from a man over the age of majority to a young woman. Significantly, the love letters that form part of the evidentiary base in these types of cases, comprising about half of all the letters consulted for the writing of this book, are written exclusively by men.

In the second category of cases, more akin to the second scenario outlined above, love letters written by women are present, lamentably. Here, the good fortune of the historian in having such a source available for consultation is only made possible through the horrific end suffered by these women at the hands of their suitors. Their relationships over, these particular suitors, like many others, one imagines, met one last time to return the love letters each had written to the other. In contrast to most failed courtships, however, here the man killed the woman before committing suicide, usually by turning a gun on himself; arriving at the scene of the crime, judicial officials collected all the letters they encountered as part of their investigations, thus preserving the letters by entering them into the official record.

Given the narrowly defined circumstances under which love letters came to be deployed as evidence in judicial procedures and, arguably, the singular nature of the cases concerned with murder-suicide, one begins to see how understanding the accident of their availability might be important to the ways we read, understand, and draw conclusions from such sources. Their presence in the archive makes apparent that many other letters must also have existed, those exchanged by men and women whose courtships proceeded relatively smoothly to marriage, for example, or those who managed to resolve their disagreements or disputes without entangling themselves in legal proceedings, or even those for whom marriage was not a particularly desirable or even realistic option. It forces us to ask questions about the circumstances that compelled people, particularly young women and their parents or guardians, even to have taken recourse to the law. How might they have weighed the disadvantages of such public disclosure of their lives, often linked to the beginning of sexual activity, against the necessity of avoiding private misfortune, such as the costs of raising a child alone or the possible diminishment of one's odds in the marriage lottery, should they aspire to take their chances in it at some later date? Alongside this multitude of personal predilections and variously constrained options must be placed the agenda of the law itself; hardly innocent, the judicial system was fully implicated in various strategies through which rule was accomplished, especially through the teaching of civic values and the enunciation and policing of various class, gender, ethnic, sexual, and other hierarchies.

The demands of the judicial system also required those involved in its formal proceedings to construct narratives about themselves as well as about their relationships, actions, and expectations. This was the case for women and men, children and their parents. As a result, women's statements to judicial officials form a central part of each of these proceedings, as do those of their suitors and parents or guardians. From these narratives, we can approach an understanding not only of the requirements of the judicial system but also of the dynamics of courtship itself, its tensions, both intergenerational and between men and women, engendered by multiple negotiations over resources and sexuality; its lived intensity as a time of promises; and its dangers, potentially capable of altering the trajectory of young lives. The prominence of the stories men and women spun before the court in shaping our understanding of courtship and the role of love letters in it makes it all the more imperative to begin with a consideration of how the structure, tone, and content of such narratives, or legal scripts, performed in front of judicial authorities might be best seen as examples of "fiction in the archives."[3]

In a similar manner, the judicial system itself was preoccupied with constructing and enforcing categories and personas. At each step in the judicial procedure in such crimes and around which the present section has been organized—beginning with the formal complaint and then moving, in the following order, to the questioning of the principals and witnesses, the gathering of evidence, the submission of medical reports and love letters, to the formal petition desisting from the complaint or the judgment, if there was one—judicial officials interested themselves in determining the legal personalities or judicial personas of those involved. Only after doing so did officials move to establish whether or not the acts they heard being recounted before them satisfied the legal criteria for the commission of the various crimes of rapto, estupro, and *violación* as set out in the criminal codes that will be discussed shortly. Understanding how the judicial system, like any process that generates an archive, gave shape to the material that comes to be located in it helps highlight the highly mediated nature of such material as well as the need to take great care in determining even the kinds of conclusions that can be reached by using such sources. Moreover, as for the law, only certain categories of individuals and families, as you will see, merited its consideration. As it is not possible to know from the documents that form the judicial archives the links, if any, that existed between judicial officials and those appearing before them or the degree of enthusiasm with which various cases were processed, little else other than the letter of the law seemed to matter.

Codes and Procedures

Far from boring or mundane, the task of drafting the first penal code for an independent Mexico must have seemed, to its framers, to have placed them at the very apogee of Mexican liberalism and patriotic virtue. Formed in 1862, shortly after Melchor Ocampo's death by firing squad, and composed of men of the "Benito Juárez generation," the commission charged with its writing had had time to complete only one book of revisions to the hodgepodge of colonial-era laws before its work was interrupted by foreign invasion. Having defeated Emperor Maximilian by mid-1867, victorious liberals wasted little time reconstituting the commission; by September, 1868, commission members were back, hard at work on the code. As Antonio Martínez de Castro, the head of the commission, glossed it—implicitly criticizing the recently deposed emperor through reference to a longer period of imperial rule, that imposed by Spain—ancient Spanish laws still in force in Mexico dated from a different era, one characterized by ignorance and absolutism. They were no longer acceptable in a Mexico that was "independent, republican, and democratic," where equality was a foundational principle, among a people who enjoyed "liberties and rights that weren't even known in the time of Don Alonso the Wise."[4]

Along with representing the triumph of liberty over tyranny as well as republicanism over absolutism, the new penal code was also meant to serve as a persuasive argument for Mexico's entry into a new club, that of modern nations, each distinguished by their own modern criminal code. For commission members, Spain, Portugal, and France, among other nations, provided important points of reference and marked Mexico as a participant in a global conversation concerning the crafting of modern judicial structures. Far from a mere copy, however, Mexico's new code, although it would come to contain many of the same dispositions as those found in other modern codes, would be modified to fit Mexico's specific circumstances. While the Portuguese code mandated, for example, that if the person responsible for rapto (abduction), estupro (the initiation of sexual relations), or violación (rape) offered to marry the woman whom he had offended and she refused without a legitimate motive, no penalty would be applied. This appeared to be a particularly dangerous precept for framers of the Mexican code, one that very well might serve as a stimulus to such behavior rather than a deterrent. After all, explained Martínez de Castro, if a man motivated either by interest or passion wanted to marry a woman, all he had to do, no matter how loathsome she found him, was to remove her from parental control and initiate sexual relations. Once apprehended, if he offered to marry her, there were only two possible outcomes:

she could agree to marry him, thus achieving his original goal, or, if she refused, he would be free to go with no legal consequence for his action.[5] You will see below how the framers of the Mexican code dealt with these and other concerns in such cases.

Taking three years to complete their work, commission members delivered the new penal code to Mexican legislators for their approval in late 1871, to come into effect in 1872. Initially meant to be restricted in its jurisdiction to the Federal District and the Territory of Baja California, with national application limited to crimes against the federation, the 1871 Penal Code, as it has come to be known, was subsequently approved by many of the Mexican states with little or no modification.[6] In the state of Chihuahua, with which this book is concerned, the 1871 Penal Code was adopted, with some modifications, in 1883 and then superseded in 1905 when the state, under Interim Governor Enrique C. Creel, decreed its own penal code, known as the 1905 Penal Code of the Free and Sovereign State of Chihuahua.[7] The two codes, national and state, were similar in organization—both were divided into four parts, or books, with the first book concerned with criminal responsibility and the application of punishment, the second with civil responsibilities deriving from crimes, the third with specific crimes, and the fourth with various categories of misdemeanors. The following year, that is, in 1906, the Constitutional Congress of Chihuahua decreed its own code of criminal proceedings in which it set out, in some fourteen chapters, the general principles for the administration of justice, covering everything from the organization and responsibilities of the judicial police to the form that criminal judicial procedures were to follow to the execution of sentences.[8] At the national level (and in some states) the 1871 Penal Code remained in force until the adoption of a new penal code in 1929. Yet despite the attempt to draft a code that would fit Mexico's changed circumstances of the late 1920s, this code, the subject of immediate criticism, was replaced by yet another new penal code promulgated in 1931, which was not only more enduring but was also meant to serve as a model for all such state codes.[9]

Most relevant for the purposes of the present study, the replacement, in 1905, of the 1871 Federal District penal code with that of the state meant that the cases we are considering as a single body of documents, stretching from the 1880s to the 1920s, were actually adjudicated under two different criminal codes. However, too much should not be made of this change. The dominant assumptions and values that structure the codes as well as the definitions of the crimes with which we are concerned, particularly rapto and estupro, remained more or less the same. In both codes, for example, rapto and estupro were delineated in the third part or book, that dedicated to specific crimes. Covering a wide array of offenses grouped into a number of sections ranging from crimes against property to those, variously, against individuals, public health, public order, and internal security, the third book in both codes also contained a section entitled "Crimes against the order of families, public morality or good customs," and it is in this section where the crimes of rapto and estupro can be found, along with offenses against the civil state of persons, against decency, outrages to public morality or good customs, the corruption of minors, rape, adultery, bigamy, and the public encouragement of crime.

Although some Mexican legal scholars in the twentieth century would subsequently describe lumping together such diverse infractions as those found in "Crimes against the order of families, public morality or good customs" as lacking in the principles of sound legal methodology, for those drafting the codes the section was far from a poorly organized collection of random offenses.[10] Rather, shared assumptions concerning the nature of authority, the place of the family as an entity within liberal law, and the importance of morality in determining who qualified for protection under the law, among other things, provided for lawmakers a powerful underlying logic that gave coherence to the section. At the most fundamental level, the codes enforce a certain vision of morality, one in which moral behavior in public, defined in the sections of the code dealing with public morality, good customs, and the sanctions against the public encouragement of crime, on the one hand, and the bolstering of the legal authority of a certain kind of family, as set out in the crimes of rapto, estupro, adultery, bigamy, crimes against the civil state of persons, and the "improper" acquisition of the "rights of family," on the other, are seen as related, even complementary categories.[11] Linking the two was a metaphorical bond that seemed to make of family and society interchangeable concepts, or the first a microcosm of the second. While I discuss the type of family the code envisioned at greater length below, at this point it is sufficient to stress that, in the face of discussion about the relationship between liberalism and individualism, and in view of attention paid to the attempts to incorporate individual rights and guarantees into nineteenth-century law, the "official family"—that is, the kind recognized by drafters of these codes—must be acknowledged, alongside the "individual," as an important fictive addressee of much nineteenth-century liberal legislation.

Rapto and Estupro

Having set out the circumstances surrounding the promulgation of Mexico's penal codes, their organization into books, and some of the categorizing principles at work in the section of the codes dealing with crimes against the order of families, public morality, or good customs, we now turn to the specific acts that, according to law, constituted the crimes of rapto and estupro, around which the rest of this section revolves.

To give face and form to this discussion of the law as well as to illustrate the common legal points joining such seemingly widely varying behavior, I began this section by describing two very distinct, yet neither uncommon, scenarios of rapto or abduction taken from the judicial archives in Hidalgo del Parral, Chihuahua. Although the first, involving the Martínez sisters, seems more like an elopement and the other the sexual assault of a minor, both ended up being adjudicated under the same section of the criminal code. According to the 1871 Penal Code, rapto was deemed to have occurred when someone, against the will of a woman, seized her and carried her off by means of physical or moral violence, deception, or seduction in order to satisfy some morally vile or dishonorable desire or to get married. It was to be punished with four years in prison and a fine of from 50 to 500 pesos. In the event that the woman had not yet reached the age of sixteen, the same penalty was to apply even if the *raptor* (abductor) had not employed violence or deception but only seduction and the woman had consented to leave with him. In other words, if a woman under sixteen years of age voluntarily accompanied her abductor, the law presumed that he had employed seduction. Regardless of the woman's age, if the abductor married the offended woman, no criminal proceedings could be brought against him.[12]

The 1905 Penal Code of Chihuahua accorded with the earlier federal code in its definition of the crime of rapto as well as in its understanding of the circumstances under which the voluntary consent of the woman could (and could not) be given. There were some differences, however. Under the terms of the Chihuahua code, the penalty for abducting a woman by means of physical or moral violence, whether to satisfy one's carnal desires with her or in order to get married, was a term of two to four years in prison and fine of from 50 to 500 pesos; abducting her by the use of seduction or deception, instead of physical or moral violence, reduced the mandated prison term to one to two years (although the fine remained the same). If, at the time of his first formal declaration to judicial authorities, the abductor refused to present the abducted woman or to give notice as to where she could be found, these penalties were augmented by one month for each day he continued to decline to do so, to a maximum of ten years in prison. In the case of a violent abduction, where the abductor made carnal use of the offended woman, the law presumed that he had done so against her will provided that copulation had taken place before the woman had been returned to a safe location. In order to proceed legally against any abductor the code required that a formal complaint be initiated by an individual, either the offended woman if she were single and above the age of majority, her husband if she were married, her parents or grandparents if she were a minor and celibate, or, in the absence of such relations or criteria, her brothers, tutors, or those exercising authority over her.[13]

For those writing both codes, at the heart of the matter in cases of rapto was the removal of a woman from those legally empowered to exercise their authority over her. In the case of the Martínez sisters, for example, it was the father who was the offended party according to the law and, therefore, the one who would be required to initiate the legal process by making a complaint. Such a requirement reflected an important distinction in nineteenth-century liberal lawmaking. Liberal law, premised upon a definition of criminal acts as those that, even though they might be directed against an individual, violated the social contract, nevertheless continued to acknowledge that some acts, rapto (and estupro) among them, constituted a greater offense to an individual victim (in the first case, Sr. Martínez) than to society as a whole. For this reason, not only was it necessary to have a legally competent individual come forward with a complaint in order to begin such a legal process, as we have seen here, it was also possible to end this process at any point in the proceedings if the offended person pardoned his or her offender and desisted from the complaint.[14] As written, the law defining rapto also reveals that a fine line existed between a criminal act and a successful courtship leading to marriage; in a sense, it acknowledged that the end justified the means: if marriage followed a rapto it concluded that no crime had taken place. Although the second example described above also involved a courting relationship, it had a very different tenor and outcome; yet even here the crime is the same, as is the legally recognized victim—rather than the young woman, it was the head of the woman's household.

Men often compounded their legal troubles by following up an abduction of a woman with the commission of a second crime, that of estupro. This the 1871 Penal Code defined as copulation with a decent and chaste woman by means of seduction or deception. Those found guilty of estupro were to receive eight years in prison and a fine ranging from 100 to 1,500 pesos if the victim were under ten years of age and four years in prison and a second-class fine if she were between ten and thirteen. Of especial significance to the collection of sources used in the present book was the following article in the part of the code dealing with estupro, as it was to satisfy the terms of this clause that most of the love letters became part of the judicial record. The judicial code mandated five to eleven months of arrest and a fine of between 100 and 1,500 pesos if the following criteria of estupro were satisfied: 1) the woman was older than fourteen; 2) she had been given a written promise of marriage; and 3) the male had subsequently refused to follow through with the marriage without just cause. In this last circumstance, the law also required that the male had reached the age of majority, that is, twenty-one.[15]

In setting out the criteria for estupro, the 1905 Penal Code of Chihuahua was again broadly similar to its forerunner in the Federal District. In regard to the special circumstances surrounding the written promise of marriage, this code stipulated five to eleven months of arrest and a fine of 25 to 1,000 pesos if the woman were older than fourteen yet younger than thirty years of age and had received from the male (who had to be of the age of majority) a written promise of marriage that was subsequently reneged upon without just cause after the act of copulation or, if prior to it, then without the just cause being acknowledged by him.[16] Legal commentators would subsequently find the privileging of a written promise over that offered verbally to have little legal merit, despite the fortuitous consequence of the preservation of love letters in the legal record. Significantly, all references to the need for a written promise of marriage to be presented as evidence in cases of estupro were eliminated when the penal code was rewritten in 1929 and 1931.[17]

Separate from estupro was the crime of violación (rape), which both penal codes defined as having taken place when someone used physical or moral violence to copulate with a person, regardless of their sex, against their will. While the code for the Federal District mandated six years in prison and a second-class fine if the person raped were over fourteen years of age, and ten years if they were thirteen or younger, the Chihuahuan code punished those found guilty of this crime with five years in prison if the offended person were older than fourteen, seven years if they were younger than fourteen but older than ten, and nine years in prison if the person were younger than ten years of age.[18]

Whereas with rapto the criminal code concerned itself with the removal of a woman from the authority of her parents or guardians, in cases of estupro its preoccupation was the initiation of sexual relations, either with a woman younger than fourteen years of age or as part of a set of special circumstances associated with courtship if the woman were fourteen or older. Dominant assumptions concerning gender and morality underpinning the penal code can be seen clearly in the legal definition of estupro. The stipulation that the woman be "decent and chaste" as a necessary precondition for the very definition of the male's behavior as a criminal act seemed to echo colonial legislation that likewise distinguished between, and mandated different treatment for, women on the basis of their perceived moral standing. Under colonial law, whereas "decent women," that is, those described as virgins, nuns, or proper and modest (*honesta*) wives and widows, could seek legal remedy against men for certain crimes, "low" (*vil*) women lost the right to take legal action.[19] Such similarities have led some commentators to regard these provisions of the 1871 Penal Code (and the subsequent 1905 code in Chihuahua) as much closer to colonial legal thinking and much less "modern" than its framers may have liked to admit. Such provisions, however, rather than serving as a measure of the code's supposed lack of modernity instead offer an excellent illustration of how so-called modern criminal codes are shot through with deeply held notions about gender and gender roles. For those drafting the penal code, to be modern was to subscribe to unquestioned assumptions about the nature of both men and women and to write them into the law.

In addition to distinguishing between deserving and undeserving women as subjects of the law, the penal codes defined the circumstances under which women's consent to the initiation of sexual relations could not be given. In separating "acceptable" sexual relations from those they considered to be unacceptable, those writing the code set boundaries around sexuality that were designed to enforce order and authority in society's basic institution, the official family. Transgressing such boundaries was, in many ways, envisioned almost as a subversive act, undermining authority both within the family and in society more generally. Those writing the penal codes were invested in providing a legal or juridical basis for the exercise of authority, both within the family and without, while maintaining the family as a model for authority relations more generally. Heads of official families, for example, those characterized by civil marriage and not informal union, could expect judicial and political officials to uphold "order"; husbands could petition officials to take action and return runaway wives to the domestic home. Rapto and estupro were both about enforcing paternal control over the marriage choice and, at least in part, the labor of children. In the event of adultery, even Martínez de Castro could not deny that, morally speaking, husbands and wives who committed adultery had engaged in the same offense. However, while a husband was punished only if he committed adultery with scandal or within the conjugal home, a wife was always subject to the full force of the law. Each merited different treatment, de Castro rationalized, because the consequences of adultery weighed differently according to gender: while the husband remained slandered by the infidelity of the wife, her reputation was not tarnished by the faults of her husband. Further, de Castro continued, the adulterous woman defrauded legitimate children of their inheritance by introducing extraneous heirs into the family, something that did not occur when male adultery produced children outside the marriage.[20] De Castro's reasoning lends additional support, were it needed, to Elisa Speckman Guerra's conclusions concerning how ideals of masculine honor, especially those premised upon the notion that any stain to feminine honor reflected on that of the men of the family, continued to inform nineteenth-century liberal law.[21]

Moving from the specific crimes of rapto and estupro to a discussion of the gendered assumptions underpinning liberal law in general serves as an important reminder that the drafting of criminal statutes about crimes against the order of families, public morality, and good customs formed but one aspect of broader changes taking place in the legal landscape of Mexico, as well as in other areas in Latin America, over the course of the nineteenth century. In her study of divorce, relationships, domestic violence, and the changing discourses that men and women in Mexico City mobilized to assert claims and construct themselves and others before the court during that century, Ana Lidia García Peña explores how liberal reforms designed to promote such values as secularization and individualism shaped legal understandings of the family and power within it. Despite claims to universality, she finds, the liberal rhetoric of greater liberty for the individual, when translated into legal codes, actually resulted in a strengthening of the system of patriarchal domination that had been initiated by the Bourbons in the eighteenth century. As she concludes, the process of becoming an "individual" as recognized by the law was highly gendered, in that husbands enjoyed an expansive judicial persona while wives were forced to subsist on the thin rations afforded by protective legislation, justified by their supposed debility and the fear, shared by liberals as well as others before them, of disrupting the family.[22] Changes set out in the 1871 Penal Code, including the increasingly contractual nature of social relations, highlight not only liberal attempts to "modernize patriarchy," as Ana María Alonso and others have referred to the process of substituting democratic, rational forms of exercising authority for violence, but also the need to align the legitimate exercise of authority in the public sphere with that in the domestic. As Alonso notes, the legal contract was seen as the epitome of reason, modernity, and free will, a concept to which I will return.[23]

Forming Couples

The liberal desire to incorporate free will into legal codes serves as a reminder that important shifts have taken place over time in the legal framework of marriage, often revolving around the role of freedom of choice within it. Under the Bourbons, a major change in the state's role in the ability to choose a marriage partner was codified with the proclamation of the royal *pragmática* on marriage in 1776. At that time, parental consent to marriage was made a formal requirement for those younger than twenty-five years of age, initially under threat of disinheritance. Proclaimed partly to reduce the authority of the ecclesiastical courts, partly to prevent the mixing of social and racial groups, and partly in response to the emergence of a society increasingly shaped by divisions based on wealth, the pragmática overturned centuries of marital practice based on freedom of choice in selecting a marriage partner. Although mixed racial groups were initially excluded from the requirement of parental consent when the pragmática was extended to the colonies in 1778, a subsequent edict, that of 1803, made it mandatory for all.[24] The 1803 edict also weakened the bargaining position of women in the nuptial market by requiring that only written, notarized promises of marriage would henceforth be legally binding.[25]

The requirement of parental consent for marriage and the stipulation that only written promises of marriage were to be binding became part of the civil codes of nineteenth-century Mexico. Whereas the Law of Civil Matrimony of 1859 reduced the age of majority to twenty-one for males and twenty for females, subsequent civil codes, those of 1870 and 1884, set it at twenty-one for both sexes.[26] Those under this age needed parental permission in order to contract marriage. In the absence of parents, the civil codes established a hierarchy of those capable of giving consent for those under the age of twenty-one to marry, beginning with the father and then moving to, in order, the mother, the paternal grandfather, the maternal grandfather, the paternal grandmother, the maternal grandmother, guardians, and the judge of the first instance.[27]

Legal descriptions of rapto and estupro in the two criminal codes we have been discussing, then, have much to do with marriage, in particular, with upholding its contractual nature and with the issue of consent, especially who had the ability to grant it. In fact, the two went together. As you have already seen in the episode concerning the Martínez sisters, the father was the victim of the crime as his daughters were under the age of majority and therefore in need of his permission in order to marry. Their status as minors meant that he was the one empowered by law to decide whether or not a marriage could take place. Lacking the appropriate consent left rapto as an option for women wishing to force the parental hand, as with these sisters, but also for men who might view it as a means of presenting the reluctant parents or guardians of their novias with a fait accompli, to which they would have no choice but to acquiesce. In scenarios like these, rapto was a form of elopement that often made of parents and guardians the biggest supporters of a speedy wedding. As you will see shortly, however, it was not always this simple, neither for parents nor for their daughters or the male suitors.

With regard to estupro, the contractual relationship that is being enforced in the two penal codes we have been discussing revolves around an exchange recognized by the law: in return for a promise of future marriage from the man, the woman would agree to the beginning of sexual relations. For this reason, the codes stipulated that the man had to be of the age of majority, that is, legally able to enter into a contract. In this regard, estupro as defined in liberal-era penal codes seemed to reprise colonial-era marriage practices, known as *esponsales*, whereby the promise of a future marriage and the initiation of sexual relations signified that a marriage had taken place, even in the absence of a formal ceremony.[28] Such an understanding of marriage necessitates viewing it not as necessarily a single fixed event taking place on a specific date but rather as a process extended over time. Certainly, there are indications in the testimony of some of those brought before judicial officials that this understanding of marriage continued to inform behavior in early twentieth-century Chihuahua. One man's insistence, for example, that another man had accompanied him in order to serve as his witness when he had abducted and initiated sexual relations with his bride (or intended, depending on one's perspective) is telling, hinting, as it does, at the many layers of publicness within which these acts took on meaning. Such behavior made a strong statement about their relationship as well as about the reputation of the woman within the larger community through a witness who stood for it while, at the same time, fulfilling the criterion of public knowledge that had been necessary for a promise of future marriage to be valid during the colonial period.[29] Finally, while it is true that the special clause of the legal description of estupro dealing with a written promise of marriage seems to acknowledge the right of a woman older than fourteen to consent to sexual relations with a man over the age of majority, men in such cases would often find themselves charged with both rapto and estupro simultaneously. In this way, the legal rights of the parents or guardians to have the final authority over their underage daughter, no matter how much a matter of form over content (as I have implied in the brief discussion of elopement), would be maintained.

Before turning to these intergenerational and gendered dynamics, however, a few additional observations are required on the subject of forming couples in order to establish the parameters within which courtship took place as well as to suggest some of the alternatives to civil marriage and the formation of the official family. In utilizing the concept of "marriageways" rather than that of marriage in his study of forming couples in Mexico, Robert McCaa means to recognize the multiple forms of union that took place in that country through the colonial period up to approximately 1900 while at the same time stressing "process over event, social interaction over ceremony, behavior over law."[30] Despite finding marriageways in the first century of independence, in general, more resistant to the historian's gaze than those of the previous century, McCaa nevertheless offers a number of conclusions that provide a context within which to situate marriage and the crimes of rapto and estupro in regard to it. Significantly, a substantial decline in the frequency of all types of stable unions characterized Mexico during the nineteenth century, leading to marriage rates in various states for women over fifteen years of age in the 1890s to range from 40 percent to 75 percent, with no state reaching as high as 80 percent. In Hidalgo del Parral (the site of the present study) in particular, the proportion of adult women aged sixteen to fifty identified as single rose from 35 percent to 49 percent between 1770 and 1930, rising to as high as 58 percent if women in consensual unions are counted as single.[31]

Women's relatively weakened position in nuptial bargaining and low rates of formal marriage, in which more than half of all women of marriageable age may have remained either single or in consensual unions, both underscore the difficult circumstances within which women made choices as well as help explain the endurance or even resurgence, in Parral, of *amasiato*, as long-term consensual unions there were known. Such unions, struck in conditions of unequal access to economic resources and opportunities, were based on an arrangement that both sides explicitly acknowledged: the woman would live with the man and provide domestic duties in exchange for her daily bread, known as the diario, earned by means of the male's paycheck. To insist on formal marriage by initiating a complaint of rapto, estupro, or both under circumstances in which most women may not have formally married must have represented something of a leap of faith or the triumph of hope over realism or, perhaps, have been a prerogative restricted to those with claims to honor and status or, alternatively, may not have been about marriage at all but rather an attempt to save face on the part of the head of the household or to enforce parental authority over children who had yet to reach the age of majority. It is necessary to remain open to all of these possible explanations.

While the hardships imposed by economic circumstance could be a powerful, although not the only, motivation to the forming of consensual unions, a woman's assent could also be compelled through violence. Returning, finally, to the example presented above of the young woman who left her parental home with her suitor only to be accosted by him at knifepoint, we are offered a glimpse at the ways in which violence could be used to circumscribe women's options. Although this case didn't lead to marriage, others involving what appears to be compulsion did. At times, men initiated sexual relations without the consent of the woman they were courting. While at the river getting some water, for example, another woman was attacked by her *novio* of three years, wrapped in a blanket, thrown to the ground, and sexually assaulted. He then told her not to say anything, as he planned to marry her, which he eventually did.[32] In this case, sexual assault seemed to serve as a brutally clumsy way of proposing marriage. In another instance, a woman who had been in a courting relationship for six months was asked by her suitor to come away with him. Along with offering her a good life and marriage, he threatened her with force if she did not voluntarily accede to his desires, convincing her, in this way, to leave with him.[33] These and other cases reveal that courtship could swing back and forth between tender promises and episodes of violence or the threat of it. Sexual relations could be initiated by assault, continue voluntarily, and eventually lead to marriage. Just as elopement might be orchestrated by women to move reluctant parents to change their minds, sexual assault could serve as a male strategy to force not only parents but also women themselves to accept marriage as, perhaps, the only remaining option. As will become apparent below, once involved in a publicly known courting relationship involving sexual relations, a woman would have been in an even weaker bargaining position in the nuptial market should she opt against marriage in the present instance.

Yet violence and economic necessity do not exhaust the possible explanations for why women chose unions, either formal or consensual. When a fifteen-year-old woman left her father's home to be with a mine laborer, she did not cite economic hardship or poor treatment from her family as her reasons for leaving. Knowing full well that her novio had already been legally married and, thus, could not marry her, she agreed to go with him as long as he had no plans to go back to his (legally recognized) wife. For her, it was enough they would live together "as if they were married."[34] Some evidence also exists that women could seek independence and satisfaction outside the bounds of legally sanctioned standards of sexual behavior. In another rapto case, a sixteen-year-old woman, in a short statement in which she denied for herself the position taken by almost every other woman in such cases located in the judicial record, turned down her opportunity for matrimony while at the same time providing the excuse that absolved her abductor. Certainly, she admitted, she had been promised marriage in exchange for the initiation of sexual relations. While agreeing to such relations, however, she rejected the marriage proposal, explaining that she had already had sexual relations with another man whose last name she did not know.[35] Admitting this would have weakened her legal case by furnishing for her abductor the "just cause" required to avoid marriage under the estupro clause of the penal code (had her abductor been charged with it), that is, her previous loss of virginity; nevertheless, by this means, she accomplished her end, that of avoiding marriage.

Criminal Proceedings

Up until this point, this section has examined the ways in which the penal codes understood and attempted to enforce the boundary between acceptable and unacceptable sexuality and family formation in Chihuahua. At work in the categorization of behavior as criminal acts were assumptions about authority, especially but not limited to that of parents and guardians over children; consent, specifically the circumstances under which it could and could not be given and by whom; and power, its nature, and its exercise. Although not necessarily contradicted by judicial officials at the local level, the assumptions of those crafting penal codes along with the results they presumed would follow from their implementation were not necessarily consonant with those that grew out of the day-to-day operation of the judicial system. While the writers of the penal codes may have assumed that they were bolstering the order of families, public morality, and good customs, they were actually bolstering the authority of those with greater access to and facility with the written word. Providing written proof of a marriage promise or something as seemingly simple as legal proof of age or of parenthood proved beyond the resources or abilities of many appearing before the court. My interest in the rest of this section, however, is not solely to contrast the letter of the law with its practice. Rather, it is to explore how both influenced people's interactions with the legal system, as well as the ways people's stories became shaped into texts.

Such a shift in focus requires a commensurate shift in perspective, one not so enamored with either the letter of the law or the intentions of its drafters. While the legal system could clearly, through various means and with varying degrees of effectiveness, act to prescribe, prohibit, or punish various behaviors, judicial norms were not always the ones by which those who found themselves implicated in it understood, explained, or justified their actions. For some of those making statements to judicial authorities, on the one hand, a certain discordant quality marks their narratives, as if they have strayed into some foreign territory where the arrangements and bargains that make perfect sense to them are no longer intelligible. Here judicial records afford us a glimpse at informal arrangements, perhaps based on verbal promises or those that, without being articulated, were understood by all, as well as the constraints and possibilities, apart from the law, that structured the choices and inclinations of a great many. On the other hand, the law, especially the rules in the penal code pertaining to promises, sex, and marriage, seemed very familiar to many others, like those women who knew what constituted binding promises or those men who knew the kind of arguments that might invalidate them. For as many who saw the legal system as a means to seek redress, a similar number must have seen it as an inconvenience, or worse, an intrusion in situations that might better be resolved elsewhere, away from officials, meddling parents, and the scrutiny implied by appearing in a court of law. Their stories are shaped by all these tensions, ambiguities, and misunderstandings.

Language itself, so laden with accreted meaning even though lodged in the political present, seems to conspire against both understanding and explanation. As you may have noted, in the last few paragraphs I have used heavily freighted language, that of "sexual assault," as a means of shaping my own explanation of, and, perhaps, your own understanding of, the relationship between courtship and violence. It seemed an appropriate reading to me in these particular cases. However, a number of years ago, when giving a talk in Austin, Texas, on rapto and estupro in cases drawn from these same judicial archives, a woman in the audience objected when I used this language. Her grandmother had been *raptada*, abducted, she explained, and, rather than as an assault, had experienced the event as highly romantic. While her grandmother may have been one of those women who arranged their own abduction and willingly left to begin married life with her novio (like the extremely gracious Martínez sisters, who have put up with being raptada for the purposes of this section for almost as long as they did to get married), it is also possible that their subsequent marriage and life together resulted in a retrospective reshaping of the story into one that could be told to one's family. This insight helped me realize that perhaps only certain kinds of stories, likewise, could be told to judicial officials, stories in which women may have felt constrained by dominant gender conventions to portray themselves in certain ways, as acted upon rather than as actors, as victims rather than accomplices, as morally fit in order to qualify for legal protection. In a statement to judicial officials, for example, one woman justified her fascination with her novio's love letters and her willingness to leave her home to be with him by pointing to the "natural weakness of her sex" as well as to her young age.[36] It may be that when thinking about the testimony in these cases we should view women (and men) as agents of narratives that, in many instances, are designed to engage with dominant gender conventions so as to sound convincing to judicial authorities. In the rhetorical strategies that women employed and in the ways they did, and did not, plot themselves into their narratives or certain parts of them, at any rate (especially the experience of estupro), women can be seen deploying, reinforcing, and, sometimes, testing and finding wanting dominant conceptions of femininity.

With these insights in mind, the new, modern criminal code in force as of 1872, and the order and morals of families at stake, let us now follow judicial officials in Hidalgo District as they set to work adjudicating complaints that came before them. I base my conclusions on transcripts of the legal proceedings found in 86 cases of rapto and estupro; 11 cases of rape (violación); and a handful of cases involving other crimes, including 3 of murder-suicide and 1 of assault, all located in the Archivo Judicial de Hidalgo del Parral and having occurred between the years of 1872 and 1929.[37] The statements, investigations, decisions, and material collected in all these cases offer insights into courtship, understandings of gender, generational struggles over marriage, consensual unions, the conceptualization of authority, and the workings of the judicial system, among other things. A smaller subset of this total number of cases includes love letters. A related task of this section, then, is to ascertain the ways, if any, in which the groups and individuals, ways of understanding, and narrative strategies in the particular group of cases where letters have been submitted as evidence differ from those drawn from the broader body of evidence. I must, however, begin this foray into judicial sources with a warning: recently rescued from deteriorating conditions in a municipal jail, the judicial archive is in both poor condition and incomplete. Individual cases do not contain decisions and entire cases are no doubt missing. As a result, I have decided against providing readers with a more detailed statistical treatment of this evidence, and against drawing conclusions concerning the frequency of such practices or the extent to which they changed over time based on such numbers alone. I offer no apologies for working with incomplete information, nor do I try to hide this fact. My goal is to offer a sense of the partiality of the judicial system (in all senses of the term), of the broader contexts and dynamics within which the formation of couples took place, and of the narratives that children and parents, men and women, and others deployed to portray themselves, others, and these events. It is only within these contexts that the use and significance of love letters can begin to be apprehended.

Moreover, not everyone agreed that recourse to the judicial system provided the best solution to what they must have perceived as the "problem" of what to do with an unwed, pregnant, underage daughter. A rifle or friends in high places (or both) might be more than sufficient to enable the father or head of the woman's household to persuade a reluctant suitor, or an innocent bystander, to agree to a hasty wedding. A plea written by a sharecropper from a small ranch somewhere near the town of Zaragoza to the Hidalgo District political boss in Parral in 1907 shows what could transpire. After his uncle's daughter had become pregnant, the sharecropper explained, and the person responsible was unable to "cover her honor," that is, to marry her, he, the sharecropper, had been held in custody, incommunicado, without any formal denunciation or initiation of judicial proceedings of any kind. His uncle's plan, he was convinced, was to make him appear "before society" as the one responsible for the family's predicament. Threatened with "terrible punishment" and "outrageous penalties" that weighed heavily upon him, he had finally broken down and consented to marry his cousin. Before he could change his mind—in fact, at that very moment—he was released from captivity just in time to meet father and daughter, or, if you prefer, uncle and cousin, who had arrived at the municipal presidency to announce the upcoming wedding to the entire society. No trace of this case exists in the judicial archives, very likely because no formal legal process was ever initiated; the details are only known to us through the sharecropper's petition, which became part of a different archive, that of the administrative record of the district-level political authority, the jefe político.[38]

Yet, the episode is telling, and for a number of reasons. Not only does it set out the sharecropper's understanding of the exchange at work in the informal arrangements at the level of the couple that were meant to result in marriage—that is, the initiation of sexual relations in return for "covering her honor" through marriage at a later date—as well as the importance of the public arbitration of knowledge, of the woman's pregnancy, responsibility for it, and the father's ability to preserve family honor through ensuring marriage; the extralegal solution also provides a concrete example of how the judicial system might be just one among a number of options for heads of families. This was especially so if, as in the present case, a close relationship existed between local political and judicial authorities, on the one hand, and the offended head of the woman's household, on the other, or, perhaps, if the bonds imposed by family could be cinched just tightly enough to persuade someone to preserve the respectability of the overall family by filling in for the missing novio of a wayward cousin. Just as formal legal processes might not be necessary to resolve such situations for the locally powerful, complaints about their abuse of authority might be most palpably expressed in an idiom drawn from and shared with the language of abduction and sexual abuse, a point to which I will return when taking up a discussion of authority.

For those without such connections or, perhaps, without the ability to impose their will through force or by other means, appearing before judicial officials to present a formal complaint was the first step needed to initiate criminal proceedings of rapto and estupro. As explained earlier in the section when discussing the assumptions of those framing the penal codes, in crimes that constituted a greater offense to an individual than to society as a whole, as did these, no criminal investigation could take place without an individual identifying himself or herself to judicial officials as the victim. After the complaint had been received and recorded, the next step was for judicial officials to seize both the young woman and the man accused of rapto, estupro, or violación, depositing the woman in a house of respect (*casa de respeto*), that is, a household in the community known for its high moral standards where her safety and honor could be protected (although, as you have already seen, even these walls might not be sufficient to staunch the tide of desire) or, at times, back with her family, and taking the male into custody. Each was then separately questioned by judicial authorities in hopes of getting at the facts relevant to the case, with their answers, as well as pertinent personal information—age, marital status, occupation, and residency—taken down in writing by a scribe or clerk (after being transposed into the third-person format common to judicial proceedings) to form part of the written record of the case. Should any accomplices have been involved or witnesses required, they were also questioned and their answers recorded in the same manner. Confronted with contradictory statements, as they were at times, judicial officials could then choose to carry out a process known as *careo*. Here, the young woman and the accused man faced each other directly in an attempt to sort out areas of discrepancy in their testimony. These statements were also transcribed and formed part of the judicial proceedings.

Essential to the successful prosecution of the legal case was the next step—providing legally recognized proof of the status, relationships, and ages of those involved in the proceeding. The person initiating the complaint, for example, needed to prove their civil status as the parent or guardian of the young woman as well as demonstrate that she had yet to reach the age of majority, a prerequisite for protection under the law in many of these crimes. This was usually accomplished by means of a birth certificate, a document that could also be used by judges to determine the severity of the penalty to be imposed on the man should he be found guilty, as penalties, as you have also seen, were of greater or lesser weight depending on the age of the woman. This was much more difficult to accomplish than it may sound to us, accustomed, as we may now be, to requesting such information from distant governmental departments. Many of those who found themselves in Parral, Chihuahua, around the end of the nineteenth century or during the early years of the twentieth, however, were not *originarios*; that is, they had not been born there. Because they comprised a growing mobile and floating population that rode the expanding rail lines in search of wage labor, perhaps combining stints of such labor with access to a small piece of land, theirs was a temporary, transient presence in many cases. Furnishing such documentation might be accomplished only by extensive time away from work, perhaps necessitating a return to Zacatecas or some other part of the republic, jeopardizing income and job. As a result, as you will see, many cases collapsed on just such a legal technicality.[39]

In cases of estupro and violación, judicial authorities also required medical experts to question and examine the woman and then submit a medical report documenting whether or not physical evidence confirmed that a crime had been committed. The testimony of doctors appears as part of the judicial record in many such cases beginning in the 1880s. At a time when the regular medical inspection of women by doctors appointed by governmental authorities was associated with the regulation of prostitution, such an exam was seen not only as intrusive but also as something akin to guilt by association. At least a few parents openly described the exam as an affront to their honor as well as that of their daughter, while one or two refused to allow it to take place. The court's interest was in documenting through medical science physical evidence of recent sexual activity on the part of the woman, assuming that the truth of her claims would be registered on her body and providing medical backing that the terms of the contract between the couple had been fulfilled, that sexual relations had followed the offer of a written promise of marriage.

Proving the existence of such a contract or promise of marriage was accomplished in court through the submission of love letters at this point in the proceedings.

At any time in the proceedings, the person who had initiated the process by making a formal complaint could bring the entire proceeding to a close by appearing before judicial authorities and formally desisting from the complaint. Like the statement initiating the criminal case, the terminating statement was copied into the judicial record, usually as the last entry in the file. Regardless of what had transpired, no criminal action could be taken against a man once the complainant desisted. As the court record often ends at this point, it is difficult to know the outcome of many of the cases if some indication of what had transpired or was to transpire, perhaps marriage, for example, was not stated in this final document. Those cases in which the complainant did not formally desist continued until a judgment was rendered.

For those who found themselves before such officials, however, the story was somewhat different. Many were interested in avoiding marriage, jail time, or both. Others simply wanted to get married or begin adult life in a consensual union with their chosen partner. Some were preoccupied with questions of honor, either their own or that of their families. All told stories that, they hoped, would get them what they wanted. At times, these stories had little to do with the legal criteria that judicial officials relied on to evaluate their acts. I always keep in mind the response that one young man gave to judicial authorities when questioned as to why he thought he had found himself enmeshed in a criminal proceeding for estupro. He stated he didn't know. Judicial authorities pressed further: "You don't know that you are accused of committing estupro?" they asked. "No," replied the young man, "I didn't know what estupro meant as I'd never heard the word before."[40] Others knew full well what was required by the judicial system to get them what they wanted, having taken care of either securing and placing in safekeeping a written promise of marriage before leaving home or writing one out to satisfy the terms of the legal exchange with a young woman. Those involved in these particular cases manifested a profound awareness of and engagement with the terms of the law as expressed in formal legal codes.

My point here is not that officially recognized norms of behavior as spelled out in the criminal justice system were unevenly spread across Chihuahua society but rather that understandings different from those institutionalized in penal codes concerning such things as courtship, sexuality, honor, and family formation can be drawn out of the testimony found in the judicial archive. Readers are confronted, then, as they turn to these documents to try to comprehend the meaning of values and behaviors, not only with assumptions and practices that may be at odds with those underlying the judicial system but also with scripts or stories that men and women used to shape their behavior and portray themselves in compelling ways. To refer to the statements of those who found themselves before judicial authorities as scripts or stories is not meant to be derogatory, nor to contrast stories with truth, fiction with fact. It is merely to acknowledge that turning acts into texts is a process of meaning-making and that this process is not innocent of power or interest. Those participating in the judicial process—judges, fathers, and mothers with grievously offended senses of honor; women who ran off with their novios; men who changed their mind, along with many others—portrayed themselves and their behavior in ways that they felt would be most to their advantage within the boundaries not only of their own understandings and imaginations but also of what they understood to be appropriate to their age, gender, and place within the community. It is to their stories that I now turn.

The Complaint

Out of the total number of cases of rapto and estupro in Hidalgo District in which a complainant—that is, someone in a position of authority over the young woman who had been abducted—can be identified, some seventy in all, half were initiated by women and half by men.[41] Of these thirty-five women complainants, fourteen described themselves as widows and a further five as single mothers. More than a quarter of all complainants, then, nineteen out of seventy) were women who headed their own household. Six additional women identified themselves before judicial officials as mothers, giving no further information about the presence of males within their households, making it possible that more than one-third of all complaints (twenty-five of seventy) were initiated by women heading their own households. One additional woman initiating a complaint stated specifically that she was acting in the place of her absent husband; two additional mothers initiating complaints explained that they were living with males in consensual unions, which they referred to as amasiato. Of the remaining seven cases in which women initiated judicial proceedings, four women had raised the young woman who had been abducted in the absence of birth-parents (two were elder sisters, one a grandmother, and one an aunt) and three women were commencing judicial proceedings on their own behalf (a fifty-year-old, a twenty-year-old, and a fifteen-year-old). As they subsequently found out, those under the age of majority acting on their own were not legally empowered with the right to do so, and neither were those over the age of thirty.

Of the thirty-five proceedings initiated by male complainants, all but four described themselves as the father of the young woman in question. Out of the four who were not, two were surrogate fathers who had raised the women involved in the cases since they were small; one complaint was initiated by an older brother (in the absence of the father), and another by a husband whose wife had left him for someone else. Nine of the fathers stated their civil status as married, five described themselves as widowers, and three stated at some point in the testimony that they were in relationships of amasiato. Thirteen men felt it sufficient to describe themselves as the father of the young woman with no further explanation as to the composition of their household. One complaint initiated by a father might better be described as a joint complaint: in this instance of parents presenting a united front, the mother also provided a statement of complaint to judicial officials immediately following that of the young woman's father.

Among the points that can be made about those initiating complaints, perhaps the most noteworthy is the large number of cases initiated by women who headed their own households and the near-complete absence of currently married women. That a large number of complaints were initiated by women who headed households, especially widows, suggests that the criminal justice system was seen as an option for upholding the position and honor of those heads of families who may not have been as able to take matters into their own hands, while the absence of married women also seems to indicate that it was expected that husbands, should they be present, would serve as the interlocutors for the family with the judicial authorities. To describe the judicial system as the recourse only for those who could not act on their own behalf, however, would be to go too far. After all, fully half of all cases were initiated by men, who must also have regarded the judicial system as a suitable venue for pursuing their aims, whether it be repairing their offended honor or punishing the man responsible for its loss. Hidalgo District, then, seems to present a contrast to Rio de Janeiro, Brazil, at this same period in time. There, for example, the father of the young woman was absent from the household in 73 percent of the cases of rapto and estupro that were initiated.[42]

A significant number of the men in Hidalgo District, often those who were single, widowers, or working, did, however, feel compelled to explain to authorities why they could not be present in their households at all times to monitor the behavior of their children. Six explained that they were working in various capacities, either in the mines or as watchmen, or that they had had to go out for various reasons. Offering such an explanation enabled them to indicate that they shared with judicial officials an understanding of how authority was supposed to be exercised—in short, that they were to rule within the household—while at the same time providing an explanation for their failure to do so in this particular instance. Other men may have felt that no such acknowledgment of how authority was supposed to work was needed, that doing so would be superfluous given that the very term "father" entailed commonsense assumptions about exercising authority in the household. Parental prerogatives, however, also came with obligations and responsibilities. "Father," in fact, as we will see shortly, could be a contested term, implying more than the right to exercise power and authority in the household but also the obligation to do so in certain ways. As fathers themselves realized, their executions of these duties could be evaluated and found wanting, by children and, they feared, by judicial authorities as well.

Another characteristic of interest to judicial officials was the occupation of those initiating complaints. These ranged from the humblest single mother who depended on public charity to survive to a well-off large-scale male merchant (comerciante). The single largest occupational category was that of agricultural worker, with six men described as agricultural laborers (labradores), another two as hacienda workers, and six more living in rural, predominantly agricultural communities. A further complainant identified himself as a farmer (*agricultor*), meaning that fifteen of the thirty-five men initiating complaints were most likely agricultural workers of some sort. Given that Hidalgo District was a boom-and-bust lead-silver mining zone with a number of towns dedicated principally to mining, those working in the mines are also well represented among complainants. Four men were identified in legal records as mine workers (*operarios*) and another four as miners (*mineros*), a category usually implying more skill and responsibility that could include organizing and supervising the work of operarios and *peones* (unskilled laborers). Another five of the men initiating complaints were from communities dedicated almost solely to mining, for a total of thirteen of the thirty-five. Too much should not be made of these occupational distinctions, however, as a great deal of movement existed between the agricultural and mining sectors. Labradores and those with access to small pieces of land might engage in mine work during slow periods in the agricultural cycle. A number of artisans also featured among the complainants, including a carpenter, a barber, and two others identified in the legal records as "dressed as if they were from the middle class."[43] Two men stressed their poverty, stating that they lacked the resources required to pursue the judicial inquiry, which usually involved paying a small fee for stamps to be affixed to the legal documents.

The occupation of the woman initiating a complaint was not information that judicial officials considered relevant or pertinent. Although statements found at various points in these cases reveal that women made ends meet by doing such things as selling meals in the street, performing domestic chores for other households, or simply having to "work," with no further information offered, judicial authorities limited themselves to inscribing the woman initiating a complaint into the documents according to her civil status (single, married, widowed), age, and place of residence or origin. Those rare occasions when the activities of women, both those initiating complaints as well as those on whose behalf the complaint had been made, are indicated, it is usually to describe them as concerned with household chores (*quehaceres domésticos*; *labores domésticas*; *ayudante de cocina*), performing work "appropriate to their sex," or without profession or occupation because of their sex (*sin profesión por razon de su sexo*). Of the thirty-five women initiating complaints, five stressed their state of impoverishment to judicial authorities, as a statement of fact or as a reason for being unable to pursue the judicial process, or, possibly, in hopes of receiving a more favorable hearing. One had witnesses testify as to her inability to afford the fifty centavo stamp—not an inconsiderable amount given that the daily wage of unskilled male mine workers might have been one and a half pesos—required as part of the costs of the judicial proceeding.

For those initiating criminal proceedings of rapto and estupro, both men and women, the formal act of stating their complaint afforded them the opportunity to frame events according to their own point of view. This was in stark contrast to subsequent stages in the criminal proceeding, where those appearing before judicial authorities had no chance to set the agenda or the terms of the discussion. Men accused of crimes against the order of families, the underage women involved, and any witnesses, should they be required, could only respond to questions posed by judicial authorities, their answers rendered into the third person and then recorded in writing by court clerks or scribes. As the true "victims" of these crimes, the mothers, fathers, and other heads of household initiating complaints enjoyed the privilege of expressing themselves in the first person, a tense that also represented an acknowledgment, on the part of judicial authorities, of their status as agents acting on their own behalf rather than as subjects being acted upon by the criminal justice system.

This is not to suggest that those involved in the judicial process had no role in shaping either the form or content of the formal complaint. The inclusion of references to specific sections of the penal code as well as the apparent care often taken to ensure that all aspects relevant to satisfying the criteria of rapto and estupro as legally defined betray the judicial presence. So does the very language being used, echoing, as it does, that found in the penal codes. Yet, the outrage, fears, and understandings also expressed in these formal complaints often had little to do with legalities and much to do with feelings as well as with the public presentation of self. When judicial officials rewrote these formal complaints, as they occasionally did, or when they asked those initiating proceedings for further statements—transposing both kinds of text, once again, into the third-person official language of the court—such statements were often omitted, perhaps because they were regarded as irrelevant to the legal task at hand. It is to this excess that I now briefly turn.

Although sentiments could vary according to the specific circumstances of each case, complainants, a great majority of them the parents of the underage women, sought to portray themselves to judicial officials as responsible parents or guardians, if within the confines of their economic and cultural resources. While a few (eight) relied on the legal rights accruing to them by virtue of their status as the "legitimate" or even the "natural" mother or father of a daughter who had yet to reach the age of majority, and even fewer claimed their right to exercise *patria potestad* by virtue of their parental status (five), many more took great care to demonstrate that their parental obligations, rather than just following from a legally recognized relationship, had been met in practice. Even when daughters disappeared from homes to which their parents had loaned them—whether to provide labor for and live with another family, to help out that family at a time of need, in exchange for instruction in some skill, or as part of what seem like webs of relationships characterized by client-patron ties—parents, nevertheless, stressed their due diligence. One complainant explained that he had been moved by humanitarian considerations as well as by the respectability, gentlemanly qualities, and religiosity of the person requesting such help when he had given permission for his daughter to live and work in the household of another family in order to help take care of the husband's sick wife.[44] In two separate cases, mothers who had given permission for their daughters to be in the homes of others, one to do some sewing and the other to keep a man's wife company, stressed not only that the gentlemanly qualities that had persuaded them to allow their daughters to be there in the first place had been falsely represented but also that their own trust had been betrayed.[45]

When daughters disappeared from the parental home, fathers often felt compelled to explain why they had been unable to control what had happened there, that is, why they had been unable to exercise their authority there. Citing duties that had taken them from the home so that they might fulfill their other family obligations, especially those of work, going to the market for provisions, changing residencies, and attending union meetings, fathers described events in such a way as to remove any suggestion of their own negligence or inattentiveness in what had transpired. Having discovered their daughters missing, fathers then stressed the rapidity of their response: "Immediately I proceeded to look for her"; "As soon as I noticed the crime that had been committed in my home . . . I asked the jefe político of the district for the aid of the police in order to obtain the apprehension of those responsible"; and "My children and I went out and looked for her."[46] Appearing in order to initiate a complaint before judicial officials, another father explained that that he hadn't brought his daughter's birth certificate because "of the pressure of time, as losing a moment of it will make my just and legitimate investigations fruitless and enervate the actions of justice."[47] The sense of urgency on the part of parents searching for missing teenage daughters is certainly understandable and, in many cases, no doubt heartfelt. However, as you will see in the next part of this section, children sometimes told very different stories about the treatment they received at home and the degree to which fathers and mothers had fulfilled their parental obligations and responsibilities, as they defined them.

Parents also took great pains to justify their own actions and decisions by situating them within the context of narratives of their own creation with which they expected all to agree. This was especially the case if they had to set out not only the details of the case at hand but also explain their delay in pursuing judicial redress. Having waited a considerable period of time to see whether the men would follow through on their promises to marry their pregnant underage daughters, a number of parents finally appeared before judicial authorities to initiate complaints, indicating perhaps, all else having failed, the depths their desperation had finally reached as well as the extent to which a judicial proceeding might represent an avenue of last resort. While the mother in one such case explained her monthlong delay in reporting her daughter's abduction as a result of the fact that she was a very poor widow who was unable to appear before judicial tribunals, fathers often took a different tack. Finding himself in the difficult position of justifying why he had waited more than a year to initiate his complaint, a merchant in Parral penned perhaps the longest statement initiating a complaint in the judicial record. Weaving evocative detail, powerful adjectives, and parenthetical remarks into a rich tapestry, this narrative served substantially as a means for the father to embroider his own paternal persona before judicial authorities. Having granted his daughter permission to work in the house of another (only after being assured that she was accompanied by persons of her own sex), the father deftly juxtaposed in his statement the building of an altar of veneration to the Virgen del Refugio, confirming, of course, his own piety and religious respectability, with the receipt of a letter ("with surprise and sentiment") from his daughter, announcing her fall from grace. As was only natural, he stated, after having learned this, both he and members of his family compelled the man responsible to confess as well as to ("solemnly, firmly and irrevocably") promise to marry his daughter. Given his word (in writing as well) as a gentleman that marriage would ("immediately") follow after a brief mourning period, as the offending man's wife had just recently died, there was little else, he explained, that he could do. After all, he continued, the only condition imposed by the offending man was that if these events became public knowledge and a scandal, with his name being ridiculed by all, no marriage would take place. Despite the injury that had been inferred upon him, "as a father," he stated, "I had to put up with these pretensions" and accept the stipulation because, he said, "I well understood and they made me understand that this was the only way to repair the dishonor caused in my wretched daughter."[48]

In his concern with honor, this father was far from alone. In their initial statements of complaint, parents returned often to the theme of honor, whether that of their daughters, themselves, or the family in general. "Honor" was a complicated concept, then, with plenty of it at stake in different ways for different individuals and groups. When referring to their daughters in front of judicial authorities, parents commonly stated that what was required of the man who had abducted their daughter or initiated sexual relations with her was that he "cover her honor," that is, that he marry her. In this understanding of honor, the young male suitor had usually "taken" the daughter's honor, either by means of removing her from the parental home or, more commonly, by convincing her to begin sexual relations with him in exchange for promising to marry her. "Honor" in this sense, then, is the woman's virginity, something that will later be covered with the blanket of legitimacy afforded by formal marriage. In another sense, "honor" refers to one's good name or reputation. According to many fathers, it was their own honor that was the true victim in crimes of rapto and estupro; one father demanded that judicial authorities deal severely with those who had "perpetrated crimes against my honor and reputation."[49] Yet honor was not a commodity in which only men could trade. Mothers, as well, complained that their honor had been infamously or vilely outraged or offended.[50]

In addition to that of mothers, fathers, and daughters, the honor of the family itself was at stake for a significant number of complainants. "As soon as I discovered that a crime had been committed in my home, and against the honor of my family, I came to the jefe político for help," stated one father. Another described how his family had been "dishonored and seduced," while a third asked for harsh penalties against the man accused of impregnating his daughter, so that it might serve as an example to others and "in order to satisfy Society that feels itself outraged in such cases that touch on that which it holds as most sacred, the honor of the family." A mother also cited the need to set an example with her case, so that others would not be tempted to "commit crimes against the order of families." While it might be argued that, in these examples, the father stood as the implied representative of the family, or that, as this section of the criminal code was concerned with crimes against the order of families, it was in the interest of complainants to make this connection, something else is also going on here. In fact, a broader discussion about the nature of legitimate authority and the right to rule was being broached.

For many complainants, it was but a short step from a discussion of the legitimate exercise of authority and rule within the family to an evaluation of the legitimacy of authority and rule within society more generally. One mother specifically linked the willingness to violate the good order of families with the corruption of political authority, stating that the man responsible was "violating my daughter, deceiving her, society, and the

Laws, perhaps through the sovereignty and protection that the Señores, sons of don Marcos G., enjoy before the authorities in San Antonio del Tule."[51] For others, it wasn't even a step at all, so closely did they see the two, legitimate authority in the family and legitimate rule in their community, as interrelated. Referring to the two brothers who had abducted his daughters, a father pointed to the fact that they were "shielded with the money that they can lay out and that gives them the means of committing crimes at any moment, given that their hearts are already corrupt and filled with all kinds of vices and crimes that offend the Law and the Society." Their actions against his daughters, he continued, took away the honor and repose of his family while also attacking his liberty as a father as well as public order.[52] As a final example of these links, a mother from the state of Durango but then living in Parral, Chihuahua, contrasted the legitimate exercise of authority in Parral with what had taken place in Carmen, Durango. "Sr. Z. is used to committing abuses and violations of greater or lesser importance in El Carmen," she stated, "where surely they respect authority when it's in their interest to do so and that no matter how serious their violations should appear, almost always the guilty remain unpunished." "He doesn't understand," she said, perhaps hoping to compel judicial authorities to live up to the liberal rhetoric of equality before the law, "that we're not in the lonely spot of El Carmen anymore and that here judicial affairs are dealt with according to their merits."[53] Protecting the authority and honor that mothers and fathers could legitimately exercise and enjoy in their families could become both a test of and a metaphor for political authority, its exercise, and legitimacy more generally.

The Couple

Although basic information was not always gathered in every judicial procedure, even ones that appear in the archive to be more or less complete, and while little more than partial records or summaries are available for others, it is possible to confirm that the great majority of the cases dealing with rapto and estupro, as well as some of those defined as violación, involved a courting relationship and that, in these cases, the young woman involved was most often between fourteen and twenty-one years of age.

Depending on how one counts, this is the age of the woman in 58 out of the 67 cases involving a courting relationship in which women's ages are available; in 6 of these cases, the woman is older than twenty-one, and in the remaining 3 cases she is under fourteen. Too much faith need not be placed in the exactness of these figures, however, for a couple of reasons. Perhaps it is worth reminding readers once again that even determining what constitutes a courting relationship is far from straightforward. To arrive at the total number of courting relationships, I include in the category of courtship only those cases where both the male and the female forming the couple characterize their relationship as such, at least at a certain point in time if not consistently or, necessarily, to judicial officials. The term they usually use is *"relaciones amorosas"* (sometimes *"relaciones lícito-amorosas"*), or relationships premised upon love, although this may be a legal euphemism, a category that simplified relationships for those interested in taking statements and making legal decisions. Doing so means not only ruling out a number of the rapto and estupro cases in order to arrive at the total number of courtships but also including a number of the violación cases as part of that number.[54] At times, judicial authorities described as rapto or estupro acts that, at other times, according to the criteria set out in the penal codes of the time, would seem more aptly considered rape (violación). Likewise, some of the behaviors described in narratives concerning cases of rape (violación) seem very much like aspects of a courting relationship that are usually treated at other times in the judicial process as cases of rapto and estupro. In a small number of cases, judicial officials, acting on the complaints of heads of household, initiated judicial proceedings of estupro and violación simultaneously for the same unique offence. This reveals the categorical confusion to be the result not only of the distance imposed by time and changing understandings of what constitutes sexual assault but also of the difficulties contemporaries could have imposing legal definitions on behaviors that could be contested by those involved in them and in which sexual violence and courtship were not always necessarily mutually exclusive.[55]

While the total number of cases that can be categorized as representing courting relationships is a matter of interpretation rather than mere enumeration, so too was determining the age of some of the young women who found themselves involved in such proceedings. A number of parents and heads of household erred on the side of youth when stating the ages of their daughters to judicial officials. The ages they gave in statements initiating complaints often differed from the ages given by the young women to judicial authorities as well as from the ages given even by these same parents or guardians in subsequent formal statements before judicial authorities.[56] Whereas parents may have been motivated to lower ages initially in an attempt to compel judicial authorities to act swiftly to locate their daughters and return them, women hoping to be allowed to marry or form households may have found it advantageous to add a year or two in hopes of convincing judicial authorities to support their desires. While such strategies may be plausible as explanations in some cases, in others it is simply the case that precise ages were neither known nor considered terribly important, neither to parents nor children. One woman stated so directly. To overcome this imprecision, and because the severity of the penalty in these cases varied according to the age of the woman, judicial procedure required that official documentation verifying the woman's age be produced by the person initiating the complaint and included in the legal record. Medical authorities adopted a different strategy, at times even giving their own estimation of the woman's age rather than accepting her statement of it.[57]

The men facing legal proceedings of rapto, estupro, and violación that appear to have occurred within the context of a courting relationship are not concentrated in one age cohort. Of the 77 courting couples represented in the archive, the male had not yet reached the age of majority in 10 instances. In the remaining 67 cases, the age range was as follows: between twenty-one and thirty in 33 cases, between thirty and thirty-nine in 11 cases, between forty and forty-nine in 2 cases, and between fifty and fifty-nine in 1 case. The age of the male was not available in 20 of the 77 courting relationships. With regard to civil status, 6 identified themselves as married, a category that had serious implications, both in terms of the relationships between men and women and of those between generations. Many of the cases of rapto, of estupro, and even some of violación (as you will see shortly) revolved around the desire to marry, and (as you have already seen in the case of rapto) if marriage followed abduction, it was determined that no crime had taken place; however, such an option was not available to married men.[58] Judicial officials identified most of the men facing legal proceedings in terms of occupation, with agricultural laborer (labrador) and mine worker (operario) the two most common categories, each containing eleven men. An additional five men can be identified as unskilled mine or agricultural workers (jornaleros, mine workers), ten men were listed as artisans of some sort (tailors, carpenters, shoemakers, bakers, blacksmiths), five merchants (comerciantes) made the list, and so did three mineros (a category usually reserved for those who organized work crews and supervised the various tasks necessary in mining). A telegraph operator and a member of the philharmonic also found themselves before judicial authorities, as did a traveling bookbinder, two watchmen, a tobacco roller, an army officer during the revolution, and a car chauffeur, an emerging occupation by the 1920s. Twenty-four men were not identified by occupation. Depending on how one does the counting, perhaps thirty-three of the men held laboring jobs, either in the mines or in agriculture (although, as I have already indicated, the line was not always so rigidly drawn between these two endeavors), while eight were fairly well-off merchants, miners, or agriculturalists. Artisans often aspired to be recognized as among the gente decente, or new middling groups, like the two bakers who made off with two sisters in 1910; they are described by judicial officials as dressed in the "clothes of the middle class," by which they meant cashmere jacket and pants, dress shoes, and a felt hat, all in black.[59] A number of the other men, including the telegraph operator and the philharmonic musician, might also be placed in this middle category, bringing it to a total of twelve. In short, those men accused of one of the crimes against the order of families in conjunction with a courting relationship represented a fairly broad spectrum of northern Mexican society, ranging from merchants to rural laborers, and were drawn not only from Chihuahua State but from mining and other regions throughout the north, as was not uncommon in a mining district.[60]

In contrast to the ability of those initiating complaints to do so in their own terms, the men and women who comprised the courting couples had to respond to a series of questions posed by judicial authorities, forcing them to follow, rather than set, the investigative agenda. This agenda, limited to information deemed pertinent to the judicial process, which operated to render everyday language into the formal, third-person prose of the court, although not always completely or successfully, seemed designed to turn into black and white portraits circumstances and understandings that one imagines were almost always a lot more subtly rendered in shades of grey. As far as judicial authorities were concerned, relationships, rather than infinitely complicated, could be only either licit or illicit, and women, either virgins or "of the world." Sexual intercourse was safely contained within the euphemism "he made use of my person"[61] and explained as a consequence of one's inexperience and lack of knowledge, in the case of young women, or as the result of exclusively masculine desire, about the nature of which all were meant to agree. In particular, judicial authorities enjoined young women to spell out the nature of their relationships with the men whom their fathers, mothers, or guardians were accusing of crimes against the order of families; to set out specifically what had taken place, including whether their participation had been voluntary or coerced, the nature of the promises that had been made to them, and the forms such promises had taken (especially whether they had been in writing); to specify their understandings of the terms of the bargain in which varying degrees of compliance with male desire often characterized their part of the exchange, including whether or not money had mediated such transactions; and, at times, although not always, to characterize the nature of their relationships with their own families, especially the treatment they received at the hands of parents and the degree of parental opposition to their own wishes. The men were then mandated to address many of these same issues, including the nature of their relationship with the woman, the promises that had been made, especially in writing, and the terms of the sexual bargain from their perspective, including, at times, their evaluation of the state of the woman's virginity, an essential component of this exchange.

As much as the controlled and directed format of judicial proceedings shaped the answers given by men and women, dominant gender conventions and scripts inflected the public presentation both of self and of the actions of the men and women appearing before judicial authorities. Women, for example, in addition to characterizing their amorous relations as "licit," framed sexual congress within an idiom that stressed their own passivity, describing their role in such episodes as that of "lending their bodies" so that men could make use of the them, the supposed "natural weakness" of their sex in agreeing to such acts, and their inexperience and innocence in such matters. As one young woman stated to judicial officials, "Without me realizing how, he seduced me."[62] Given the centrality of virginity to the very definition of "*decencia*" in women, to negotiations over marriage, and to the ability for women to even qualify for legal recourse in cases of estupro (as you have seen above), women insisted on their status as *doncellas*, señoritas (sometimes "legitimate" señoritas), or "*casta*" (chaste), or that they enjoyed the "state of a child," all synonymous with virginity, when describing themselves and their actions to judicial authorities. This often placed them in the difficult position of having to insist on their previous virginity while admitting to court officials that they had had sexual relations with this particular man. Removing themselves from the bounds of decency, family, and law could be explained only by means of the combination of their "natural" weakness and inexperience on the one hand with male insistence and promises of marriage on the other hand. Before agreeing to ride off on horseback with her abductor in 1888, for example, Jesús María pointed to the repeated and insistent nature of Remedios's proposals: "I hadn't wanted to accede," she explained to authorities, "but finally after so much tenacity I acceded with the understanding that we would be married."[63] Another young woman, an eighteen-year-old seamstress, was careful to explain that each and every one of the six times she and her intended had had sexual relations it been proceeded by a promise of marriage.[64]

Men, although not burdened with such preoccupations concerning their own virginity (although one labrador is unique in being described in judicial records as "*célibe*," the only male in the entire archive to be characterized in terms of sexual experience[65]), equally traded on dominant assumptions concerning gender when characterizing their own actions as well as those of others. Perhaps more typical an expression of understandings of masculine sexual desire can be seen in the following statement of a man accused of rapto: when asked by judicial authorities whether he had had sexual relations with the woman he abducted, he responded of course he had, that is why he had carried her off. Another used the term *"conquistado"* to refer to his taking of a young woman's virginity.[66] Yet another expressed the idea that his masculinity would have been threatened had he not agreed to rent a room at a local hotel and have sexual relations with the woman who had accompanied him. Instead of virginity, however, it was trust in a man's word that formed the stuff of masculinity. "Don't worry, we'll marry," the phrase one male used to reassure his hesitant partner, may seem simple and straightforward enough. Implied in it, however, as it equally was in the many promises of marriage in these documents, was not only the understanding that a man might give his word and be held to it but also that the woman believed him to be a man who possessed such moral character, someone to whom she could surrender her virginity in the knowledge that such promises would later be fulfilled.

As unconcerned as they were with regard to their own reputed virginity, men were fundamentally preoccupied with proving to their own satisfaction that of the women whom they planned to marry or establish long-term relationships. Although close to four decades separate the events set out before judicial officials by Leonardo, a tailor accused of estupro in 1888, and Feliciana, a young woman on the edge of a nervous breakdown in 1924, the centrality of a woman's virginity to the negotiations over marriageways remains remarkably consistent. As Leonardo explained to judicial officials, during the eight months he and Maria Francisca had been involved in "amorous relations with the goal of marriage," he had come to learn that she had already lost her virginity prior to their relationship. In hopes that he would be convinced otherwise, he continued, Maria Francisca had offered to give him a "proof" of her condition, that is, to leave with him and agree to the initiation of sexual relations, so that, once he was reassured, marriage could then take place.[67] Turning to the later relationship, it is apparent that Feliciana had been asked to shoulder the same burden of proof. As she framed the narrative of her experience for judicial authorities, after nine months of a courting relationship, Joaquin, her intended, began saying that he knew she wasn't chaste and insinuating that she should prove the contrary to him. In view of the written marriage promises that he had given her, she continued, she had agreed to do so, only once, by means of sexual intercourse.[68] While not all couples were as forthright in spelling out the significance of the woman's virginity to the agreements being negotiated, numerous references in the judicial record to the initiation of sexual relations in exchange for promises of marriage make it possible to infer that a large number of such cases involving a courting relationship hinged on this issue.[69] The fact that ten of the young women involved in these cases were either pregnant during the judicial proceedings or had already given birth to a child provides another measure of the importance of virginity, even if only indirectly, to the bargain being made, that of the confirmation of virginity by means of the initiation of sexual relations in exchange for the promise of future marriage.

If men required proof of women's virginity before following through on their marriage promises, denying its existence before judicial authorities could seem, for some of them at least, a compelling and convincing pretext for calling the whole thing off. In fact, one of the main axes of contention between men and women and around which many of these cases turned was the sexual status of the woman at the time of the initiation of sexual relations. In at least twelve of these cases men commented on virginity explicitly, citing the failure of sexual relations to yield proof of the woman's virginal status as the reason they were now no longer interested in marriage in ten of them. The fact that, in half of these ten instances, men subsequently agreed to marry the women despite making such accusations gives one pause when interpreting the meaning of such statements, however. Rather than their evaluations of the woman's sexual status, such statements are almost a kind of gendered reflex, a reversion to a default position that not only blames the woman for her "failure" to hold up her side of this exchange but does so within the terms of the logic established by the law. In short, it was a good excuse. After all, the "without just cause" clause of the Chihuahua State estupro statute may have been interpreted, both by those writing it as well as those charged under it, to refer to virginity. Men also questioned women's sexual status in other ways, referring to the women they abducted and initiated sexual relations with as "mujeres libres" (free women), "*mujeres del mundo*" (women of the world), "*mujeres malas*" (bad women), and even clandestine prostitutes, all categories that implied sexual experience and the loss of virginity.[70]

While the woman's virginity formed a primary axis of contention around which many, perhaps most, of these cases and, indeed, marriageways, revolved, it was not the only one. In explaining to judicial authorities the terms of the agreement or bargain they believed they had struck with one another, men and women might also contest the type or quality of commitment they felt they had entered into, with men emphasizing its more contingent and fluid nature and women a more absolute interpretation of what was being promised in any exchange. Although proof of virginity certainly figured prominently in their understandings of the overall bargain being struck, men and women, through the gendered narratives they told to judicial officials, went beyond this aspect of the exchange to reveal another major axis of contention, that centering on the force and meaning of pledges, including a contested understanding of the contractual nature of obligations and promises. This is complicated in that, despite the fact that the law was only interested in enforcing contractual obligations in the form of written promises of marriage given under a specific set of circumstances, men and women nevertheless revealed in their statements to the court a much broader understanding of how couples might be formed and the role of various manners of promise in that process. In addition to being offered in written form (or rather than being offered in this way), one's word of marriage (*palabra de casamiento*) could be given verbally instead, as it was in approximately thirty of the cases under consideration. As if sensing that such verbal promises alone might not sound all that compelling to judicial authorities, women often went on to stress the solemnity with which they had been given (*solemnamente comprometido*); the number of times, as seen above, they were reiterated, as if that served somehow to enhance their seriousness or the weight they should be given; the fact that such a verbal promise had been sworn to (*bajo juramento*) or perhaps witnessed by someone else;[71] or their formal, even though verbal, nature. From the perspective of those men involved in these thirty cases, upon questioning only eleven agreed that such a verbal promise had been given; a further seven, once pressed, agreed to marry at a set date in the future, even if some of them initially characterized their relations as illicit or not implicated in courtship (as did two additional men); two men promised, instead of marriage, to sustain or maintain the woman and an additional three insisted that no promises had been made at all; finally, five men were not available to respond, having fled from judicial authorities.

For many men and women appearing before judicial authorities, neither marriage nor formal marriage proposals, whether written or oral, entered into the terms of the negotiations that were meant to lead to a life together. In thirteen of the cases having to do with marriageways or the formation of a couple, the woman reported that before her leaving her parental home or agreeing to the initiation of sexual relations either the man had not made any offers whatsoever or that he had agreed only to maintain her, to provide her with a house in which they could live together "as long as they both should want" or "as long as they both found it convenient," or to "live in her company and sustain her." As already discussed, men who had already been married had few options in this regard (although so important was the appearance or form of marriage to one of these men that he made use of the written word, as we will see in the next section, to craft a legally fictive state, that of "as if they were married"). Once again, however, we must not be in too much of a hurry to take statements made to judicial authorities in these or any other cases at face value. It is possible to infer from testimony in which the man expresses surprise that he finds himself involved in a judicial process or attempts immediately to make a deal with the father to marry the woman later, or from other asides present in the testimony, that women's insistence that no promises had been given could be a strategy, in a situation of trust or desperation, or perhaps both, of protecting the man from judicial action with the understanding that a private arrangement would follow the termination of such proceedings.[72]

Although the very definition of the crimes of rapto and estupro made it legally impossible for some young women to grant their consent to leave the parental home or to form a couple, those involved in such judicial proceedings nonetheless often framed their narratives and explained the choices they themselves had made, as well as the actions of others, with reference to "will," a central, if contested, term in many of these proceedings. Of course, this was partly at the prodding of judicial authorities, interested as they were in determining whether physical or moral violence, deception, or seduction had figured in the commission of these crimes. As a result, more than fifty of cases involving courting couples involved some discussion either of will or of the nature of or circumstances under which consent had been given. In a minority of cases, some nine in total, women and men differed fundamentally in the way they framed the woman's decision to leave the paternal home or engage in sexual relations, with women stressing physical violence, threats, moral coercion, force, or intimidation as the reason for their actions while men stressed spontaneous consent or the woman's free will. Even in the majority of cases, however—those in which women and men agreed that the woman had given her consent or acted of her own will in the actions that had led the men to face criminal charges—women almost always stressed the contingent nature of consent or will, linking it to a promise, usually of marriage, on the part of the man. Men, on the other hand, almost always describe will in absolute terms; that is, they insist that the woman had granted her will or consent to being abducted or to sexual relations without situating her decision within any broader exchanges or sets of expectations.[73] Moreover, whereas judicial authorities may have located "will" within the legal register in an attempt to adjudicate criminal intent or behavior, men and women, as you will see, often saw in "will" the very measure of commitment in a courting relationship.

Some women stressed the difficulty of their home lives and of their economic circumstances, seeing few options other than consensual unions. The phrases "to give her her house" and "to live together as long as they both should want" were commonplace not only in testimony in crimes against the order of families but throughout the judicial archive. They served to encapsulate the understanding at work in consensual unions, known as amasiato, where the man agreed to provide daily sustenance, often called the diario and usually obtained through laboring for a wage in or around the mines, in exchange for domestic duties on the part of the woman.

Such phrases also hint at the economic responsibilities that forming a couple entailed, responsibilities that characterized not only consensual unions but understandings of marriage as well. Being able to provide a place to live and the resources to set up housekeeping and establish a residency seemed to be an important measure of adult status, even a prerequisite to constituting life as a couple. While this gendered obligation is spelled out most clearly in the terms of the amasiato relationship, another measure of its importance is that a number of men facing judicial proceedings in these cases asked for a period of time during which they could husband resources before complying with their promises to marry. Fourteen men asked for such a term, ranging from one to five months, citing, variously, their need to wait until "their circumstances should permit it," "when they get the resources," "when he had the money," "when he has the means," and once his father had given him the money so that he could marry; another was reported to be selling cured hides in order to raise funds for married life, and yet another borrowing money in order to fulfill the obligations he was about to undertake. Three additional men were clearly using the idea of a waiting period as a pretext to avoid marriage, perhaps altogether. A year after initiating sexual relations and following the subsequent birth of his child, for example, one man still found it necessary to request a two-month delay in order to come up with resources to begin married life. While, no doubt, most of those requesting a delay had good financial reasons for doing so, asking for a term also underscored the contingent nature of men's promises. For one man in particular, promising to marry once his circumstances permitted it seemed like a last-ditch attempt to avoid the inevitable, given that claiming illicit relations, that the woman had not been a virgin when they slept together, and that he had paid money, the diario, in exchange for the initiation of sexual relations had all failed to deter the young woman's mother from continuing the legal action against him.[74]

Promising to fulfill one's word of marriage within a certain period of time was often enough to convince most parents or guardians to desist from the complaint with which they had initiated legal proceedings. It was not always sufficient, however, to diffuse the tension between generations, another major axis of contention in these cases. While it might be expected that abducting a daughter or initiating sexual relations with a young woman outside of the institution of marriage or the custom of consensual union would provoke hard feelings if not outright hostilities between parents and the offending man, contention between the generations informed the dynamic of these cases in other ways as well. In all, of the seventy-seven cases concerned with courtship in this archive, twenty-two contain a specific mention of some form of intergenerational conflict. In eight of these twenty-two courtships, the refusal of parents or guardians to grant the permission required for their underage daughters or charges to marry compelled the younger generation to take matters into their own hands. As one twenty-one-year-old woman stated, in the face of parental opposition, she and her novio "were forced" into running away together; another regarded abduction as the best way to "overcome parental difficulties."[75] Testifying not only to the discussion that must have gone on among the work crew but also to the large gap between general knowledge and parental ignorance with regard to the amorous relationship of one young woman, one miner's peones reported that another miner had stated he would "carry off" the miner's daughter if he didn't agree to let her marry him.[76]

Faced with such a scenario, parents and guardians, formerly opposed to the match, usually came to see marriage as the only way to cover the honor of the young woman and themselves. In these cases, abduction acts as a form of elopement, which worked to overcome parental opposition because it announced the relationship of the couple and the fait accompli of sexual relations to the entire community; the daughter's shame, and, by extension, that of the family, as we have seen, now demanded that marriage take place.[77] The sense of reluctant resignation on the part of one mother in accepting the de facto elopement of her disobedient daughter is clearly captured in her statement to judicial authorities: "I, as mother, even though my heart has been torn to pieces by the conduct of my wretched daughter, can't do anything other than send her a 'God Bless You.'"[78]

One abductor, however, saw the flow of honor and dishonor differently. Rather than himself, he blamed the girl's father; as for marriage to the young woman with whom he had initiated sexual relations, he saw it as not only desirable but also an absolute necessity in order to cover the dishonor that the girl's father had thrown over them by attempting to shame them through initiating a judicial complaint, that is, through making their situation public knowledge.[79] Although every case of the abduction of an underage woman by a man interested in achieving marriage did not necessarily end with that result, as you will see shortly, the expectation on the part of most, including judicial officials, was that it would, especially when the woman expressed the same desire for marriage. While parents might be slow, even reluctant, to pardon those who had offended them, they usually did, given the logic outlined above; one father, however, simply refused to cooperate in the elopement drama, insisting, instead, that his daughter marry her previous suitor, with whom she had broken off relations a month earlier by means of a letter. Whereas most cases involving a courting couple desiring to marry were resolved fairly quickly, this particular father was still demanding that judicial officials act on his complaint nearly two and a half years later, not only in punishing the abductor but in returning his daughter to his side. Underpinning his long statement to judicial authorities was his insistence that an underage daughter simply did not have the legal right to give or grant her consent to marriage, especially when under the influence or will of her abductor, an argument about parental control that judicial authorities were also interested in upholding. Although covering honor usually trumped parental rights, this particular episode stands out in its exception to this general tendency.[80]

Nor were the parents of underage daughters the only ones whose opposition to marriage was thought possible to overcome through abduction. When the parents of a nineteen-year-old tailor from Parral refused to grant permission for him to marry, a legal requirement for males as well as females, he decided to abduct his intended as a way of changing their minds. As the eighteen-year-old woman recounted to judicial authorities, the tailor's plans were that she would first leave with him, abandoning her home, so that his parents, especially his mother, "wouldn't make any difficulties about their getting married."[81] Although the outcome in this case is not known, the tailor's plan was not as far-fetched a scheme as the understandings of the allotment of honor, as we have outlined them here, would seem to indicate. It is possible to catch glimpses, in the various statements made as part of the judicial proceedings, of the male's father (and not only of those males under the age of twenty-one) at work in the background, perhaps advocating on behalf of their son with the offended head of the woman's family, perhaps serving, by their very presence, to locate the offending male within a family context, with the concomitant values that implied. In cases where a son was reluctant to honor his commitment, a father might nudge him along to "do the right thing" and marry the woman.[82] The weight of expectations and the role of families, not only the woman's but also the man's, in enforcing them helped make abduction as a form of elopement work while attesting to the persistence of such shared values and understandings.

The remaining fourteen cases in which tension between the generations is stated specifically all focus on the young woman, although they do so in different ways. In eight of these cases, it is confusion about the status of the young woman that prompts both the man's actions and the subsequent legal wrangling. Forced by economic circumstances to fend for themselves or threatened with physical abuse or with being thrown into the street for continuing in their courting relationship, some young women confronted a future with few options, all of them difficult. As one fifteen-year-old woman explained, her decision to leave home and live with a mine worker was because, as her stepfather did not bring home enough money to feed both her and her mother, she could not be certain from day to day that she would even have enough food. As her new partner had already been married, he promised only to maintain her at his side.[83] Another, without a father and whose mother lived on public charity, fled to Chihuahua City to try to improve her lot; two others faced difficulties with their grandparents, with whom they lived, who refused to permit them to marry despite being unable to support them.[84] When disputes—often having nothing to do with their own courtships but engendered through new relationships of amasiato undertaken by one of their parents—or basic lack of sufficient food on a daily basis forced them out of their homes in search of other options, with or without parental consent, the status of young women became less clearly defined.[85] In such cases where parental authority was not particularly apparent, men stated that they thought they had been dealing with a "*mujer libre*," that is, with a woman free from anyone who might initiate a complaint.[86] The existence of such a category in popular understanding helps us make sense of the great lengths parents and guardians sometimes went to in their complaints initiating judicial procedures to assure authorities that their parental presence was real if, at times, stretched by the demands of making ends meet.[87]

Whether the parental presence was real or simply a pretense was something about which daughters often had much to say. In place of form or word, where honor accrued simply by virtue of one's position as parent or guardian or was merely asserted, daughters often evaluated its content and practice, the actual carrying out of parental duties and responsibilities and the degree to which they had been fulfilled or found wanting. At times, their descriptions of the practice of parenting could be damning. When two sisters under the age of consent in Parral agreed to leave their home to live with two brothers, they admitted that, rather than marriage, they had been offered only a house where they could live in freedom. Rather than in negative terms, however, they saw this as a great improvement over their current family situation, where, they explained, their father had abandoned them to the care of his *amasia*, who, treating them like "used furniture," had turned them over to the charity of others to the point where they found themselves forced to beg for their daily bread. They chided their father, who now claimed that his honor had been sullied by their abduction, for failing in his parental duties, forcing them into the street, as the sisters put it, without as much as a cigarette. As far as they were concerned, when it came to their father, honor was little more than a *palabra hueca*, an empty word.[88]

Even though judicial proceedings could become a forum for deflating the airs of the older generation and a place where family tensions might be discussed and even formally inquired into, as they were in this case, judicial authorities were usually reluctant to overturn generational authority and hierarchy in the family, despite what the case of the ignored elopement might suggest. Even when one young woman begged not to be returned to the authority of her grandmother, who despite not being able to provide for her would not permit her to work outside the home, her pleas were ignored.[89] In fact, rather than undermining parental authority, the questioning format of legal procedures could be used as a means of instructing young women in proper deference and behavior toward their parents or guardians. In a case that revolved around the claim of "free woman" status being asserted by a young woman and her novio, judicial officials specifically questioned the young woman on the reason she had failed to comply with the duties she owed to her grandfather in his capacity as guardian. Admitting failure in some respects, this young woman refused to accept all the blame: it was she who had been thrown out of the house, she stated, because she had wanted to enjoy her liberty as, according to her, that was the way that life worked.[90] Another, asked whether she understood the damage or harm she had occasioned by leaving her home clandestinely, again hedged her admission of misbehavior with a claim to the right to make choices on behalf of a chance at her own happiness. Sixteen years old and facing a life of hardship and privation in the house of her grandmother, who refused to grant permission for her to marry, she stated that she believed she would be happy with the man she had chosen for her husband.[91]

In at least five of these twenty-two cases involving tension between generations, it was the fact of courtship itself that provoked a response on the part of parents or guardians. An uncle and a father, for example, not only refused their permission for marriage but threatened to kill a fourteen-year-old young woman if she agreed to married her suitor; another was so afraid that her mother and uncle were going to do the same thing after she left with her suitor the first time that she felt she had no choice but to leave with him yet again.[92] As yet another young woman explained, in the absence of any other protection, which she referred to as *amparo*, she had little choice but to marry her abductor.[93] Faced with an impending medical examination to confirm a suspected pregnancy, a fourth woman reported that she had been threatened with a beating, with being thrown into the street, and even with jail, should the exam confirm parental suspicions.[94] Two additional young women, after accepting a ride home from a party in the mining town of Santa Bárbara with two men with whom they described themselves as cultivating relationships only of friendship, described themselves to judicial officials as the victims of sexual violence. So great, however, was their fear that family members would find out about what had happened and attribute it to their own frivolousness or lewdness that they voluntarily abandoned their homes, convinced that they would be thrown out of them anyway, without asking for or even desiring the support of the men who had assaulted them.[95] These and other examples offer but a glimpse of the broader role that threats and physical violence against young women played in enforcing adherence to decorum or compliance with parental wishes as well as the degree to which the fait accompli of sexual relations could severely limit women's options.

Up to this point, we have seen how those initiating complaints of rapto and estupro enjoyed the privilege of expressing themselves in their own writing as well as how all subsequent statements gathered as part of the judicial procedure, like those by the men and women we considered in this part of the section, came in response to questions from judicial authorities who, in effect, set the agenda. In and of themselves, however, statements and responses, rendered into the third-person written format required by the legal process, were insufficient. To obtain a favorable judicial decision, the complainant also needed to be able to provide proof of the many claims being made, especially those concerning the age of the young woman, the complainant's relationship to her (either of parentage or guardianship), the existence of a promise of marriage, and, in some cases, physical evidence of recent sexual activity. All these could be accomplished only with further recourse to the written word, in the form of official, legal documents such as birth certificates, written promises of marriage, and written medical reports. A pillar of what Angel Rama has referred to as the "lettered city"—that coming together of writing, power, and the urban center in Latin America—the judicial system was premised upon the primacy of the written word.[96] It is to the submission of such evidence that I now turn.

In Writing

Rather than as "supporting" evidence, documents such as birth certificates, written promises of marriage, and medical reports need to be seen as constituting the very substance of these legal cases. Despite the considerable time and effort dedicated to the taking of statements from complainants, the couple, and any witnesses who might shed light either on the events or the moral character of some of the principals, failure to provide such documentation ended the possibility of obtaining legal redress, no matter how convincing individual narratives might be. Even decisions initially rendered in favor of the complainant could be overturned at the last moment by their failure legally to prove their relationship to the young woman, something about which not even one person ever disputed in any of these cases. Nor were such official documents always easy to obtain. One young man, frustrated with the fact that two months had elapsed since official documentation of his unmarried status from a neighboring state had been requested, with no reply in sight, decided on abduction, perhaps in hopes of speeding along the paperwork and thus his marriage. No doubt many complainants, some drawn to the mines of Chihuahua from other mining areas in Mexico, faced the same delays in obtaining birth certificates to attest to the ages of their daughters or their relationships to them. Even when they were obtainable, the failure to fill out such forms correctly could invalidate them as evidence, as the complainant from a smaller community in Hidalgo District, whose surname had been inadvertently left off the birth certificate, found out.[97] In short, of the twenty-two of these cases to reach the stage in which a final judgment was rendered, a full nine foundered on the failure to provide such legal proof of the young woman's age or a relationship of parentage or guardianship to her.[98]

An additional seven cases faltered on the basis of medical reports that purported to be able to determine the truth of a woman's sexual history after a single medical examination or, in other kinds of cases, failed to find adequate physical signs of a struggle. In these cases, mostly dealing with estupro (although one case initiated as violación is treated as an estupro case), it was not the fact of sexual intercourse that judicial authorities were interested in documenting (as they were in the fact of parentage or age) but rather the chastity of the young woman preceding it. As written in both the Federal District as well as the state criminal codes already discussed, estupro was defined as copulation with a decent and chaste woman. To determine such a state "scientifically," judicial authorities turned to doctors, illustrating their belief that a woman's sexual history was inscribed upon her body in signs recognizable to medical experts, making such practitioners into arbiters of the woman's reputation. Medical reports stating that the woman "had not been a virgin for some time," that she had "not recently been deflowered," as well as reports that testified to sexual experience, or even those that were unable to determine precisely when "deflowering" had occurred, resulted in dismissal on the grounds that prior chastity had not been proven.[99] Nor in cases in which a child had already been born or in which the complainant had waited too long to initiate proceedings (one judgment determined that the signs of recent "deflowering" were apparent for up to twenty days) could the corpus delicti be substantiated through expert medical examination.[100] In such cases it was lack of medical evidence of prior chastity that served as grounds for dismissal.

Cases of rapto, however, without a similar need to establish the chastity of the young woman, employed a different standard in the use of medical evidence, even in those instances in which copulation had followed her abduction from parental authority. In one of the few cases in which a male was actually sentenced to a prison term for either rapto or estupro (the outcomes of these cases will be discussed shortly), the complainant, the mother of the young woman, refused to consent to the medical examination of her daughter, citing the need to avoid the "natural shame" that her daughter would experience during the process and arguing that such an examination was unnecessary in any event given that the accused male had already admitted to having had a "carnal act" with her daughter. While the mother stressed that all involved had already admitted to engaging in sexual relations, the fact that the criminal charge brought forward was that of rapto and not estupro, even though it seemed both had taken place, made expert medical evidence of the daughter's prior virginity unnecessary in this case.[101] Finally, in a case that seemed to be about both estupro and violación, while authorities dismissed the charge of estupro on the basis of medical evidence that was unable to verify the exact timing of the woman's "deflowering," that of violación was placed in question by the failure of medical experts to find "signs of external violence," the ultimate means, according to the court, through which women could prove the commission of violación (despite women's testimony of being threatened with knives and pistols if they failed to go along).[102] What is most compelling about the use and abuse of medical evidence is that, in desiring to know the "truth" of a woman's sexual history, judicial authorities and young men in search of a suitable partner shared a compelling mutual interest, if a different set of investigative tactics. One cannot help but wonder at the ways in which each reinforced the other, at the very least helping to underwrite a conception of power premised upon the body that transcended any supposed private/public divide.

It was also at this point in the judicial proceedings that love letters entered the judicial record, submitted in order to prove the existence of a written promise of marriage, as mandated by the criminal code in cases of estupro that met the specific criteria outlined earlier. Of the seventy-seven courting relationships documented in these cases, twenty-four make specific mention of the existence of a written promise of marriage. Some do so only in passing, as when such letters were discovered by parents or described in conjunction with specific stages of a courting relationship, or when it was stated that, having thought the relationship over, someone had burned them—a not-entirely-convincing explanation and perhaps a means of claiming the materiality of a written marriage promise where none existed. In nineteen of these twenty-four cases, complainants, or perhaps their daughters, submitted to judicial authorities the love letters they had received in hopes of satisfying the terms of the estupro article of the legal codes calling for a written promise of marriage. Although, as explored further in subsequent sections, some of these written promises were direct and to the point, others were not, leading women to turn over to the authorities, rather than a single letter or document, their entire amorous correspondence or a substantial part of it, hoping, in this way, to establish that theirs was a courting relationship destined to culminate in marriage, if only by implication and the weight of expectation rather than in so many words.

Separating out and considering as a single group those cases involving courting relationships in which written promises of marriage, usually love letters, are either included as evidence or acknowledged to have been exchanged yields the same diversity of backgrounds of those involved—their motives and situations, and the narratives that they presented—as the broader body of evidence from which they have been drawn, that is, the total number of cases involving courting relationships. In short, there is little evidence to suggest that those cases involving the use and exchange of letters differed fundamentally from the broader context of legal cases involving rapto, estupro, and violación of which they form a part. The young women's age in this particular subset, when known, ranged from fourteen to twenty-six, with most being from fifteen to nineteen years old; the ages of the men accused of these various crimes range from nineteen to fifty-nine, with 3 under twenty-one, 8 between twenty-one and twenty-nine, and 1 in each of the deciles thirty to thirty-nine, forty to forty-nine, and fifty to fifty-nine. Similarly, whereas more than half of those men in courting relationships accused of these crimes in the total number of cases were described as laborers of some kind (33 out of 53 whose occupation is known), more than half in this subset also fit this category (10 out of 18). Here, it is worth noting that, rather than being equally represented as in the overall totals, mine workers (operarios) outnumber laborers (labradores), perhaps reflecting a slight urban bias in engagement with the written word. Given the (already noted) fluidity between these sectors, this may not be all that significant, as laborers and agriculturalists are certainly found among those exchanging letters. Whereas just under a quarter in the total number of cases were artisans or middling groups (12 out of 53), it was just under a third for those involved with written correspondence (5 out of 18). Likewise, the same rough proportion held in both groups for those men who were relatively well off (8 out of 53; 3 out of 18). Clearly, the use of written correspondence, especially love letters, was not limited to the elite but, rather, fell within the purview of a much broader range of social groups, at least as measured by occupation.

Likewise, just as the entire set of courtship cases revolved around a number of intersecting axes of contention, so too did the subset of cases involving letters. Of the 24 cases that included written promises, 9 grew out of and attempted to overcome parental opposition to the courtship or prospect of marriage. In 2 additional cases, men who had already been married, and thus could not offer a promise of marriage but only the chance to build a life together "as if they were married," as one stated it, found in letters a powerful means of convincing their partner to leave the parental home. Nearly half of this subset of cases, at least 11 or 12, had to do with the initiation of sexual relations in exchange for a promise of marriage, in writing, often revolving around the now-familiar understanding that this exchange would be contingent upon proving to the male's satisfaction the previous virginity of his intended (this is mentioned specifically in 5 cases). In all, it is possible to conclude that, while these 24 cases did result in the amassing of some 50 love letters in the judicial record, they are in no other way distinguishable as a group from the larger body of cases I have been considering.

If we add to this total, as I think we should, 4 additional cases of courtships that resulted in judicial proceedings, 2 of which concerned murder-suicide, the other a homicide, and the fourth where information other than the letters is not available, 49 more love letters become available, bringing the total number of love letters to nearly 100, including 30 sent by women. While murder-suicides within a courting relationship are certainly at one extreme in the spectrum of behavior associated with courtship, they do, nonetheless, form part of that spectrum. It is worth noting that the ages and occupations of those involved in such cases situate them squarely within the courtship dynamics that have been traced out in cases of rapto and estupro—both involved men in their early twenties (twenty-two and twenty-three), one a mine worker and the other a white-collar employee (*empleado*) from a family of merchants, and women between sixteen and eighteen years of age, one whose father worked in the mines (operario).

Not much, then, separated those who knew their way around the lettered city (or at least were familiar with some of its neighborhoods) from those dwelling outside its paper-thin walls in less literate locales. Although written promises of marriage, medical reports, and official documents like birth certificates served as the only recognized mediums of exchange in one of its main institutions, the judicial system, they were a peculiar kind of currency—while their absence guaranteed that there would be no legal consequences for those accused of rapto and estupro their presence seldom led to the opposite, the conviction of those responsible for such crimes. In turning now, finally, to the resolution or at least the termination of the judicial processes I have been considering, the end results seem as much as anything else to highlight the need to reevaluate our understandings of the role the judicial system was meant to play in such generational, as well as gendered, wrangles.

Outcomes

It seems difficult to accept that all this narrating, gathering of evidence, and effort on the part of parents, police, and judicial authorities in these 77 cases of rapto, estupro, and violación involving a courting relationship led to only 4 men being found guilty of any of these crimes, with 1 of these guilty verdicts overturned at the level of a higher court.[103] Certainly, the problems discussed in the previous section took their toll—parents found it difficult to provide written proof of their status or of the ages of their children; medical reports failed to confirm virginity or pointed to the lack of signs of a struggle; and written promises of marriage (or even marriage itself), while tremendously important from a legal point of view, weren't always regarded as such by those making life's decisions. Even if, however, we add to the 4 guilty verdicts the 9 cases that failed because of missing documentation, the 7 that were undermined by medical reports, the 3 turned over to a higher court (including 1 of the original guilty verdicts), and the handful of men still at large, for a total of 25, still unaccounted for are slightly more than 50 cases, a large majority of those I have been considering. It seems that there were few legal consequences for men who perpetrated crimes against the order of families, public morality, or good customs.

Perhaps, however, the number of guilty verdicts is not the best indicator of the success or failure of the legal system in resolving such issues. Appearing ineffective when measured in terms of the formal penalties it meted out, the judicial system, nonetheless, did have an important role to play in resolving these disputes, although that role is not always apparent from the documents themselves. Readers will remember that, just as cases of rapto and estupro could only be initiated by the complaint of a parent or guardian, so too could they be stopped at any time point during the proceedings should the offended party, that is, the parent or guardian of the young woman, choose to desist from their complaint. As stated earlier, the law recognized these crimes as a greater offence to the individual than to society as a whole, the entire premise by which the complainant enjoyed these rights. It is particularly telling, then, that nearly half of all the cases I have been considering, some 33 in total, representing 36 courting couples once pairs of sisters are included, were brought to an abrupt halt when the complainant exercised this right to desist from the legal proceeding by making a formal statement to judicial authorities to that effect, attaining, in this way, a private end to a private crime while at the same time hinting at the possibility that legal proceedings had brought some pressure to bear on the parties or, at the very least, bought enough time so that these issues could be worked out extralegally.[104]

The formal statement of desisting, a separate and recognizable phase in the legal proceedings, came complete with its own formalities and politics, revealing constructions of personal honor and generosity, if not always the fate of the courting couple. Perhaps it is only fitting that, having been initiated only by means of the formal voicing of a complaint by a clearly identified offended party, these cases were often brought to an end in the same manner, giving the last word to the main figure around which this legal drama turned. Just as in the introductory statements in which the complainant was accorded the possibility of expressing their grievance in the first person, later rendered into the third-person language of the law, formal statements of desisting seem often to fracture the formal legal grammar, reintroducing the "I" once again, as if signaling a departure from the world structured by the demands of the penal code and a return to that of everyday relationships and understandings. Yet, for many, this sojourn into the lettered city had undoubtedly been worthwhile, even if no judgment had been rendered—after all, the time and space provided by the legal process had given both impetus and opportunity for those involved to resolve their disputes among themselves, often on the basis of informal arrangements drawn from much closer to home.

No doubt, legal forms and conventions helped shape such statements as well, although the great variety of postures adopted by those choosing to desist as well as the ways they framed themselves, their offenders, and the larger public within which such roles took on meanings betrays a great deal of leeway in their crafting. Some, for example, often but not uniquely female, complainants reported that a "private arrangement" had been arrived at, usually an agreement for the accused to marry the young woman or provide her with a dowry (discussed further below).[105] Others, often male complainants, while pointing to the same solution, that of marriage, stressed not the fact of the arrangement itself but the way it served as a means to a larger end—that of repairing the offense that had been done to them. "Having married my daughter," stated one father, "and being repaired in this manner the offense that caused me to initiate my complaint, I ask the judge to place the expressed [offender's name] at liberty."[106] Still others, both male and female alike, stressed that the rights they enjoyed under the law, both to initiate and desist in such cases, made no explanation of their motives for doing so necessary. "Making use of the right that is his right to exercise, that he possesses as the father of the young woman, he withdraws the accusation," stated one father in terminating a legal proceeding. In halting another, one woman simply stated she had done so "for reasons that aren't pertinent to set out here."[107] Finally, a few complainants stressed the economic hardship that taking the time to pursue a legal judgment imposed on them, citing their penury or their need to work in their statements of desisting.

The public nature of legal proceedings and the visibility they implied weighed differently on those involved in these cases. Some fathers, chagrined at seeing their daughters implicated in such proceedings, even if they themselves had initiated them, hastened to bring them to an end.[108] Another father situated his deliberations over his course of action or options in the case within the public or community context from which it had originated: "Yielding to the promptings of the wise counsel and the observations of respectable persons I see myself as having the obligation to pardon Don Manuel, and I do so, of the offense that he has inflicted on me, consenting so that the marital engagement with my daughter can take place."[109] Such grudging forgiveness, elicited with the help of one's peers in the community, served to highlight simultaneously both the tremendous generosity of the offended father in forgiving the man responsible for the attack on his honor and the father's membership within respectable society, the ideal venue he called into being with his statement in which the event and all those involved were to be adjudicated.[110]

In addition to forgiveness and magnanimity, statements of desisting could also be about reconciliation, even, at times, the rehabilitation and reincorporation into respectable society of those accused of such crimes in the first place. After all, some of those initially accused of criminal acts were now family, as resolution had come about through the marriage of the courting couple. In such cases, concern for honor extended to that of former abductors, as a rewriting of the past and a retrospective reshaping of the significance of events began to take place: by the end of the case, initiating a formal complaint against the men who abducted his daughters had become "an error originating in unfounded appearances," stated one father, the result of "the natural zealousness of a father for his daughters." His formal statement of desisting, as much directed at those he had formerly been accusing as at judicial authorities, was an attempt to "repair the offended reputation" of those he had accused with his complaint.[111] Another emphasized his daughter's willingness to go along with her abductor, framing the episode within a context of elopement or romance rather than violence or assault: "Sr. R. made use of my referred to daughter, with her full consent, and not desiring in any way to harm this gentleman I withdraw completely all petitions and actions that in these affairs the law concedes to me and request that he immediately be placed at liberty."[112]

The issue of the woman's will is a complicated one, however. In other statements of desisting, will is not used to absolve the accused male but, in and of itself, as the very basis for terminating legal proceedings. "Having been restored to the bosom of her family," stated one male complainant, "and freely manifesting her will (voluntad) to marry her abductor and obtaining the consent required, I desist in all form of the interposed complaint."[113] Here, one can only imagine that, given the absence of such will, a statement of desisting would not have been forthcoming. In other words, while the criminal code recognized parents as the only ones able to exercise consent and express will, parents often granted such agency to their underage daughters. Perhaps, in rare moments, so too did judicial authorities. In an unusual final statement, made only after the father had desisted in his complaint given that the abductor had agreed to marriage, the fifteen-year-old daughter stressed that she had changed her mind, that is, that she no longer possessed the "will" to go through with the promised marriage. Stating that she no longer had "regard" for her abductor, she asked for nothing from him, given the fact, she explained, that she herself had very spontaneously agreed to leave with him. Given her lack of will to see the marriage through, the court decreed that, in the only mention of such an instrument in all these proceedings, the guarantee (*fianza*) making an unidentified third party responsible for the civil and criminal consequences should the abductor not go through with the marriage be suspended, an outcome the young woman acknowledged and agreed with.[114]

Two additional statements, both by women, implicate will as well, but in a slightly different manner. Here, the attempt seems to be to arrive at a consensus in order to achieve reconciliation. Shifting to the plural in both cases, mother and daughter speak together, with the will of both being taken into account, as in the following: "We have agreed to desist as we are desisting in all forms of the law."[115] In the second of these two cases invoking the plural female "we" instead of the singular male "I," the man accused of estupro expressed his agreement with what the mother and daughter were saying as part of the legal proceedings; the case ended in marriage, with the man having the final word, participating in as well as verifying their statement of desisting or, perhaps more importantly, turning the entire legal system into a witness to his agreement to marry while highlighting both the women's forgiveness as well as his deliverance from criminal to honorable status.[116] In this last case, the statement of desisting becomes a surrogate written promise of marriage, obtained only after the fact at the end of judicial proceedings; ironically enough, the absence of such a written promise would have guaranteed that no legal consequences would have been forthcoming for his actions.

Whether or not they included such endorsements on the part of the offending man, statements of desisting, by their very existence, confirm that the various generational and gendered issues, or at least those that seemed to matter most, had been worked out by the parties involved. In the cases of half of the courting couples in which desisting occurred, some 18 out of the 36, marriage can be confirmed. In a further 16 cases, an arrangement had been reached that may have included marriage, although the complainants in these cases refused to state why they were ending legal proceedings with their statements of desisting. Such an arrangement could also have included the paying of a dowry, as can be confirmed in an additional two cases from the statements of desisting. Originating during the colonial period as the ecclesiastical solution to broken marriage promises, where it was seen as both punishment for the man and compensation to the woman for the harm done to her, the dowry survived as a custom into the twentieth century.[117] In recompense for enticing an underage woman out of the parental home to live with him, for example, one mine worker, who had already been civilly married and thus could not cover the honor of the woman by that means, agreed to pay the girl's family one hundred pesos—half immediately and half later in the month—a substantial sum for a worker in 1905.[118] In another case that took place shortly after the violent decade of revolution in Mexico, in 1923, a laborer explained to judicial authorities that he had struck a deal with the mother of the woman with whom he had had sexual relations: he would pay the dowry and she would desist from all accusations.[119]

In those cases of rapto and estupro involving a courting relationship that did not include statements of desisting, not a single marriage or the payment of even one dowry can be confirmed (although marriage may have resulted in cases where the outcome is not known). Rather, in the cases of these supposedly courting couples (some 41 couples located in 40 cases in total), either the resolution of the case is simply not known, as in some 12 of these proceedings, or, even more likely, the case was dismissed owing to the failure to provide written evidence in support of either parentage or a written promise of marriage, or the failure of medical reports to document prior chastity, the case in some 14 proceedings; an additional 2 were declared not guilty (and in yet another the decision was pending the arrival of proper documentation), and 2 more were turned over to a higher court. As stated above, 4 men, all found guilty of the crime of abduction (rapto), were sentenced to prison terms of between one and two years and fined between 50 and 100 pesos, although one of these verdicts was subsequently overturned. Three men remained at large, having fled to avoid the proceedings, and a handful of cases involved women who did not meet the age requirement. One father refused to give permission for his daughter to marry, even though everyone else involved in the case seemed to desire it.

Finally, although statements of desisting serve to distinguish those cases in which an arrangement was arrived at from those that continued through the judicial process—seldom to an official end that would provide some satisfaction to the complainant—they are not similarly distinguished by the presence or absence of love letters. That is, of the 33 cases (36 couples) that end with a statement of desisting, 11 are characterized by the presence of love letters or at least contain a mention of their exchange. Of the 40 cases (41 couples) not ending with such a statement, 13 similarly include or make mention of such correspondence.

Conclusion

Despite their common grouping within the relatively narrow section of the penal code dealing with crimes against the order of families, public morality, or good customs, and despite the unity suggested by the category of "courtship" used to describe the scenarios at work in them, the legal cases of rapto, estupro, and violación upon which this section has been based are characterized by a great deal of diversity. Perhaps it would be to repeat a cliché to say that all relationships are unique, yet there may be something worthwhile revealed by such a remark in the present discussion. Though I had hoped to draw some general conclusions concerning the dynamics of courtship on the basis of these documents, I have instead found it necessary to be attentive to the multiplicity of voices within them and to the many and varied circumstances that led to their creation and within which the narratives that emerge out of them might be situated.

Testimony in the cases of courting relationships I have been considering is partial, cacophonous, and mediated through the lens of the legal process and the apparatus of writing it was premised upon. My hope is that suggested here has been the great variety of experiences, understandings, and contexts that contributed to the length of the present section and at times seemed to demand an almost case-by-case treatment, and that some of the narrative strategies for constructing self, place, and courtship within them have been glimpsed, hopefully making of this grouping of stories more than the sum of its parts. You have seen that not only could the end desired—whether marriage, living together in amasiato as long as they both should want, domestic duties in exchange for support by means of a paycheck, or sex—vary from couple to couple and even within a single relationship but also that family dynamics, individual circumstances, and the contingencies created by the dynamics of a relationship could vary substantially as well. Moreover, numerous conflicts, at some times located within the couple, at others between generations, and always gendered—those concerned with, for example, demonstrating virginity, the contingent versus more absolute framing of the type or quality of commitment or promises being made, overcoming parental opposition (on either or both sides), and the status of the young woman as either subject to or free from parental jurisdiction—formed some of the primary axes of contention that shaped relationships in particular, often unique, ways.

I hope that, in addition to drawing attention to such diversity, I also have helped bring into focus some of the common narrative strategies around which self, couple, and courtship were imagined. The construction of paternal personas in statements of complaint and of desisting; the complex equations by which honor, initially lost, was regained, for men and women, children and adults; the mutual constitution, and contestation, of authority in family and community; and the gendered language of "naturalness" in the conventions and scripts of both men and women in their statements to judicial officials all drew on as they defined understandings of self and couple. It was "will" (voluntad), however, perhaps more than anything else, that served as a particularly dense and productive discourse for the simultaneous construction of self and couple. Inasmuch as "will" was a legal term that was recognized only in those empowered by the law to possess it, parents, guardians, and those forming young couples, men and women both, nevertheless also found in it a means of expressing their most profound wants and desires. "Will" was what women exercised when deciding to leave home to be with their novios; it was what parents often sought to support in their daughters when they desisted from their complaints and agreed to allow marriage to take place; and it was what men asked women to demonstrate, along with their virginity.

This section has attempted to establish two things. First, it has sought to explain the circumstances under which love letters became lodged in the judicial archives and, thus, available to historians. Love letters offered a means of satisfying the legal requirement for a written promise of marriage in certain cases dealing with the courtship of women under the age of majority. They can be read as belonging to the history of legally binding promises. Second, it has also sought to explore whether or not such cases involving love letters differ from the broader context from which they have been drawn, that is, the total number of cases of rapto, estupro, and violación dealing with courtship in the archive. After evaluating the occupational groups of the complainants and the men accused in both sets of cases, as well as the ages of the young women and the ultimate resolutions of the cases, it is possible to conclude that there were few if any differences distinguishing the cases including love letters from those that did not. Letters can be found in cases involving mine workers and agricultural laborers as well as in those in which artisans, miners, and more substantial merchants are involved. As a result, rather than limit to those cases that contain letters the discussion that follows about courtship and other matters concerning the sentimental anatomy, I will often draw upon the broader number of cases.

Separating the cases involving courtship from those that clearly do not (not always an easy task) is not designed to downplay or hide the fact that sexual assault and violence were one important context within which courtship, like gender relations more generally, took place. In fact, the evidence presented in this section suggests that "courtship" itself was a contested term that implied a range of behaviors, some of them violent. Men could cover with a promise of marriage acts that read very much like sexual assault; sexual relations, initiated violently, could end in marriage—they could be, in fact, a means of proposal under circumstances in which women were left with few other choices. Parents, as well, used corporal punishment or at least the threat of it to police the boundaries of decency and enforce parental prerogatives, leaving daughters who had been victims of sexual assault, according to their recounting of events before the court, reluctant to return home lest they face further violence there. Leaving the parental home, no doubt a highly romantic act and the ultimate expression of will for many young women, could turn violent for others and, as we have seen, leave them without much hope of obtaining retribution under the law. Often, as well, their decisions to leave seem to have been made, at times, in situations in which few alternatives presented themselves, a form of economic violence in and of itself. Even the bargain that led to the formation of couples—the initiation of sexual relations in exchange for a written promise of marriage—seemed to be hedged in, despite the emphasis on "will," by the potential for violence. However much a scar across the face of "happily ever after," such violence was not as terminal as the lethal literality of "until death do us part," the murder-suicide of the novia/novio, the extreme end of the continuum of violence within courtship.[120]

The legal system was not particularly effective in punishing those men carrying out such violence nor those charged with the crimes we have been considering. However, guilty verdicts may not be the only measure of the role judicial structures were meant to play in such affairs. Given the number of complainants who desisted, it seems that judicial structures lent sufficient weight and gravitas to the situation to enable the families involved to resolve these issues, whether through marriage or the paying of a dowry or some other, unspecified means. Given that the parents or guardians were considered to be the true victims of these crimes, their authority—or at least the authority of those who exercised it in the official family as constituted through written texts like birth certificates—was nevertheless recognized in these cases, situating family authority within the context of power and political authority writ large. In the same way, the law itself reflected, even as it lent its force to, unquestioned assumptions concerning gender. Not only did women qualify for protection under the law only if prior virginity could be medically substantiated but the writing of the clause on estupro dealing with love letters seems tacitly to support the male quest to verify virginity, even giving such a proof the added luster of a medical or scientific backing. The criminal code, then, sought to uphold the informal pact linking the initiation of sexual relations with the exchange for a promise of marriage, even if giving men considerable leeway in escaping their obligations.

This was the case only, of course, if the promise of marriage came in written form. One reading of love letters, then—indeed, the one offered in this section—is to situate them within the lettered city, that place of power premised upon the circulation of the written word through arteries of communication like the press, the novel, and the judicial system. Here, love letters, birth certificates, and medical inspections form part of the apparatus of power, providing support to the official family and persons who could substantiate and exercise their judicial personas in written form. Yet those individuals sending and receiving love letters, one imagines, must have hoped they would be read in a different light, one in which the arteries of circulation sustained a sentimental anatomy rather than the official body. Before turning to these engagements with the written word (the focus of the final section of the book), however, we need to know more about the broader contexts within which writing took place and in which its meanings might be made apparent, the task of the next section.

The Lettered Countryside

That neither could read or write seemed not particularly to matter. In hopes of persuading his fifteen-year-old novia to leave her home in the small agricultural town of Huejotitan in the southern reaches of the northern Mexican state of Chihuahua to be his partner (*compañera*), Liberato had sent a series of love letters to María. Essential to the matchmaking was Doña Dolores, Liberato's sister, who had acted both as messenger, delivering the letters to his intended, and interpreter, reading her brother's (or, more accurately, someone else's) heartfelt prose to his credulous, though hesitant, true love. It had not been Dolores, however, who had been responsible for penning these missives—her skills, she admitted, were limited to reading, and reading printed letters at that, not those written cursively. The task of writing (or, more accurately, printing) the letters had been left to another relative, Liberato's brother-in-law, who was married to another of our suitor's sisters, and who made ends meet, as did Liberato himself, through agricultural labor on the same small rancho in southern Chihuahua in the waning years of the nineteenth century.[1]

As for María, she had good reason to be hesitant. She knew that Liberato had already been married, making him unable to "cover her honor," that is, to marry her in the not-too-distant future if she would agree to the initiation of sexual relations in the present, an exchange that, as you saw in the previous section, was designed to provide for the man a demonstration of the woman's will and virginity. For a man of Liberato's imagination and creativity, however, this was only a minor setback to be overcome with further recourse to the written word (the first had been his love letters). María insisted that among the correspondence she carried with her when she left her home had been an official-looking document, boasting actual government stamps, in which Liberato had obligated himself to live in her company and maintain her during their life together. Liberato himself (or, at least, Liberato's letter writer) expressed what that document was meant to accomplish in yet another letter, this one to María's eldest brother, her legal guardian and head of her household, who, incidentally, testified he could not read or write either. In this third recourse to the written word, Liberato explained that he regarded this faux-marriage certificate to be the same as a legal proof (a *constancia*, as he called it) that would protect and defend the young woman (that is, grant amparo to her) until the day he died, "the same as if we were married." This letter is a triumph of form over content. Although it is written as a *carta de pedimento*, a formal petition commonly composed in order to ask for the woman's hand in marriage, it could accomplish everything but that: Liberato's previous marriage made such an outcome a legal impossibility.[2]

As you might imagine, neither María's brothers nor judicial authorities were impressed with Liberato's formalistic legerdemain, his attempt to cover his illicit activities with a thin veneer of legalese. Liberato ended up before judicial officials to answer for the crime of rapto when, his letters having had their intended effect, María gathered up her clothes and correspondence and left her home to accompany him to the house of his letter-writing brother-in-law. Yet, I find Liberato's once-removed (and, perhaps, at times, even twice-removed) correspondence and the meanings and actions surrounding it to be particularly impressive, and for a number of reasons. While designed to overcome a specific impediment, that of Liberato's previous marriage, these strategies nevertheless point to the particularly striking relationship between certain kinds of reading and writing practices on the one hand and courtship on the other. They draw our attention to a number of engagements with the written word, all by people who achieved literacy only in cooperation with others, each possessing varying degrees of literacy skills or access to them, potentially complicating our very understanding of the term "literacy" itself. In short,

they make of literacy a problem to be investigated rather than a preconceived category of analysis.

As for María, her insistence on maintaining in her possession an officially stamped document masquerading as a certificate of marriage as well
as Liberato's promise-laden letters may, for some readers, evoke the image
of an earlier woman, her namesake or *tocaya*, Doña María Josepha Pérez de
Balmaceda, living in mid-eighteenth-century Havana. In order to maintain
her honor in the face of an unfulfilled promise of marriage, this earlier
María had continued, for the rest of her life, to wear around her neck on
a chain a crumpled piece of paper upon which a promise of marriage had
been written (if subsequently left unfulfilled).[3] As much as the familiarity
of their behavior lodges the couple in the colonial past, Liberato's use of
government stamps and fake marriage certificates locates them squarely in
their contemporary present, an era marked by the survey and subsequent loss
of village land in the agricultural communities of southern Chihuahua, as
elsewhere in Mexico, and by a bevy of new regulations, issued increasingly
by appointed rather than elected municipal- and district-level state officials.
His letters and conjured marriage certificate contributed to the flurry of
written documents, some more official-looking than others, circulating
with ever-greater frequency by the late nineteenth century, documents
attesting to land ownership, the payment of taxes, business transactions,
the inspection of brothels, cantinas and billiard halls that, I can assure you,
fill district and state archives in places like Parral, testifying not only to
the presence of a Mexican state attempting to arrogate power to itself but
also, increasingly, to the documents it generated as a source of legitimacy
and authority.[4]

The increase in both the number of documents as well as the velocity
of their circulation in places like the mining towns and agricultural communities of Chihuahua has been seen as part of a project that was intended
to discipline, transform, and make abstemious and productive citizens out
of all Latin Americans, Mexicans included. In this supposed triumph of
the written word over the oral culture of the countryside, as Angel Rama
characterizes it, the expansion of writing made possible the collection
and use of oral traditions, often as part of projects of national imagining,

a process that simultaneously destroyed the very unwritten traditions and oral communications upon which such invented traditions were being premised. One of Rama's main contributions in his book *The Lettered City* is to identify the close relationship between power, the ability to manipulate the written word and other signs, and the urban center in Latin America. For Rama, the lettered city was the site where the extensive production of texts took place, texts like the criminal codes discussed in the previous section, through which the independent countries of Latin America were brought into being and ruled, and through which that rule, along with the hierarchies and values essential to it, was justified.[5] What needs always to be kept in mind, however, was that, by the end of the nineteenth century, the lettered city was still a fairly small neighborhood, one that, in Mexico, was as much aspirational as accomplished, a place that might one day be populated by suitable residents if only the current ones could be made over or convinced to move out.[6]

This section is concerned with another kind of writing, even if just as much implicated in questions of power, the creation of hierarchies, and their justification. Leaving the urban center with its close connections to circuits of official power, it focuses instead on the writing and exchange of personal correspondence among people like Liberato and María (and their relatives), men and women of more humble origins than those of many of the letrados considered by Rama. If, in the previous section, the circumstances under which love letters came to be part of the judicial archive were set out, this section takes as its subject the writing and reading practices of, as well as the exchange of love letters among, men and women of the mining camps, rural communities, and smaller towns and villages located in Chihuahua during the last two decades of the nineteenth century and the first three of the twentieth. I argue that, by the late nineteenth century, the countryside was also increasingly lettered, especially with written missives about love (as did the city no doubt pulse to the rhythms of oral cultures[7]). Here, I use "countryside" for effect, even polemically, as, given the movement and circulation of people between the rancho and the mine, the center of the country and the north, as well as between Mexico and the mining and railroad camps of the southern United States, the idea of an isolated or unchanging countryside in much of northern Mexico was more the device of novelists and historians longing nostalgically for a past they were helping to invent than a description of reality. Focusing on such writing has forced me to rethink my own understanding both of the meaning of literacy as well as the easy dichotomy that links the city with command of the written word and the countryside with oral communication. Rama anticipated as much. Employing a literate/oral binary, although to great effect, Rama nonetheless notes, although fails to explore, that the project of the letrados, far from simply eradicating previously existing cultural forms, made possible new patterns of rural culture, often representing a combination of written and oral forms.[8]

The love letters gathered in this book belong simultaneously to both the oral and the literate realms. Although written, many of them must be seen as essentially conversations in written form, more a part of than separate from the world of everyday speech. Some of the letters are understandable only when read aloud, a process that makes clearer where accents and punctuation marks along with natural breaks in ideas and trains of thought can be found. A few are impossible to comprehend without joining together into words sounds that have been expressed in writing as separate syllables or by separating the last syllable of one word to read as the beginning syllable of the next. Others are farther removed from the world of everyday speech, more closely attuned to the conventions and forms of the lettered city. Love letters, rather than joining distinct cultures, one premised upon orality and the other on literacy, reveal the boundaries between the oral and the written to be porous or fluid rather than firmly fixed. They make it difficult to answer the question I most often get asked—"What percent of the Mexican population at that time was 'literate?'"—by complicating the meaning of the term literacy itself.

In this book I view literacy, and its impact on society, as a subject for analysis rather than as a reenactment on the Mexican set of a familiar production already staged in many other venues. Not all would agree. In his far-reaching and influential work, for example, Walter Ong argues that fundamental and all-encompassing changes accompany the shift from oral to writing to print culture, a process he describes as the technologizing of

the word. "More than any other invention," he argues, "writing has transformed human consciousness," leading to the isolation of the self and to the
opening of that self up to ever increasing introspection and self-analysis.[9] In
addition to changes in the nature of individuals or of personhood, scholars
adopting this perspective have argued for literacy's role in fundamentally
transforming social structures and cultures, often positing a dichotomy
between societies characterized by literacy and those where it is absent.
In contrast to this point of view, Niko Besnier and David Barton, among
others, reject the claim that there are universal attributes of literate societies,
arguing instead for the need to view literacy as a multifaceted phenomenon
and, consequently, for the need to determine such things as who has access
to what type of literacy and in what social context each literacy activity is
learned and used. They propose an "event-centered" approach to literacy,
focusing analysis on one particular social setting or context, such as personal letter writing, to ask how such a literacy, in each instance, derives its
meanings from the broader context in which it is practiced. Their interest
in understanding the cultural ways of utilizing literacy leads to a concern
not with literacy, but with literacies, each associated with different domains
of life, different social groups, different institutions, different genders, each
shaped by and helping to shape power in different ways.[10]

In what can only be called a model study of the event-centered approach
to literacy outlined above, Laura M. Ahearn focuses on the writing of love
letters to explore the social effects of literacy in rural Nepal in the 1990s.[11]
Increasing female literacy rates during this decade, enabling the writing and
exchange of love letters, resulted in new courtship customs and, especially,
a transition away from arranged and capture marriages and toward more
self-initiated marriages like elopement. Yet, love letters also both reflected
and helped shape other fundamental transformations under way, in such
things as conceptions of agency, the ways in which residents conceived of
themselves and their own actions, understandings of romantic love, notions
of personhood, gender ideologies, and ideas associated with development.
Drawing on development discourse to compose their love letters, villagers
in Nepal increasingly came to associate romantic love with success and
autonomy in decision-making, making love itself into an agent of change

in many aspects of their lives. The strength of Ahearn's work is that each of these interrelated areas is the subject of investigation and analysis rather than presumed to follow from the supposedly inherent transformative power of "literacy."[12]

The gradations and fine distinctions in the reading and writing skills of those appearing before judicial officials in cases that involved the writing and exchange of written correspondence in Chihuahua, especially but not limited to love letters, are seldom so directly discussed as they are in the case of Liberato, María, et al. What can be documented, however, is the circulation of love letters, along with other kinds of writing, among men and women who describe themselves as artisans, including carpenters and tailors, mine workers (operarios), agricultural laborers, like Liberato and his brother-in-law, and women concerned with their household chores (quehaceres domésticos). At times, as in Liberato's case, such writing represented a profound engagement with the norms and forms (the architecture) of the lettered city, the amparos, constancias, and certificates that were, simultaneously, its progeny and progenitors. Part of the written transcript in another legal case taking place at about the same time as that of Liberato, the missive that Ismael penned to Atanacia, which reads more like a promissory note than a love letter, offers further testimony to the reach of the documentary state into private correspondence: "In Hidalgo del Parral, 28 October 1890. Whereby I draw up these lines to the Señorita Atanacia N. I give her my word that I'll marry her as soon as I get the money and so I sign. 28 October 1890. Yours, Ismael M."[13] Some letter writers even managed to express the most private of sentiments and desires as they offered formal commitments that might later be used against them in legal proceedings. Writing in 1903, for example, José pleaded with Libradita, "Libradita: This letter is the last in which I swear to you and obligate myself to marry you if you accept my desires this very same day today I'll wait for you at the time you decide and I hope no one will know what is going on. I swear to you that as soon as what I desire happens we'll get married and we'll be happy as I've already told you. Libradita today I wait for you to do the right thing. Yours. J.Y."[14]

Not all letter writers were so enamored with the need to obtain official recognition for their relationships, whether from representatives of the state or the church. Writing in 1910 to Romanita, his young novia, twenty-five-year-old Teofilo, another mine worker (operario), after greeting her, stated, in no uncertain terms:

> [That] we don't need witnesses at least not a single living soul to sanction our friendship because why would we need the señor Jefe or the señor priest [cura] as you say to me what is it that you want that these men should do with us or is it that you think that with the word of these men we'll be happier or what are you talking about because I believe that neither of these men will lead me to look out for your happiness only one God can guide my thinking only before Him can I humble myself and in this world I'll give to no one what I've given to Him not even for your love will I humble myself to people who you tell me to not even with the exception of those two and I'm telling you this because I believe that our friendship is completely independent of them.[15]

The message, certainly self-serving, or at least convenient, given that Teofilo's previous marriage made it impossible for him to do so yet again, seems also to attest, if measured by the shrillness of its protest at any rate, to the degree to which the edifice of the lettered city could rest on couples, despite their attempts to distance themselves from it.

If one of the bricks used in the construction of the lettered city was the judicial system, with its formal requirements for documentation as outlined in the previous section, and as illustrated in the fake marriage certificate and legal language of Liberato and the formal promises of mine workers (or even their adamant expression of their refusal to do so), other materials deployed in its composition might include literature, especially the novel, and the new, sensationalist mass press, the venue where novels often first appeared in installments. Running through both the novel and the press was the letter form, not only in the case of the epistolary novel but also with the inclusion of letters and other texts within novels more generally, and, in the case of the press, in the reporting of correspondents, a kind of implied letter, along with the publishing of actual suicide notes and other such texts, often taken from judicial processes like those about which you have been reading.

As each genre of the production of texts often implicated and referenced the others, the letter ran through them all, deployed to different, if at times overlapping, ends. My interest in this section is in this body of writing, what I'm referring to as the lettered countryside, in at least two senses of that term. The first is with the corpus of writing or genre of the letter as constituted by some of the many forms of letters that were circulating in the late nineteenth century. If letters could serve as legal evidence and help constitute the judicial persona, they could also, when deployed in novels and in the press, help bring into being various kinds of publics, those sharing a common sense of time, those transcending space through an emphasis on the immediacy of events taking place elsewhere, and, perhaps simultaneously, those sharing common sentiments that these very texts were meant to engender. It is this sense of an emerging public or publics being called into being that the phrase "lettered countryside" is intended to evoke.

If the letter in the press or the novel could be put to a number of uses, helping to constitute various kinds of publics, this writing might also offer models for those penning their own letters to draw from as they themselves helped shape existing understandings or codifications of the letter form. Such codification and the rationale for it could be found in etiquette manuals, like that of Carreño, as well as in more popular love letter–writing manuals as published by the Vanegas Arroyo press and sold in the streets. Letters, as will be discussed further, could be didactic, designed to teach the very values and categories they were intending to bring into being. My concern is also with this body of writing in a second sense—the form and meaning that the letter could take in the practices of courtship at that time and in that place. Here, as men such as Liberato and others, as well as a number of young women, took up the pen or had others compose letters with them, letters could be designed to accomplish many things. As much as letters could be written to be informative or newsy, meant to enable communication across space, they could also be written to bridge emotional divides as well as those obstacles lovers imposed as a means of securing ever-increasing commitment and trust to a courting relationship. As you will see in the next section, love letters were also, in a sense, performative; that is, they brought into being the very thing they were discussing—as symbols their arrival initiated a courtship while their mutual return or destruction pronounced its conclusion.

Whether these engagements between the written and the oral are described as new cultural forms, as in the case of Rama, or as a clash between dominant and vernacular literacies, as others have characterized it, the point that needs to be stressed is that, in the face of a body of literature that claims for literacy in the singular the power to transform individuals and selves, one that is often premised upon the presumed existence of a great divide between the oral and the literate world, people participate in and are characterized by many different literacies, each with their own sets of assumptions, power relations, gendered practices, and consequences. Each literacy, in short, has its own history, and it is to the history of the reading and writing practices associated with love and courtship that I now turn.

"Cartas y cartas, compadre. . . ."

That Liberato and María along with artisans, mine workers, and other rural dwellers should be exchanging letters would probably have come as little surprise to Manuel Payno, author of *Los bandidos de Río Frío*, a novel published in monthly installments in periodicals as it was written between 1889 and 1891, about the same time that Liberato and his relatives were composing their missives.[16] Payno's inclusion of love letters in this novel, including those supposedly penned by plebeians, makes it an especially useful starting place for our discussion of the relationship between writing and courtship while allowing us, as well, to situate such writing within the broader reading and writing practices of the time. Beginning here also helps to remind us that the novel, especially a sentimental novel like this one, and the letter, along with other forms of writing, could share many similarities, including the privileging of emotion, an emphasis on self-reflexivity and introspection, forms of narrative and emplotment, and the writing into being of a certain kind of subjectivity, both of self and other. Both the novel and the letter could be intertextual and dialogic, a conversation between a self and a presumed reader who is often even addressed directly and whose reaction is imagined or anticipated.[17]

A potboiler that kept people on the edge of their seats waiting for more; an imaginative yarn based on true crimes and real events in the history of the republic; a foundational fiction whose characters knit Mexicans together both through their common speech, customs, and habits and in their movements across the range and breadth of the country; a meditation on the past and the future through an insistent focus on inheritance, legacy, birthright, destiny, and fate, both of the characters that trample across its pages and of the country they inhabit; and, it seems, the very embodiment of Rama's argument concerning the incorporation of rural orality into the service of the lettered city, *Los bandidos de Río Frío* lends itself to many readings. Implicated in, if not central to, all these readings is literacy, or literacies, manifested not only in Payno's preoccupation with charting the myriad ways that Mexicans of all classes in the nineteenth century participated in various reading and writing practices but also in his incorporation of the predominant genres of writing of the time, especially those associated with the newspaper, the legal system, and the letter, among others, into the novel.

As Payno's explicit concern is with forms of writing, the conventions and understandings associated with them, and the transformations they were undergoing, it is not by accident that the novel is littered with letrados. Three lawyers serve as main characters, moving the plot along by means of their activities while providing Payno with a pretext to include extensive discussions of the reading and writing practices associated with criminal investigations, other legal proceedings, the exchange of letters, political pronouncements, love notes, and the reporting of all such activities in a burgeoning press. The novel begins with a newspaper report of a cause célèbre, a criminal case concerning the sensational murder of a woman by her novio, one that generated two thousand pages of legal testimony and supporting documents gathered into three large *expedientes*. It ends with a letter supposedly written to the author belittling his writing ability while filling in the reader on the fates of the many characters in an imagined future that has supposedly taken place since the end of the events covered in the novel. In between, one lawyer, Bedolla, who becomes a criminal judge responsible for protecting "the honor of families" and presides over the kinds of crimes written about in the first section of the book you are currently reading, gains and loses political influence on the basis of his own incompetence in handling the criminal case that begins the novel, while another, Lamparilla, searches for the legal documents that will prove that his client, Moctezuma III, is the legal heir to extensive properties and haciendas, a patrimony that has been denied to him. A third, Olañeta, uncovers the errors or helps resolve the work of the previous two, protecting the various protagonists at the same time; it is Olañeta, as well, who finally brings the entire criminal conspiracy from which the novel takes its title to an end, a task he accomplishes while simultaneously engaged in an inner struggle, which often takes place in his library, between his romantic feelings, or what he refers to as fleeting sentiments, on the one hand, and his learning, the timeless wisdom gleaned through hours of engagement with the yellowed parchment of his books, on the other hand. All the while, an increasingly sensationalist press trumpets these and other events in newspaper articles and anonymous broadsides to a growing public that its very activity of publishing is helping to bring into being.

The presence of such a public, or publics, in the novel, recognizing themselves in the newspapers and becoming aware of and judging the actions of similarly positioned readers, now fellow constituents at the court of public opinion and members of an expanding public sphere, makes apparent that letrados were not the only ones engaging with the written word. In fact, Payno takes great care to spell out the reading and writing abilities of almost every character, regardless of whether or not they are lawyers or members of the aristocracy. Whereas these and other characters of higher social standing are often portrayed ensconced in their libraries, adept at manipulating the forms and formulas of literate society, those from the popular classes are almost always shown as in the process of learning to read and write (if they don't already know how to do so), incipient or potential, if not already fully, residents of the lettered city.

As a result, scenes of reading and writing, especially associated with the teaching of literacy, abound in the novel. A poor boy, finding himself a servant in Olañeta's home after being abandoned in a garbage dump, getting rescued, and then subsequently running away from the lathe-turner to whom he had been apprenticed, is seen diligently applying himself to "reading and writing Spanish grammar in the library" under the kindly lawyer's supervision, the continuation of an education that began with informal lessons in reading and math in the marketplace and during his stint in the poor house. (Readers themselves are ushered off to the library to read about the history of this institution![18]) Two rural *curanderas* responsible for his abduction—more likely than not to be cast at the time as the epitome of rural, feminine ignorance and superstition, perfect foils to urban, male medical knowledge—instead exchange curative roots and herbs with a schoolteacher at a nearby municipal school for women in return for lessons from a spelling book, a transaction that takes place on the street corner where they sell their wares. Another woman, the cook in the house of one of the main criminal masterminds in the latter part of the novel, seals the legal fate of this character by including as part of the recipes she writes into her recipe book the detailed evidence that she has incriminating him. As for Moctezuma III, heir to the patrimony of his ancestors and resident on a rural ranch far from the city, Payno states, "Of course he knew how to read, and he wrote in a stubby but completely legible hand."[19]

Comfortably situated within the genre of the foundational fiction, that novel of nineteenth-century Latin America that crafted the nation discursively by bringing together love of country and romantic love in mutually reinforcing allegory, *Los bandidos* clearly links literacy with national imagining. Here, all characters are literally reading on the same page of the novel of the nation; likewise, they experience the passage of time as national time, that is, simultaneously, something achieved not only by means of the form of the novel itself but also through its intertextuality, that is, the inclusion of letters and newspaper articles (even the original manuscript of the Enabling Act of the Republic hanging in a gold frame is featured, should Payno's point about writing the nation into existence be missed).[20] At critical junctures in the novel, however, the bricks and mortar of the lettered city—those legal documents, wills, marriage banns, deeds, newspapers, and letters plastered into its pages—are revealed as little more than a crumbling façade through which can be seen the way things really work. The character Bedolla, for example, law degree in hand and serving in the esteemed position of criminal judge, regards the documents generated by the criminal justice system, the declarations, the testimonies, the evidence, as so much blather (*mucha paja*). Having gained the ear of the president of the republic, he owes his influence to his sycophancy rather than to his wisdom or education, which he has completed, as Payno puts it, "without managing either to read with punctuation or to write even a single line without misspellings." It is likewise this same Bedolla ("who didn't write and who, as a matter of fact, had never been able to piece two sentences together"[21]) who came to control the supposedly independent Mexico City press. As for Lamparilla, one of the other lawyers, all the legal deeds and certified documents in the world are not sufficient to recover Moctezuma III's lost patrimony—it is only through making use of important personal connections in the judicial system along with applying brute force (the seizure of these lands by means of force of arms), that this is accomplished.

Just as the forms of the lettered city are not always sufficient for the task at hand, the written word itself is often found wanting and gives way to orality or the spoken word in various places in the novel. Even as the servant Juan puts his new knowledge of literacy to use by reading about himself in the newspaper delivered to the home where he works, the lawyer who is teaching him to read learns the truth about Juan's past when he overhears a conversation taking place in the kitchen, allowing him to chart a different destiny for the boy (although, simultaneously, clearly linking orality with the feminine and spaces such as the kitchen and reading with the masculine, especially in such venues as the library). Similarly, although the main criminal mastermind, a man known as Relumbrón ("Flash"), is assured of criminal prosecution because of evidence written on recipe cards, it is only by means of eavesdropping on the conversation between this figure and his father that the cook has managed to gather such detailed information in the first place. Referring to yet another character, a member of the aristocracy, the lawyer Oñate describes him as a person whose word is as good as a written contract.

More than simply a convenient device for moving the plot along or resolving actions, the centrality of orality at various points in the story serves rather to highlight the profound engagement between the written and spoken word that takes place in the novel more generally. It is not by chance that the novel is often described as being "chatty" in tone—in fact, it is as much a conversation with the reader in written form as it is a novel, a point the author, as well as his critics, makes. At many places in the text, the reader ("patient and curious") is interpellated and directly addressed (as she is in this book), at certain times to be asked for forgiveness, at others to be assured of the truthfulness of the tale, and at still others to have the novel's purpose explained to them. Moreover, along with national customs and national types, typical Mexican popular expressions and manners of speaking are incorporated into the text, allowing readers at the time to see in written form what they might hear in the streets in their everyday activities. In this regard, the novel itself is similar not only to many of the fictitious letters included in it but also to written correspondence more generally, as will be discussed shortly. The novel, written in monthly installments and published in the press, as well as marriage banns, wills, and letters, could be (and were) read out loud, often to those whose levels of literacies precluded a solitary reading. In fact, the properties of the novel that resonated with listeners have proven particularly enduring, as *Los bandidos* was still being read to children in Mexico a century after its writing.[22]

Payno's focus on customs, costumes, and the quotidian, especially forms of speech, as well as the conversational tone adopted in the novel, seems as much designed to critique the conventions of the lettered city as it is to capture orality in its service; at the very least, Payno, with his writing choices, brings into question, perhaps even breaks down, the sharp distinction usually posited to exist between these two realms. A number of hybrid forms of text are presented, in which, much as in the novel itself, the spoken and the written, literate and popular, are interfused. Near the beginning of the novel, for example, the written portion of an ex-votive image (itself an example of a genre that represents the coming together of written and pictorial forms), usually composed to give thanks for divine intervention, instead mocks the inability of a highly trained doctor from Mexico City's prestigious medical academy to cure a rural patient, a woman who had been pregnant for eleven months. As already mentioned, a humble cook writes out recipes that result in Relumbrón's just desserts. Barbers and other tradesmen know of crimes because of the newspapers they have read or the broadsheets they have heard hawked in the streets. The use of double-entry accounting is mocked when it is used by elite passengers on a stagecoach to tally up the supposed benefits of having been robbed rather than their losses ("the numbers don't lie" states one of the book's robbery victims, or, perhaps better, "beneficiaries," according to the new method of reckoning). At the heart of the book, rather than separating the letrados from the unlettered and isolating the threats to civilization in the barbarous wilderness inhabited by the illiterate in Río Frío, is Payno's vision that, perhaps, Río Frío is not so very far from the capital, that supposedly respected and well-off residents in Mexico City, at the center of the lettered city, can be corrupted by money and the developmentalist version of progress (as implied by the name of the criminal mastermind, Relumbrón, "Flash," or the ostentatious one). Although, it might be argued, this is only accomplished by making all Mexicans potentially residents of the lettered city, it is a lettered city in which the new neighbors are loud, boisterous, and unruly.

One of the forms of writing in the novel that Payno identifies as increasingly characterized by the intermingling of the written and spoken word is the letter, especially that associated with love. While in the novel letters of all kinds, formal and informal, genuine and forged, are central to carrying out business, both of the aboveboard and Río Frío variety, as well as to arranging everything from matters of state to those of family, it is the love letter, penned by men and women, from the most aristocratic to the most humble, that makes possible relationships that transcend social barriers, even if only with difficulties. Here, Payno's point seems to be that the heart cannot be controlled, that love, when it strikes, is blind to barriers of social class, status, and age. It is through love letters, for example, that the son of an hacienda overseer and the daughter of the most wealthy and conservative aristocratic family can aspire to, and finally succeed in forging, a life together. Another main character from the popular classes, Cecilia, receives love letters, read into the text of the novel by the lawyer

Lamparilla, one of Cecilia's suitors, from men located on various rungs of the social ladder, ranging from a humble butcher to a small store-owner/ black marketeer, the district's political chief, and, finally, the wealthy son of one of the region's largest hacienda owners.

If all lovers, like all countrymen, were joined by their common ability to dominate the written word, if not their hearts, the meanings and understandings associated with both the writing of love letters and their exchange could vary. For those with only the most tenuous grasp of the written word, letters, according to Payno, rather than serving as an integral aspect of courtship, usually followed it. Addressed to the head of the woman's household instead of exchanged between the courting couple, such letters pleaded for forgiveness for an act already past—the unauthorized abduction of the woman from her household, or a rapto—rather than planned for a future act, that of formal marriage. Forgoing in this manner the written trappings of official family formation—the banns, the certificates—an omission that Payno characterizes as laziness and that results in the formation of a couple in every sense except the formal one, an engagement with writing is, nevertheless, maintained. For most other courting couples in the novel, love letters themselves are essential, either to develop the courtship or to overcome the distance and circumstances that make it impossible for the couple to communicate in any other manner. In this courting correspondence, as in other cases of letter writing found in the novel, the written word generally, and letters specifically, are assumed to reveal the fundamental characteristics or qualities of those writing them. Commenting on the letters he is exchanging with the Marquis of Sauz holding him to his previous promise to marry the aristocrat's daughter, the suitor—highly honorable yet presently impoverished—remarks that each letter corresponded to the true character or nature of the person writing it. While the aristocrat's letter revealed his harsh and snobbish character, the suitor's frank and likable disposition was immediately apparent simply by reading his response.

In a similar manner, the love letters written to Cecilia, mentioned above, offer direct access to the inner character, qualities, and even the social standing of those composing them. That from the butcher, written on business stationary from the "Dwarf's Bacon Shop, of the great city of Chalco," seems to conjure, out of the form and content of his missive, the very letter writer himself. The fat and twisted letters scrawled on the yellow-tinged stationary smelling of butchered hogs; the misspelled words; the rendering into written form of an essentially spoken Spanish ("pamí" instead of "para mí," "quentra" instead of "que entra," "mitá" in place of "mitad"); the sexual innuendo and double entendre; and the concern with demonstrating economic resources sufficient to undertake marriage along with his embarrassment at approaching the subject directly, in face-to-face conversation, rehearse not only the butcher's character but offer a visual, aural, and even olfactory portrait of its writer and perhaps of stereotypes about the artisan world at the same time.[23] So, too, does Payno manage to capture, not only with this letter but also in the discussion of Cecilia's entire correspondence, the fundamental situatedness, one within the other, of the written and the oral. As Cecilia explains, much like the María from Havana mentioned earlier, she keeps the love letters in order to have them as proof or evidence should some busybody want to talk about her; as such, and apart from their content, they are physical tokens to be deployed in an oral public sphere in which respectability and reputation are asserted and contested through such means as gossip. She also gives her word, and keeps it, that she will marry Lamparilla, the lawyer courting her, only once he has triumphed in his legal quest to obtain formal written title to the lands claimed by Moctezuma III. Along with many of the characters in the novel, Cecilia not only negotiates in matters of the heart but over the very manner in which, orally or in writing, such transactions are to take place.

While the love letters from those suitors higher up the social ladder may be less colloquial than that of the butcher, they are no less revealing. The letter from the local political prefect, for example, on glossy paper newly imported from Paris expressly for the purpose of writing of love letters, came emblazoned with a little Cupid furiously shooting his arrows at a fat heart and looking more like a street urchin than the symbol of love; its prose exposed him to be similarly badly formed—a hypocrite as well as a bully, the prefect reveals himself in the letter as a man accustomed to getting his way by means of the arbitrary exercise of authority while simultaneously terrified by the powerful hold a woman had over him.[24] By contrast, that written by the storeowner was steeped in the gendered values of middle-class respectability, its concern with frankness in manners of speech, its preoccupation with reputation and honor, both his own and those of the object of his affection, and its attention to propriety. It has little to say about love, envisioning their marriage instead as a business partnership in which the pooling of resources would lead to ever more lucrative dealings, both in the store and in his sideline business of running contraband alcohol. Framed in terms of rational self-interest rather than as an appeal to emotion, the bargain as set out in this letter nevertheless included the expectation that Cecilia would act as the mother of his seven children, a circumstance that, in her opinion, promised no end of argument and domestic discord, even if highlighting women's roles as mothers, both of the family and the nation, in his middle-class discourse.[25]

If the letters from the butcher, the prefect, and the storeowner give expression to characteristics, preoccupations, and values commonly associated with these figures, turning them almost into "types" or stereotypes that are meant to represent classes or social strata in the same manner as other characters in the novel represent regions, so too does that from the son of a powerful hacienda owner portray the values associated with his social position, enabling Payno to explore the highly charged zone where the discourse of equality and chance in matters of the heart runs headlong into the fixedness and inequality of position when it comes to family and social standing, the single most dominant tension that structures the novel. In contrast to the previous relationships, this one, at least initially, seems to be one of equals, that is, if equality is conceptualized in terms of their mutually felt desire rather than in social standing. Cecilia clearly articulates her physical attraction to Don Pioquinto, drawn, she states, to his youth, to his body, and to the promised pleasures of the flesh, in much the same terms as he expresses his longing for her in the opening lines of his letter, prefiguring, in his hopes for a glimpse of her body through the curtains as she bathes, the culmination of their desires. Unable, however, to conceive of a concomitant social equality to match that of their desire, Don Pioquinto spends the rest of the love letter outlining his elaborate scheme to bring the two lovers together while maintaining intact social hierarchy and inequality. To avoid the scandal that would follow from the marriage of such social unequals yet nevertheless satiate his desires, he proposes that Cecilia come to the hacienda he will be in charge of administrating in the position of cook, offering her the (relatively) lavish wage of six pesos a month plus five and a half reales as a weekly ration, a sum that, in addition to the excess she could skim in the purchasing of supplies, would allow her, in his calculation, to put aside some twenty-five or thirty pesos a month without his father being able to complain in the least. Despite Don Pioquinto's attempt to shroud with a cloak of morality the dubious arrangement, by offering a vision at the end of his letter of the couple kneeling together at a private mass in the hacienda chapel, as if happily ever after, he can accomplish, much like Liberato with his writing, only the form and not the substance of holy matrimony—the implication that Cecilia will be his mistress, not his wife, is impossible to miss.

Cecilia's response is also worthy of consideration, turning on its head, as it does, the supposedly unassailable social hierarchy assumed by Don Pioquinto (and perhaps by readers as well). Whereas, in response to the previous propositions, Cecilia resolves matters verbally—either by sending a message through one of her female servants or by means of a conversation in person with the suitor, a perfectly acceptable option offered explicitly by these earlier correspondents (who, interestingly, all acknowledge her ability to respond in writing but respect that she may not choose to do so)—in this case, a formal written response is forthcoming. In both form (the use of writing) and in its content, the letter is an insistent assertion of equality and, simultaneously, a challenge to the social and gender hierarchy through the skillful use of analogy. "If you are hungry," she tells Don Pioquintito (addressing him now in the diminutive), "I can give you a job carrying fruit in the market for a salary of eight pesos a month and a real daily for your ration." Moreover, mocking him as well as the manner he proposes for her to make additional income, she offers to pay so that he can eat every day at *agachados*, booths where vendors heat up the scraps of food and leftovers purchased from the kitchens of the rich, a variation on the arrangement he was suggesting she accept. In this brief letter, she asserts that she is his equal in every way—as an owner, a patron who can provide employment and food, a person who commands, and a writer.[26] It is as if the social blindness that is meant to characterize love both contributes to as it is structured by another assumption—that all are equal in their ability to write love letters. Equality, or at least the ability to disregard social barriers in love, draws sustenance from as it is premised upon love letters as an exchange between equals; it makes of love letters a potentially radical venue for the leveling of hierarchies of social class and of gender.

The positioning here of Cecilia as Don Pioquinto's equal, achieved by means of demonstrating her ability to manipulate the written word, contrasts strikingly with the role she has been assigned in much of the rest of the novel, that of the verbal pole in an oral/literate binary comprised by her relationship with Lamparilla, one of the many lawyers in the novel. While Lamparilla lives in the world of contracts, deeds, wills, statements in judicial procedures, and political pronouncements, that composed of "letters and more letters," the phrase uttered about him that I have borrowed to frame this portion of the present section, Cecilia is grounded in the local, the particular, the popular, the everyday, the subsoil from which that which is uniquely Mexican has been nurtured and grown. A voluptuous fruit vendor, she is the very embodiment of the bounty of the land, preparing its most savory, and specifically national, dishes, rooted in local tastes, ingredients, and means of preparation and described in local parlance and manners of speech that all, letrados included, can partake in, enjoy, and praise. Their constitution as a couple presents Payno with almost endless opportunity to mediate or negotiate across this local/letrado divide, with orality becoming a shorthand for the particularly and specifically Mexican and Cecilia its most important spokesperson. When Lamparilla proposes, for example, Cecilia gives her word that she will marry him only once he has successfully recovered Moctezuma's patrimony, an oral promise that she honors. When Lamparilla waxes poetic about the "sublime," the apogee in a geography of sentiment brought into being by the spectacle of nature, Cecilia counters that the poor were born to work and, unlike *licenciados*, did not have the head to think of such things. When he writes verses to attempt to woo her, she reads them through the lens of her own experience, transposing his references to literature and history to the register of daily life, to local figures she knows, to the particular and specific, before expressing her hope that the words he has written might eventually be made into a song and accompanied by guitar (a prospect that he relishes rather than rejects).

In the book, Payno makes a complicated argument that resists being reduced to a conflict between the oral and the literate, even though that binary is indeed employed at numerous points in the novel. Much of it has to do with his assumption that it is place itself that generates unique qualities, characteristics, traits, and types, perhaps in the same manner that Melchor Ocampo envisions by naming his own estate Pomoca, an anagram of his own name. If Payno often employs orality as the predominant means for expressing the local customs, characteristics, and types that come together to form what is uniquely Mexican, it is in no way meant to deny the concomitant local command of literacy. As you have seen, although Cecilia continually returns to ground all explanations and understandings in various forms of orality and the spoken word—not only in her relationship with Lamparilla but by apologizing continually for her inability to spell correctly or for not understanding literary or other references or for not understanding what she is signing when she becomes involved in a judicial procedure—she is more than capable of asserting her own equality, as a writer and as a person, in her written correspondence with Don Pioquintito. Despite the fact that all characters in the novel, from the humblest curandera to recruits for the army to the daughter of an aristocrat, are portrayed as learning to read and write, if they do not already do so, and thus are cast as potential if not already current residents of the lettered city, its forms and formulas are presented as far from an unalloyed good for Payno. In fact, the novel can be read as a profound critique of the lettered city, its incompetent lawyers, its inaccurate and sensationalist, even compromised press, its forgeries, its titles and deeds that are useless unless backed by force, its flawed bookkeeping, its yellowing and dusty parchment, its fake library that serves as a false front for hidden treasure, the sugarcane crop dying while its supposedly enlightened administrator sits in yet another library reading the latest methods for growing cane while ignoring local knowledge, its triumph of form over substance. Despite the fact that the destiny of every character in the novel is mediated through some kind of written form—the love letter, the discovered note that reveals true identity, titles and deeds, judicial decisions and evidence, recipe books, the newspaper column—such technologies can also be employed by the criminal enterprise of Relumbrón linking Río Frío to the heart of the republic, in this instance in the form of written notes made by one of his accomplices and submitted to Relumbrón in which were specified potential victims of robbery, their habits, and any items of worth, information that then circulated through the network of thieves facilitating its work.[27]

Payno continues nevertheless to hold in tension the oral and the literate, the local and the national, tacking between these poles depending on the task at hand, at times to praise the local as the essence of the truly Mexican, at others to argue for its improvement; at times to ridicule prejudices that disdained local knowledge and ways of doing things, at others to advocate bringing over the latest breeds of cattle and sheep from Europe; at times to mock double-entry accounting and privilege local bookkeeping premised upon experience and local needs, at others to privilege phrenology, European science, and mesmerism. Increasingly enmeshed in the forms of writing that characterized life at the end of the nineteenth century, for better or worse, and situated in an imagined future where all are reading on the same page of the novel of the nation, the novel's characters nevertheless continue to give expression to customs, characteristics, and the local in oral form. In doing so, Payno expresses neither a longing for the past nor a yearning for the modern, but brings the two, simultaneously, into being, placing his characters resolutely at home (or not at home) in both, oscillating between these poles that increasingly structured people's lives, holding out the promise of a future nation premised upon the combination of long-standing ties to place with its newly acquired common literacy. However, while all might equally be producers as well as the products of the texts of their times, an equality the consequences of which are imagined most radically in the exchange of love letters, differences in manners and morals not only reestablish hierarchies of gender and social position but justify the role of a select few in guiding the entire process.

Having, in the penultimate chapter of *Bandidos*, resolved the various plots that structure the novel as well as relieved readers of their suspense by revealing the fates of those characters, and especially those courting couples, to whom they had become attached, Payno, in the book's final chapter, situates himself in the novel's present, as the actual author who had just finished writing the novel, while, simultaneously, reiterating how many of its events and personalities had been premised upon an actual episode in Mexico's history, the operation of a criminal ring by a certain Colonel Yáñez, a high-ranking figure during the time of Santa Ana.[28] In this chapter, Payno, describing himself as the lone guest in an isolated hotel in Normandy, France, ponders the lives of the fishermen and their families whom he has been watching from his room as he has written the book, noting how profoundly they had been shaped by this place and the sea.

In the midst of this scene before him that encapsulated in the present the same process that the historical scenes he had just finished recounting accomplished in Mexico's past, a (fictitious) letter arrives from a dear friend of the author in Mexico. Whereas other texts produced in Mexico and circulating in Europe remarked upon in the novel serve only to confirm European prejudices and underwrite calls for intervention by portraying Mexicans as backward, barbaric, and in need of being saved from themselves, this letter points to the future rather than the past. Overturning some of the conclusions presented by the author in the penultimate chapter, the letter updates the author (and reader) on the fate of some of his characters and their relationships, revelations, the author warns, that readers can choose to "swallow" or not. Despite the humor and playfulness captured by the idea that a friend of the author could know the fate of the characters being written about, an idea that seems to collapse history and fiction (in that some of the characters may have been historical figures and others inventions of the author), this intervention from Mexico more importantly establishes a trajectory into the future, an ongoing future brought into being by this past in which the characters continue to go about their lives. While Payno is adamant that the novel is meant as a legacy, presenting Mexico's customs and practices to present and future generations, its project, like the lives of its characters, is ongoing, as much forward-looking as it is nostalgic—documenting that which is particularly Mexican, even if changing or disappearing, becomes the raw material for the creation of a national literature that, if generated out of Mexico's past, will write the future nation into existence.

Presented as the final chapter, the letter, along with the author's reminiscences and the establishment of the actual historical setting from which many of the events and personalities of the novel are derived, serve to make apparent the author's own voice and the constructedness of his text, highlighting the need for the reader to beware not only of the conclusions the author presents but of the forms used to present them. Locating himself overlooking a beach in Normandy, pondering the lives of the fishermen and their families as he writes, Payno highlights his own authorial presence as he destabilizes it, the historical nature of the material as he fictionalizes it, and the finality in the relationships of the fictional/historical characters that have been resolved in the penultimate chapter as contingent, up for grabs, one point of view among others that may be contradicted in a letter, newspaper story, or in some other form, along with the grounding of his "chatty" prose in the world of the oral. Collapsing genres, authorial authority, even time, serves in no way to diminish the impact of the work—in fact, it may do precisely the opposite. Combining all these forms serves to write into a being a broad audience that can read (or hear) itself as "Mexican" while simultaneously receiving an education as to the forms of sentiment, feeling, and self that might be appropriate to inhabit such a category of belonging.

Just as I have read *Bandidos* through a lens very much shaped by my engagement with love letters and judicial archives, I now propose to reconsider various forms of writing in light of some of the issues suggested in my discussion of the novel. While the image of every character in the novel reading on the same page of the nation, current or potential residents of the lettered city, is more a letrado dream of national imagining than a description of life in many communities in late nineteenth- and early twentieth-century Mexico, the various forms of writing with which the novel engages—the reporting of an expanding sensationalist press, judicial writing generated by criminal cases, various kinds of government correspondence and reports, the letter, along with the novel itself—were indeed becoming more and more a part of the fabric of everyday life in Chihuahua, as elsewhere in Mexico, at that time.

Literacies in Porfirian Chihuahua; or, Dramas de
la vida pasional (Dramas of the passionate life); or,
Mañana daremos detalles (Details tomorrow)

The tragedy that took place in the Hotel Palacio in Ciudad Chihuahua in late January 1906 may not have generated two thousand pages of testimony and other legal paraphernalia, as did the fictitious cause célèbre around which much of the plot in *Bandidos* is structured. However, the mode of its reporting in *El Correo de Chihuahua*, the paper of record in that city at the time, as well as the manner in which readers were addressed in such newspaper writing about this and other "sensational crimes" and "passionate dramas," shocking events that appeared ever more frequently in their columns in the first decade of the twentieth century, would have been very familiar to readers of that novel.[29] As in many of these bloody dramas, as the press dubbed them, jealousy was to blame. Having left Mexico City to travel to Chihuahua City in order to see the woman with whom he had been living perform in a theatrical benefit being held there, Manuel Algara, a person who was "very well known and belonging to one of the principal families of the metropolis," shot María Reig before turning the pistol on himself. Both initially survived the trauma, Reig for nearly a week before succumbing to her injuries while Algara took until nearly the end of February to die, precipitating yet another opportunity for mass-mediated scandal, this time over the decision to transfer him to the care of the physicians at the Hospital "Porfirio Díaz" rather than leave him in the hands of his own doctors at the Hotel Palacio, where his recovery, it was said, had supposedly been progressing nicely.[30]

My concern here is not with the particulars of this case but with what seems to be the growing fascination with such sensational reporting as well as with the techniques used to render these events textually. In short, I am interested in understanding why writing about these crimes seems to have been particularly productive, that is, useful for producing a certain kind of affect, a particular type of reader, a specific sense of time, in a text that, like the novel, combined the written and the oral, addressing readers directly, conjuring a verbal public sphere in printed form while simultaneously bringing into being a public or publics of readers and listeners who were consuming such writing. Although I will often come back to the texts generated by the tragedy in the Hotel Palacio to make my own argument, readers should remember that, in 1906 alone, *El Correo* carried several stories about the killing of women, not only in the state of Chihuahua but in Puebla and Mexico City as well, and even a sensational case in Havana, Cuba; numerous columns about the suicides and suicide attempts, both of women and of men who, having dared to take a chance at love and lost, found that they could no longer go on; and a handful of other stories about crimes of passion, especially murder-suicides like the one at the Hotel Palacio.[31] A common thread running through all these columns was a particular understanding and construction of love, a theme to which I will return.

Although unfolding in Ciudad Chihuahua, the tragedy in the Hotel Palacio was anything but local news. Given the social status of the participants and their place of residence in the nation's capital, the story was quickly picked up in Mexico City, where it appeared in *México al Día*, a column featuring daily events there, especially as they pertained to respectable society, and one that *El Correo* received by telegraph from Mexico City and published regularly. In fact, *México al Día* seemed to specialize in reporting crimes of passion, carrying similar stories later that year about a terrible drama of murder-suicide in Puebla (which the column likened to the earlier affair in the Hotel Palacio); details of a sensational crime in Havana, Cuba, in which a husband had murdered his family; and stories about suicides, especially if the person was well known or from the right social circles, as in that of the female singer who had performed in many of the plazas of the republic, as well as that of an "elegant" woman. Common to all these stories were their "sensational" nature, a description that the columnists never tired of repeating, usually with a different adjective (*"sensación tremenda"*; *"sensación . . . profundamente horrible"*; *"grandísima sensación"*); an emphasis on the degree of feelings manifested on the part of "all society" as well as by distraught relatives, especially grieving mothers; and the use of graphic (and often bloody) details to evoke the specifics of the crime, the condition of its victims, and the particulars of each episode as gleaned through rumor and local discussion, or, in the absence of actual information or gossip, through the filter of locally accepted commonsense understandings of what was likely to have taken place.

Perhaps it was only fitting that readers in Chihuahua were learning, at least in part, the details of the Hotel Palacio and other affairs from a columnist based in the country's capital city. Not only did such crimes and their reporting seem to be particularly associated with life in the big city rather than in the rural areas where novelists often staged them, but, as well, the juxtaposition of local, national, and, at times, transnational voices and perspectives served to highlight that the readership being constructed was also similarly envisioned. While an extensive literature attests to the centrality of the press in imagining the nation into existence, making newspapers, in the idiom of the novel, one-day bestsellers, reporting on crimes of passion was only intended to intensify this sense of national belonging: the extensive use of specific details in such reports served to highlight not the unique nature and circumstances of each case but rather the fundamentally similar values, feelings, and sentiments, rooted in family, emotion, and social standing they were meant to evoke as well as the expectation, shared throughout the country, that a common lens existed through which to view them.[32] As one editor in Chihuahua glossed it, "When it came to the Algara-Reig tragedy, everyone from the First Magistrate of the Nation to the last citizen was hanging on the slightest details."[33] One of Payno's characters could not have said it better. Crimes of passion in Puebla were like those in Chihuahua, which were like those in Mexico City, that is, useful in creating a community of sentiment premised upon shared feelings as well as, simultaneously, similarly shared sensations of horror and fascination. So useful were the details of such events in evoking such responses that crimes taking place elsewhere, outside the national frame (as in Havana), could nevertheless be used to call forth, even demand, as well as produce, common sentiments at home.

Yet, this was only part of the story. Along with México al Día, correspondents, including one signing himself "El Corresponsal," also submitted stories for publication in *El Correo*, many similarly concerned with violence against women, crimes of passion, murder, and suicide. Focusing on the existence of these two types of contributors helps make apparent, firstly, that, far from speaking in a monotone, every edition of the local paper comprised a number of distinct voices, from columns by various kinds of correspondents to editorials and letters, including brief reporting of factual matters, and, secondly, that each of these voices drew differently on already-established genres of communication as they helped craft some of their own. In this second regard, México al Día and those articles contributed by El Corresponsal were quite similar, with both borrowing many of the characteristics of the letter, even though both may have been submitted by telegraph. While a salutation to a "Dear Reader" was not explicit, an implied reader was often imagined or, at times, even directly hailed in these columns, as the assumed representative of the community being brought into being around common feelings toward these events. The date of its composition is also made clear, not only on every page of the newspaper itself but also at the top of the column. In El Corresponsal's description of the horrible crime in Ciudad Camargo, Chihuahua, for example, after setting out the date, "*sociedad camarguense*" is identified as the addressee right from the first line of writing and, of course, each story is signed "El Corresponsal" at the end.[34]

If reading a column by El Corresponsal was very much like reading a letter one had just received, the column must also have seemed very familiar to readers of novels like *Bandidos*, the writing techniques of which columns and other newspaper writing no doubt helped forge. With respect to the events in Ciudad Camargo, the brutal stabbing of a young woman (she was sixteen and working as a maid in one of the hotels in the city) who, along with her killer (a painter who was her former amasio), had arrived from Parral a few months earlier, El Corresponsal crafted, in a few short paragraphs, a dramatic portrait of events grounded in the realm of the spoken word and the specifics of the compelling detail. Not only did the use of phrases such as "it is said" and the explicitly stated task of sifting through multiple versions of what had supposedly happened serve to locate the correspondent at the very scene of the crime while acknowledging the processes of community judgment and meaning-making that were taking place around it, they enabled the writer to evoke in print the feelings, sentiments, and morals of such a world, as in a novel. "It seemed like she knew in her heart something was going to happen," states El Corresponsal, playing, perhaps, on popular understanding of fate and the role of premonition, "and as these last words crossed her lips, as she was going to get her bedcover because she was afraid and wanted to stay with some of her friends," it was then, just upon entering her room and striking a match for light, that she was killed. In a follow-up story a few days later, more details emerged, again presented through dialogue: "Nobody makes a fool out of me," the murderer stated, adding, as well, that he was a "respectable person."[35] "Nothing else is being talked about," the writer of México al Día assured readers in the aftermath of the Algara-Reig tragic affair, when both still clung to life.[36]

Likewise, when discussing yet another crime—the "horrible tragedy" that had occurred in the populous Colonia de Santa María in Mexico City in February 1909—the paper presented two slightly different versions of what had transpired when a young husband murdered his wife by shooting her five times.[37] In the first, the one the paper chose to give credence to, the husband, possessed by extreme jealousy and having made marital life miserable for his wife, shot her when she left the house to go to the store next door. In the second, much less believable according to the writer, the wife was described as the lover of a certain individual, specifically named in the story, a wild idea, according to the paper, given the social distance between the two. A few days later, following up on the initial story, the news writer reported that he had interviewed the supposed lover, who denied his involvement with the murdered woman as insistently as the popular voice was proclaiming it.[38] What is more interesting, however, was the proliferation of versions to explain the tragedy, some more or less absurd, according to the paper, to which the "truly sensational" event had given rise. While the article began with the usual statement—that the theme of every conversation in the capital was, at present, that of the terrible tragedy—it went on to mention that a long caravan of curious onlookers had formed where the murder had occurred, in order to, as the paper stated, forge a thousand stories out of the few passing phrases they managed to gather on the way by. Attesting to the multiple versions of the event that circulated orally not only situated the writer at the heart of what was taking place, defining the local by the extent of the reach of the conversations, it also created an even larger community of readers who could eavesdrop in print on these events and perhaps discuss them themselves wherever they might be as their means of participation and entry into the same community of readers, speakers, and listeners.

As the twists and turns in sensational dramas provided the opportunity for follow-up stories, the writing of these news columns could turn them into what must have seemed like pithy chapters in much-abbreviated novels, which themselves had often first appeared as installments in the periodical press. The passage of time and its marking by means of daily installments in the press ushered in a novelistic time of simultaneity: "It is almost certain that at the hour these lines are being written, he could have disappeared forever from among the numbers of those still living," the paper wrote about the fate of someone who had tried to take his own life. The writing was also anticipatory and enticing. "We will provide details tomorrow," promised *El Correo*, when readers, finding cautious optimism in the fact that Señora Reig seemed to be recovering from her wounds and following her medical progress in the paper from day to day in the week after the shooting, learned that she had died just as the paper was going to press. "We will continue reporting on any new developments in this affair," the paper continued the following week, after describing the convulsions that Algara had experienced the previous night, and that, despite now having survived for ten days from his self-inflicted wound, he was still far from out of danger.[39]

By the end of the decade, editors and columnists had hit upon a new technique for subdividing the text, even in these already brief news stories, into easily graspable fragments while highlighting the sensational nature of the material. Although subheadings were not new, the separating of the last clause or few words of the preceding sentence and placing it in bold font as the next subheading was. A much different read is produced, one that is reminiscent of how current-day students respond WHEN I INCLUDE MY COMMENTS IN CAPITAL LETTERS WITHIN THE BODY OF THEIR PAPERS OR THESES: "Why are you yelling at me?" I have been asked. Likewise, in *El Correo*, the separated text printed in bold delivers the same type of additional emphasis, as the reader's internal voice stresses the highlighted material. Those reading out loud would have also found it an effective device for summarizing the main points or organizing concepts, especially when combined with another common reason for employing subheadings—to identify the major figures or principal actors in the dramas, as in the use of "The trial," "The witnesses," "The lawyers," "The audience," "The proof," and the important dates, as did the story on a sensational trial for that took place in El Paso, Texas, in September 1909, in which the governor of Chihuahua requested the extradition of a political opponent to face charges of rapto and estupro in Chihuahua.[40] Yet another strategy was to use questions as subheadings then offer the reader answers to these questions in the paragraph that followed or, at other times, to provide no answer at all. Readers with inquiring minds would have little choice other than to purchase the next day's paper.

The story that followed the headline "ANOTHER WAVE OF BLOOD!" utilized all these devices and more.[41] Reporting the attack on a woman with a sharp object by a man whom the paper initially believed had been her lover, the story began by setting the stage—the time and place of the drama—and then described the scene: "The red blood that in abundance flowed from that wound, had bathed the poor woman, who was taken to THE PORFIRIO DIAZ HOSPITAL."

Subsequent sub-headings presented the main actors in the drama, setting out the identity of the woman and the location of her wounds as the topic of one section and utilizing a rhetorical question to introduce a section on the identity of the attacker. In fact, in the absence of any real information, the entire paragraph on the attacker is filled with rhetorical questions that nevertheless frame this particular event as one more enactment of an all-too-common and recurring plot: "Did this episode have its origin in jealousy? Was spite to blame? Are we dealing with cruel revenge? Who knows!" The paper concluded that the judge would be the one to unravel the details of this crime. New details received just as the paper was about to go to press were included as part of the story under the heading "At the last minute." Now identifying the attacker as her brother rather than her lover, the paper once again promised further clarification as the authorities sorted things out. Addressing "readers of *El Correo*" directly, the paper underlined its self-proclaimed responsibility to present all notable details in this (as in every other) affair as it invited readers to embrace a particular sense of time, one in which the gap between the event itself and the publication of the particulars (its rendering into text) that characterized it was meant to be as small as possible if not virtually nonexistent.

In addition, the extensive reporting on the medical condition of those who lingered after such crimes is striking, providing more evocative detail to go along with the number of times stabbed, the trajectory of the bullet, and the extent of the anguish of family members, only in this instance, it was the language itself that was the message, conjuring the modern, as well as Chihuahua's own place in it, through a kind of medicalized abracadabra.

Where the language of medicine offered a prognosis on the place along with the patient while the use of dialogue invoked the everyday world of rumor, gossip, and an oral public sphere of the nation to which all belonged, even if only in print, the inclusion in columns and news stories of actual letters from these dramas of passion contributed yet additional voices. As newspaper accounts, fictitious love letters, legal proceedings, and other kinds of texts were incorporated into *Bandidos* and other novels, actual letters and suicide notes, along with dialogue and medical and legal opinions, found their way into various news stories, forging an even closer link between the kind of writing carried out by correspondents (like El Corresponsal), that by novelists, and that found in personal correspondence as carried out by means of letter writing. Revealing that it was through the arrival of a letter that the paper learned the details of a suicide attempt in Ciudad Camargo in 1906, this same column carried the actual text of a letter recovered from the scene, one of a number of papers found on the twenty-five-year-old musician who had attempted to take his own life on a park bench in the main plaza by putting a bullet through his heart. The published letter was addressed "To my very dear friend Sr. José E." and left to him his clarinet and viola and to his young daughter his auto-harp, so that she should have a "memento of a friend of yours who when he was living in the world remembered her on the last day of his life," and in hopes that his friend would provide for his mother until his brothers could return home from the United States; some of the other letters, summarized for readers by the columnist, were addressed to the young woman who had spurned him.[42]

The arrival of a letter was also the means by which *El Correo* learned the details of the hair-raising (*horripilante*) mass murder that had taken place in the Andrés del Río district of Chihuahua, where, in March 1910, an amasio had used a machete to hack to death his amasia, their children, and two other members of her family.[43] The letter is referred to explicitly a number of times in the brief story, serving for *El Correo* as a seemingly reliable source of information not only for details about the crime and a compelling explanation of the circumstances that had led to it but also as kind of a "scoop," that is, as information of which others, especially governmental authorities, might not even be aware or admit to being aware, thus affording them an excuse for inaction. Because the letter writer, the paper explained, did not know whether the appropriate steps had even been taken to capture the killer, identified by name in the column, the paper was able to position itself as a kind of crusading voice that could use information obtained independently to hold the government accountable for the delivery of justice and to mete out punishment. In a sense, the letter sent to the paper was much like the letters or statements through which many judicial processes could be initiated, a similarity that the paper acknowledged with the headline "Se nos denuncia a un criminal" (A criminal has been reported to us). Along with the bloody details, *El Correo* could serve up moral indignation while carving out a role for itself in an emerging public sphere where justice, whether for mass murderers or for those suffering from abusive political authorities, was in increasingly short supply.

In many ways the news column, much as a novel, contained many of the textual elements found in a judicial investigation, only this time marshaled toward sentimental or emotive, rather than culpatory or didactic, ends. It included the particulars, setting out the ages and occupations of those involved as well as a description of the scene of the drama while also corroborating details, including the path of the bullet, the caliber of the pistol, and the opinion of the medical examiner. In addition to the text of one of the letters, the column about the suicide in Ciudad Camargo even included a statement that the wounded musician had supposedly made to the investigating judge, one in which he said that he had wanted to take his own life and that absolutely no one else was responsible for his death. For this columnist, like others writing for *El Correo*, the suicide attempt provided more grist for the sensationalist, and moralistic, mill. Stressing how the attempt had left the mother and two young sisters submerged in affliction and without support, the columnist pointed to the "true horror" he felt in being the bearer of such bad tidings, behavior that was hardly possible for "people in their rights minds or even among animals" and thus doubly reprehensible in creatures to whom "the Supreme Being had given the gift of understanding." Elsewhere in the paper, turning the tragedy in the Hotel Palacio to his own ends, the editor of *El Correo* lamented not only what he referred to as the progressive increase in the incidence of "crimes of passion" but also the vice of idleness—the one thing that all "*matadores de mujeres*" supposedly had in common—and one of the absolute staples, along with the evils of drinking, gambling, and prostitution, of the moral reform discourse so prevalent among the gente decente at the time.[44]

Cacahuate, Camarón, and Cachivache: Love, Twentieth-Century Style

If the means of generating stories, increasingly filed by on-the-scene reporters and local correspondents in forms that drew much from the genre of the letter, as well as the choice of topics considered to constitute "news," ever more frequently evincing a concern with crimes of passion and other sensational dramas wherever they might occur, heralded the arrival of the modern press in Mexico as elsewhere, so too did the growth in the use of graphics, especially photographic images and lithographic engravings.[45] Here, as well, the presence of the letter could be felt, not in its form—those means of salutations, closings, and addressing the reader—but rather as a symbol, at some times, of the epitome of a modern existence and, at others, of its very opposite. Such was the case in the advertising campaign of the El Buen Tono cigarette company, a pioneer in the use of images and other techniques to create a consumer culture and sell its products in late nineteenth- and early twentieth-century Mexico.[46] In a series of humorous advertisements published (or republished) in *El Correo* after the turn of the century, serial drawings accompanied by text, much as in the form of a comic, presented readers, and, thus, potential consumers, with variations of essentially the same story line—that of how discovering the wonders of smoking a particular brand of cigarette has reversed the fortunes of a formerly forlorn protagonist. In many ways, the narratives set out in the ads mimic the rags-to-riches story the press deployed to describe the results of winning a lottery, an activity also increasingly sponsored and promoted by this and other cigarette companies as another means of advertising. Although much more could be said about these ads, it is sufficient for the present purposes to stress that they brought into the same frame as cigarettes other "modern" consumer products, especially beer produced by the Moctezuma brewery and the Vulcano bed. They did so while explicitly referencing the centrality of the new means of circulating such messages, the mass-circulated daily newspaper, as well as its status as a similar kind of commodity—a number of the comics feature, either in the background or through having a character reading it, the newspaper *El Imparcial*, the first mass-circulated, low-cost daily paper in Mexico, from which *El Correo* obtained its cigarette advertising. There was nothing quite like a cigarette made by El Buen Tono, it seems, to find one's way in the modern world, if more often than not as a consumer of modern products and the narratives generated around them than as the grand winner of a cigarette company lottery.

In the same way that business failure might be overcome, persons injured in car accidents resuscitated, and even the end of the world narrowly averted through timely resort to a puff or two on a Buen Tono–brand cigarette, so too might true love find a way to triumph if helped along by the cigarette's powers of persuasion. In fact, love features prominently in these ads (as do love letters), offering an easily recognizable plot or series of plots that lend themselves to, if not divine, then at least somewhat miraculous intervention. Yet not just any type of love would do. Just as the ads themselves herald a world of consuming modernity, replete as they are not only with beds, beer, and cigarettes but also with bicycles, automobiles, and hot air balloons along with references to the latest silent film of a trip to the moon, romantic love as well, along with the reading and writing practices associated with it, was meant to be modern. As much as movement, on bicycles and in cars, and attire, especially new forms of fashion and clothing associated with new occupations and pastimes like driving, reading *El Imparcial* and reading and writing one's own love letters marked off the meaning of the modern.

Far from passé, love letters serve, in a number of the ads, as the main conceit around which the narratives turn. In one, the story of a modern-day rapto, a chauffeur with the name of Cacahuate (Peanut) uses love letters to woo the daughter of a ranchero.[47] In this instance, the opposition of the father serves only to heighten the desire of the courting couple and they decide to take flight on a motorized three-wheeler. Although all the horsepower of the machine is not sufficient to escape the enraged father and the machine itself explodes, sending the couple flying when Cacahuate attempts to floor it, the rich aroma of the Canela Pura–brand cigarette accomplishes what the letters and abduction could not: not only does it calm the father's thirst for vengeance, it convinces him to support their desired marriage, shown as an accomplished fact that they all toast with a glass of Moctezuma beer in the final panel. In addition to updating the abduction narrative to include motorized vehicles and modern forms of consumption, the ad is interesting in its juxtaposition of the chauffeur, marked by his new driving hat, with the rural ranchero, sporting traditional sombrero, shown as engaged, along with his daughter, in agricultural work. Despite her *mandil* (apron) and commitment to traditional occupations, she, agricultural implement in hand, is able to read Cacahuate's love letter herself, with no need for intermediaries. And while initially, at any rate, it seems as if modernity has let the couple down, given that the father is using the wheels from the exploded motorbike to harness the couple and bring them back under paternal control, it is in the end the modern with its objects of mass consumption that triumphs, resulting not only in their marriage but in the overcoming of the rural itself, indicated by the disappearance of the father's traditional sombrero in the final frame.

Another ad features this same framing of love letters as essential to the warp and woof of modern life, this time implicated by means of modern maladies and a modern form of voluntary association as well as through the act of writing. Suffering from "neurosis," a young woman—the "lovely Elena"—swears in the first panel of this ad that she will go to her grave celibate, much to the disappointment of Camarón (Shrimp), her impassioned yet barely noticed suitor.[48] However, upon witnessing, from her balcony (which just happens to overlook the *Imparcial* newspaper building) doves carrying letters, she is so taken that she declares she will break her pledge and give her hand to any man able to use these birds to offer her his love. Camarón, in search of the doves, notices that a vulture has flown down to scoop up the butt of a Superior-brand cigarette that he has just discarded. Reflecting for a moment on the figure of the vulture enjoying the cigarette, he comes up with the idea of asking the bird to deliver his amorous missives in exchange for a package of cigarettes, to which the vulture agrees, stating that, for that price, he would go to the end of the world to do so. Interrupted at her domestic task of sewing by the vulture swooping in through her open window, love letter in beak, the young woman needs a moment to recover from her fright. Pausing briefly to ponder the situation, she comes to the conclusion that a vulture is just as good as a dove and answers Camarón's letter in the affirmative. The marriage ceremony that follows, replete with numerous toasts with Moctezuma beer and the vulture hovering in the background holding up her wedding trousseau, is a splendorous affair and soon gives way, in the final panel, to a vision of domestic bliss, with Camarón, decked out in his Masonic uniform, sitting in his rocker smoking a cigarette and reading the paper while the vulture, who now lives with them, tends to the couple's newly arrived baby.

Humorous and fantastic, the ad also captures some of the defining attributes of modern urban life while asserting, through the presence of the *zopilote* (vulture), an avowedly Mexican rendition of it. In addition to invoking the modern condition by referencing female hysteria and male voluntary association through the Masons, as well as the presence of the new mass media as represented by *El Imparcial*, the comic links writing practices to modernity, posing Elena at her desk composing a love letter to be sent to Camarón.

This is not to say that the love letter itself is always seen as a particularly modern artifact. In yet another cigarette ad, this one dealing with the effects of the 1907 financial crisis, precisely the opposite is postulated.[49] In a complete reversal of fortune, Cachivache, a former banker, finds that he has gone from handling millions of pesos to poverty, with his only possessions being an old drum and the rags that cover him. Our hero, incapable of begging (the ad is clear to state), first tries to earn his livelihood as a street musician, with unfortunate results—instead of meeting with success he is pelted with rocks and whatever else is at hand and chased off by street dogs. Undaunted, he takes up another occupation, this time as the writer of love letters for, by implication, lovers who are incapable of composing such missives on their own. Here, however, he meets with similar results. Shown sleeping in a chair beneath a sign stating "Amorous Correspondence at Prices Never Before Seen," Cachivache is visited only by mice that scamper all over his writer's desk, indicating a state of near complete abandonment and inactivity. In this case, however, it is not his talent (or lack thereof) that is to blame; rather, as the written text below the drawing indicates, it is instead that "love, twentieth-century style," no longer requires epistles. Who knows what might have happened, the ad continues, had Cachivache, his patience at an end, not happened upon and tried a discarded butt of a Superior-brand cigarette. Convinced that the product was a gold mine to be exploited, he begins selling them in plazas and at events. This time, the "god of success" smiles on his efforts, not only enabling Cachivache to return to the world of high finance, where he is shown enjoying a Moctezuma beer with fellow bankers, but also offering a solution to the financial crisis plaguing the country: drawn by the rich aroma of a Superior cigarette, the final frame shows bags of foreign currency landing in Mexico in hot pursuit of the alluring weed.

Playful and highly contemporary in being set during Mexico's financial crisis of 1907, this advertisement, like many of those discussed above and the genre in general, stages Mexico's modernity as the consumption of a basket of modern commodities. The cigarettes, beer, and beds being sold are endowed with their particular chic or the patina of modernity through their association, literally in the same frames, with the symbols of modern life, especially those associated with new forms of movement. In some, it is motorized vehicles, bicycles (or, in one ad, a flying cycle that allows the protagonist to convince a comet not to collide with the earth), dirigibles (advertising El Buen Tono of course), steam ships, and hot air balloons (even if traveling to the Moon or inflated with the smoke of a Canela Pura cigarette) that are featured. In others, science, as in the telescope, a chemistry lab, power lines, modern forms of illness (and their cure, with cigarettes serving to overcome tuberculosis in one ad), and presentations at scientific conferences are privileged. In all, modern forms of reading practices predominate, by which means readers might not only learn about new products by reading new newspapers like *El Imparcial* and *El Correo* but also plot themselves in particularly modern ways as consumers of the new products and the narratives imbuing them with meaning and as actors in the important events they learn about only by means of the press. For those producing the El Buen Tono ads, modern reading practices were those necessarily carried out by literate individuals, that is, by men as well as women who knew both how to read and to write. Thus, it is Tula's ability to read Cacahuate's missive independently and Elena's capacity to respond to Camarón by writing her own letters that mark these relationships as modern. By contrast, Cachivache's stints as scribe and street performer are of a piece, with both seeming to evoke a (hopefully) bygone world of popular custom and traditional practices no longer desired. Perhaps it was not precisely the case that love "twentieth-century style" was no longer in need of epistles but rather that such missives might be penned and perused in private, by those with suitable abilities in reading and writing, both letters as well as the narratives of modern times.

"I have taken up the pen with trembling hand"

Up to this point, this section has been concerned with some of the ways that the love letter in particular and letter writing more generally have featured in the popular imagination as represented in the works of novelists and by those creating advertisements in the mass-produced and increasingly mass-circulated press. Whether as a literary device that enabled the plot to be moved along or actions to be resolved in a novel or as the very symbol of modern love in tobacco advertising, the letter assumed its place, along with texts like testimony in judicial cases, titles, deeds, and newspaper columns, as one of the forms of writing in which life at the end of the nineteenth century and the beginning of the twentieth had become enmeshed and through which one's destiny was more and more likely to be mediated. Employed increasingly as well by correspondents reporting on sensational crimes, the letter form facilitated the creation of a community of sentiment around such acts while evoking many of the same emotions and feelings as did these other, more formally fictional, genres. Letters, fictional as well as real, from the love letters in a novel like *Bandidos* to the suicide notes, verbatim testimony, and letters published in the press, shared forms of narrative and emplotment as they were similarly dialogic, implying a conversation between self, even if imagined, and a presumed reader, definitely so. In both venues, their distinguishing and almost unique characteristic lay in the presumption of their transparency, that is, their ability to enable access to the fundamental character or qualities of those composing them, a presumption often shared by historians using them as sources.[50] For some, like Cecilia in *Bandidos*, they also seemed to offer a radical venue for leveling social hierarchies, especially those of class and gender.

If contextualizing letters has provided some clues as to the meanings they possibly held and the manner they might be put to use, it remains to take some measure of the ways that letters figured in the conduct of the lives of those courting couples encountered in the archives. If letters and letter writing, as well as the written word more generally, took on meanings within the broader context within which they took place, these contexts would have to include the spread of novels as well as the growth of the sensationalist press and other forms of writing, often characterized by the juxtaposition of various writing genres, like the letter, within a single text; the increasing presence of the documentary state, its visibility often proclaimed in written form and access to its institutions premised upon the ability to produce various forms of written documentation; and an increase in various forms of literacies, one of them associated with the writing of letters, whether individually or as part of a larger ensemble or grouping. Evidence of this latter claim is extremely thin. To be blunt, I have no way of knowing who wrote most of the love letters I was able to read. Few cases discuss the manner in which the writing, exchanging, and reading love letters had taken place to the level of detail as that of Liberato and María, with which I introduced this section of the book.

Yet it is my sense that many, including women, did acquire sufficient ability to pick up the pen, even if with trembling hands, the phrase used by Guadalupe, a fifteen-year-old young woman with whose written statement I begin this section, to characterize her own engagement with writing in the first lines of the letter she was composing to her novio.[51] To be completely fair, in this letter, included as part of a case of rapto and estupro initiated in the mining town of Santa Bárbara, it is unclear whether it is her relationship, her circumstances, or her writing skills that is engendering her physical, embodied response. What is clear is that this fifteen-year-old, writing in 1905, had attained much greater familiarity with the written word than had the previous generation of women in her family: whereas, as required by law, it is her mother who initiates the legal case by swearing out a formal complaint, it is not she who signs the document authorizing the judicial process. Despite describing herself as the "undersigned," she is so in legal name only and not in the ability to command the written word; instead, it is Guadalupe who affixes her signature to the statement initiating the case.[52] Nor were they alone in this generational change. A few years later, another mother, a widow, and her seventeen-year-old natural daughter, this time in San Antonio del Tule, displayed a similar division in their abilities to authorize, by means of a signature, their statements to judicial authorities. In this instance, as well, the ability to sign one's name seemed to presuppose a more extensive command of the written word. Here, we need to make inferences from the letters written by the man, the only ones available in the judicial record in this case: each one begins by acknowledging receipt of a previous letter from his novia and goes on to paraphrase the major issue with which it is concerned, usually, in this correspondence, the initiation of sexual relations, which both had a vested interest in keeping secret.[53]

When it came to acquiring a level of literacy sufficient for this task, a little education went a long way, in Mexico as elsewhere. Discussing working-class letter writing in the early twentieth century in South Africa, Keith Breckenridge finds that, despite the overwhelming "illiteracy" of working people there, migrants to the mines made extensive use of letters to communicate and that the vast majority of these letters were concerned with personal matters, often taking the form of stylized love letters. While much of this letter writing, involving amanuenses, was indirect and collaborative, heads of households also cultivated what he refers to as a "radically constrained form of literacy among their children, specifically organized around the mastery of the writing of the vernacular letter."[54] Interested in exploring what he refers to as the minimum conditions for lettered correspondence, he finds that the most basic primary education, like that offered through state support for Catholic schools in Mozambique in the 1930s, was sufficient to foster the development of popular letter writing among migrants working in the sugar fields of Zululand. These letters, incidentally, were described by censors in much the same way as some of those from northern Mexico I have had access to could be described, with "words split into syllables," the statements being made "difficult to connect to their context," and the letters, in some cases, "very difficult to decipher."[55]

Official reports indicate that schooling increased in places like Parral during the Porfiriato. Like the double-entry accounting in *Los bandidos*, the precision with which statistics concerning primary education attendance in Hidalgo District were increasingly rendered in annual reports by the jefe político of that district may confuse accuracy with wishful thinking. While such measures did indicate an increase in primary school attendance there after the turn of the century, both in schools maintained by the district as well as in those established by some of the major mining companies as part of the employment package, correspondence from local officials and other information emanating from various communities within the district chronicles a litany of obstacles to achieving basic literacy: whether the mobility of the working population; the exigencies of the agricultural cycle requiring the labor inputs of the entire family, children included; the reluctance of parents to send their daughters to school; fears of social mixing; or even, at times, the vagaries and vices of a small number of those employed to do the teaching, precise numbers belied the general unpredictability and tremendous unevenness in regular attendance at school.[56]

Opportunities for artisans to receive an education as well as their degree of commitment regarding the importance of doing so also grew at this time. After 1890 especially, mechanics, blacksmiths, carpenters, tailors, painters, and bakers, along with other artisans and clerical and office workers, formed and joined mutual aid societies, often with the encouragement of the Catholic Church as well as of those in power. Many attended night schools offered by these and other associations that, in addition to addressing literacy, helped found such things as libraries and sponsor anti-alcoholic leagues and other events and activities. While much of this was seen by those in power as a great improvement—substituting education and instruction for dynamite, armed strikes, and violent confrontations, as one newspaper characterized the process—such activities, along with providing increased opportunities for accessing basic literacy, helped artisans and other groups stake a claim for inclusion within "decent" and respectable society. Nor were women exempted from this emphasis on the importance of education: supporting the founding of industrial schools for young women, like the one established in Parral in 1906, became an important component of progressive philanthropy, catering, in this instance, to women who described themselves as "*todas pobres*." As for those organizations and associations that attempted to promote the instruction and advancement of the working class, representatives of literate society could only admit, albeit grudgingly and in the most paternalistic of terms, that they were imparting, albeit on a "rudimentary basis," knowledge to intelligences that lay "in the most complete ignorance."[57]

Yet, there were more ways to acquire basic skills in reading and writing than attending schools or joining mutual aid societies. Concerned particularly with understanding the relationships of those caught in its purview and the circumstances within which acts such as the initiation of sexual relations and the removal of young women from parental control had taken place, the legal system offers tantalizing glimpses at the everyday activities of young women as well as of those being reported for transgressions against the heads of their households. While much of the testimony and statements to officials have to do with the paternal household, an important subset of these cases involved women who had been placed or found themselves in households other than the one into which they had been born. This circulation of women, often to provide domestic labor, formed part of a broader pattern of exchanges between households, resulting in situations in which identical activities and duties might be framed and understood in remarkably different terms. At one end of the spectrum, the cleaning, caretaking, and cooking that women performed were understood by all parties as "work," that is, the performance of such duties in exchange for a wage. This was certainly true in the case of seventeen-year-old María de Jesús, whose widowed mother lived on public charity and whose brother took his meals at the house of the municipal president in Parral so that he would be able to continue attending school. The food and clothing that the merchant who had hired her provided, when combined with the two and a half pesos he paid every two weeks to her mother, no doubt helped keep both alive, although this did not prevent the mother from demanding that her daughter leave her job and return home, a request that judicial officials could do little other than support given the age of the daughter.[58]

Not all cases involving the loaning out of the domestic labor of young women, however, were framed in this way, nor was all work remunerated in the same manner even when they were. When fifteen-year-old María Candelaria went to live in the home of a local employee of the customs office in order to keep his wife company and, perhaps, perform domestic duties, no wages were offered or sought. Instead, such kindnesses were in recompense for the instruction that she was to receive, in sewing from the wife and in writing and accounting from the husband, lessons she had taken sufficiently to heart to be able to sign her name on her statement to judicial authorities. In addition to providing additional insight into how literacy skills might be acquired in the absence of formal schooling or participation in the activities of societies organized by workers for such purposes, the case also hinted at the ways in which the relationship between the young woman and those in charge of her adopted household might be construed, by all parties, within the realm of the familial rather as part of the world of work, or at least how metaphors of family might serve to modify or constrain the behavior of those within it. Referring to the fact that she stayed in the house day and night, "as if she were a member of the family," the young woman had attempted to fend off the senior male's advances by informing him that she "respected him as a father." For his part, the male head of household, attempting to avoid the scandal that might ensue should his behavior become known, promised that, in future, he would "see her as a daughter" as long as she didn't tell her mother what had already happened.[59]

In another example, the needs of a sick neighbor were sufficient to convince a widowed father to leave behind his fourteen-year-old daughter Luz to help out when he sought new accommodation for his family in another part of the district. This arrangement, lasting more than a year, involved the young woman carrying out domestic chores, in exchange for which she received only food and clothing. No salary was paid and Luz described herself not as an employee or a domestic but rather as a "familiar," or bound by bonds of family. So strong were these bonds that when, six months after her arrival, the son of the woman she was assisting tried to give her a love letter, she refused to accept it, stating that "she didn't want it [the love letter] because she was in his house."[60] Others found in godparenthood bonds sufficiently strong to convince the heads of households to loan out their daughters.[61] Finally, in the absence of ties of neighborliness or family, fictive or otherwise, urgent necessity occasioned by sickness or a death in the family might be sufficient to convince heads of household to part with the labor of their female charges. Such "humanitarian" gestures, as one head of household described them, might also include "considerations, security and retribution" for such service, although these were not always specified in the documents.

The letter that arrived home from one such daughter on loan described what could happen when desire or even simply availability tested and found tenuous the bonds established through such family surrogacy. Although twenty-five years old at the time, Cleofas had received permission from her father to move to the house of Don Celestino, then fifty-eight years of age, to offer whatever services she could to his sick wife. When his wife died shortly after Cleofas's arrival, Don Celestino insisted, with success, that she be allowed to stay to continue working in the household, even accompanying the newly adopted family to a small rancho to place an altar of veneration before the Virgin del Refugio, described as one of the multiple devotions of the devout Don Celestino. It was there, however, Cleofas wrote, and only weeks after his wife's death, that the don had assaulted her, using physical force to accomplish his ends while, by means of a promise of marriage, offering to "make her happy," a promise he reiterated in written form. Cleofas's letter to her father, which must have come as quite a shock, was designed to inspire a sense of obligation on his part, to compel him to take action. Here, however, the father's demands for remediation had to be tempered in light of the fact that Don Celestino also had some bargaining power—standing by his intention to marry Cleofas, he promised to do so only if her father kept the matter quiet. With any hint of scandal, he insisted, the marriage would be off. Feeling he had little choice in the matter and seeing marriage as the only way to repair the honor of his daughter, the father agreed that the marriage could take place after a period of mourning suitably sufficient to maintain respectability. Meanwhile, Cleofas returned home, eventually giving birth to a son, whom Don Celestino initially supported with a small daily food allowance; along with the rest of her family, Cleofas expected that marriage to the don would take place after the bean harvest on the rancho had been completed.[62]

Such was not to be the case, however, and when Don Celestino attempted to marry another woman, Cleofas's father had little recourse other than to go public. Before judicial officials he swore out complaints both criminal and civil, the first regarding the estupro of his daughter and the second an impediment to prevent the impending marriage. In response, Don Celestino stopped providing for his child. He also attempted to reframe the narrative of their relationship, including his presumed promises and responsibilities. Like many of those novios who offered testimony in the previous section, he cast doubt on the manners and morals of the woman with whom he had had sexual relations, describing her as a "woman of the world and of bad customs because all of her family, that is, her sisters, have been lost." This was a common refrain of those accused of failing to fulfill their promises of marriage; it was also the response of last resort of those in households into which young women had come to work. Whereas, they proclaimed, the order and morality of their own households were beyond reproach, the same supposedly could not be said for those from which many of these young women hailed. At times, this could lend a class or clientelist coloring to the temporary incorporation of woman into these households—after all, given this logic, the initial decision to do so must either have been a mistake or an act of charity to a family that was somehow lower in the social hierarchy or less well deserving in terms of reputation. Of course, such rhetoric was self-serving, designed to evade punishment, burnish reputation, or both. What is interesting is that, as in the case of Celestino and Cleofas, such inequality, whether of status or reputation, rather than stand in the way of matrimony, might provide a basis for it, although a different basis than the ones upon which most of the relationships discussed in this book are founded. As her father explained to judicial officials, Don Celestino had initially promised to marry his daughter because of the "affection [*cariño*] that he had for her and because of the gratitude he felt for the innumerable services she had given to his household over a long period."

It is not possible to know whether or not Cleofas herself had written the letter she sent to her father describing what had transpired at the hands of Don Celestino. Nor does it particularly matter. It is likely though that she did write, to her father as well as to Celestino, as she is able to send letters both when she is at home and when living in her temporary household. Although he didn't always know what to make of them, Celestino does mention receiving communications from her: "Also you ask me to look for a García but you don't tell me even a little about who she is," he states in one letter to her. In another, he confirms that he has in his possession a brief letter (*cartita*) from her blaming him for inflicting greater suffering on her mother (who seems to have died by the time Don Pablo had initiated legal action). In yet another letter to her, Celestino (or whoever is writing) adopts a format common to letter writers of the time, making specific mention of an ongoing conversation that was taking place between him and Cleofas by means of an exchange of letters. "Cleofas," he began, "you say to me that you're leaving with Andrellita." The letter itself also concerns the legal ramifications of her upcoming visit, requesting specifically that he receive assurances that no one in her house or elsewhere will take action against him as a result of it. He also agrees to show her written documents upon her arrival, perhaps having to do with their wedding: "When you come I'll show you the written notices (*oficios*) and you will be convinced."

As for Celestino's letters, distinctly different handwriting can be distinguished in them, making them the work of number of people rather than just of Celestino himself. The first letter sent by Celestino, one of those submitted to judicial officials by Cleofas in order to prove the existence of a formal written promise of marriage, is particularly striking, both in terms of what can only be described as the pained appearance of the handwriting as well as by the fact that it seems to be written on mourning stationary, a page framed on all sides by heavy black margins, testimony to the circumstances in which the new relationship had been undertaken as well as, perhaps, a harbinger of the way it would actually work out. This letter is brief and to the point, if replete with words spelled out as they sound and absent any punctuation: "Cleofas I'm sending you the blankets there I forgot them there are two don't worry I already said to don Pablo that everything with him remains arranged as I offered to you and you shouldn't worry and that's it Cels." The next letter he sent to her, this one dated November 1893, was much more neatly written and, as a result, easier to read; it not only contains periods, commas, and semicolons but also employs standard spelling rather than words written phonetically, for the most part at any rate. Here Celestino (or whoever was writing for him) reiterates his written promise, if only to explain his delay in fulfilling it: "It is almost impossible for me to leave my affairs thrown about the countryside to go and fulfill my word of matrimony that I have given to you, that it can be postponed a little like I offered to Don Pablo and he was in agreement." He closed by insisting that there was no reason for her to worry.

The next letter in order of their appearance in the archive, although dated a month and half earlier than the previous one, is, like the first brief note, written in what seems like Celestino's own hand. Citing once again the demands of his bean crop, Celestino apologizes for his absence. This is the most romantic of his letters, perhaps written soon after her departure from his household: "Receive a kiss that I send you and send one back to me where I am here I'll receive it on the wind and always your lover." The tone in his letters had certainly changed by the following year, hinting at the real reason for his failure to follow through on his promise of marriage. He wrote, "But I'm still not even 20 miles away and still you are mortifying me with your damned jealousy and I will be a thousand miles away and still even there you have to be mortifying me with your damned jealousy this will be the motive for not living well nor being able to accept your desires because if even when I'm so far away you insult me, how will we live together fighting as we have lived without sleeping the days that I have been here." Perhaps this is what Don Celestino was referring to when he confirmed before judicial authorities that he had indeed agreed to marry Cleofas, but only if she "behaved in an honest manner and mended her character," something that, given the tone of more recent letters, he clearly believed she had not managed to accomplish to his satisfaction.

Although the outcomes of the legal processes, both civil and criminal, are not available in this instance, it is more than likely that they were not favorable to Cleofas and her family. Her failure to undergo a medical examination to confirm the existence of the crime of estupro, a crime that, as you have learned, medical authorities were supposedly able to see registered on the woman's body, is the last thing mentioned before the expediente terminates. The testimony and letters do, nevertheless, highlight women's engagement with writing along with their circulation between households to provide care and domestic labor. And, whereas Cleofas seemed secure both in her command of the written word and in her ability to obtain her daily necessities, such was not always the case. The letters composed by Guadalupe, the fifteen-year-old who took up pen with trembling hand, tell a different story, one in which young women managed to acquire or gain access to some degree of letter-writing literacy despite being always on the edge of economic hardship, a step away from being unable to find ways to make ends meet, either in the household of another or by means of a relationship of some kind in which the man brought home the daily wage (diario) as his part of the bargain.

As in many of the cases I have been discussing concerning the circulation of women between households, Guadalupe's mother, despite describing herself to judicial officials as married, seemed to be managing the household on her own.[63] Originally from the state of Sinaloa, where Guadalupe had also been born, the two women, mother and daughter, found themselves resident in the small mining town of "Los Azules" in 1905. Perhaps Guadalupe's father had gone elsewhere in search of work or had simply abandoned the family upon failing to do so. Again, we don't know as no mention is made of him in any of the testimony or documentation pertaining to the case, although her mother describes herself as married rather than as widowed. What does get spelled out in the materials generated by the court are the letter-writing abilities of all those appearing before it. It has already been established that Guadalupe signed the complaint initiating the process on her mother's behalf. We also are fortunate in that her actual letters became part of the judicial process, if only by chance. Whereas, in every other case of this kind it is the woman and her family who submitted the man's letters in order to substantiate the existence of a written promise of marriage, in this instance it is Felipe, the thirty-six-year-old accused of abducting her, who submitted the letters, both those he wrote to Guadalupe as well as those she had written to him. His reasons for doing so are difficult to fathom as, legally, they have no relevance whatsoever to the case. In fact, their presence can only be explained as owing to the vagaries and idiosyncratic nature of the judicial system, whose representatives, thankfully, in this instance, also formally asked Felipe whether he had any nicknames and whether he knew how to read and write, to which he answered "no" to the former and "yes" to the latter.[64]

If judicial officials had intended to scour this correspondence in order to see what exactly had been promised to the young woman in writing, they were to be sorely disappointed. In fact, the letters that wound up as part of the judicial proceedings were only those they had exchanged most recently, after the abduction had taken place. Before the abduction in September, the relationship between the two seemingly over, Felipe had returned Guadalupe's letters, a common occurrence to mark the end of a courtship. For her part, Guadalupe, thinking the same thing, had burned them all, destroying, through this act, the evidence of the written promise of marriage that she claimed was contained within them. Those left and submitted as evidence—four from him to her and four from her to him, all written in the first three weeks of September—treat, for the most part, the fallout from her abandonment of the paternal home and the initiation of judicial proceedings, occasioned when, their relationship obviously rekindled, Felipe had abducted Guadalupe from her household and initiated sexual relations, the preliminary steps, in Guadalupe's mind in any event, on their way to married life together. In fact, if the dates on the letters are accurate and the mother's account of events is to be believed, all of the letters treat the period between her abduction on 7 September and Felipe's statement to judicial officials, which must have been just after 21 September (in order for him to have been able to provide the letter with that date on it to the authorities). Guadalupe's mother had initiated legal proceedings only a few days earlier, on 18 September. To make things even more complicated, Felipe himself doubted the authenticity of at least one of the letters, the one that Guadalupe supposedly wrote to him on 10 September, shortly after her abduction and before legal proceedings had begun, which reads as follows: "My dear and friend I am putting to you these badly formed lines [lienas, sic] in order to ask you a favor of sending me a few centavos that I need for my daily upkeep because I don't have more than 50 centavos left and it's very little for my food and send me my clothes." For his part, Felipe responded that while he couldn't refuse her anything, he doubted that the letter was from her. Pointing to the absence of details and her failure to mention the letter when they spoke the following day, he wrote back asking for a prearranged sign to be included in subsequent correspondence: "Answer me and include one of those known words from among those that we have had for greater security." Once he was sure that she had written it, he said, he would send what she had asked of him.

A secret code or password is not required to resolve the question of authorship in the case of this letter or any other of those from Guadalupe, however. Like the other three letters from her, this one is marked by phonetic spelling, the division of words into syllables, both common to many of the letters I have read, and, much more distinctively, manifests what today might be called a learning disability that involves the switching of the order of letters, making "lineas" into "lienas," "gracias" into "garcias," and "Sept. 18" into "Sept. 81," three of the many such examples found throughout her correspondence. Self-deprecating comments are also found in all her letters pertaining to her ability to write, another distinctive characteristic ("forced lines," "trembling hands," etc.). Difficult to read, as difficult as they must have been for her to compose, they are a testament to the triumph of her tenacity and determination, to her will to acquire and deploy letter-writing skills, and to the importance that letters held for her as part of courtship, or even as synonymous with it. Rather than anticipating their future together, however, as might typically be the case in a courting correspondence, these letters reveal a person attempting to come to terms with the consequences of a past action, her decision to leave the parental home to be with Felipe. In them, she asks initially, as we have seen, for a few centavos, which she refers to as the "diario," the term used in the mining zones to signify sufficient money to buy one's daily bread. Stung by his doubts as to whether or not it was she who had written to him or, perhaps, the situation in which she found herself slowly beginning to dawn on her, the reply she makes in the next letter is curt, even for her: "Dear F I don't want anything what I would like is that you should do me the favor of sending me the sewing that's in the house of Don Francisco." Mindful of her need to find a way to sustain herself, she continued: "Because I'm going to serve in a house and that's all there is to say to you with tears I see your answer because I can't bear so much." She also let him know she was sick and didn't know how she was going to get to the house where she was supposed to work.

Felipe was less than sympathetic. After the standard and formulaic introductory lines acknowledging receipt of her letter and reiterating some of its main points—her sickness and that she was about to start work—the real message begins: "I'm of the belief that if you hadn't shown such wretchedness [*infame*] you wouldn't have to suffer and if in the present and in whatever happens you are suffering you don't have anything about me to complain about." As a matter of fact, as far as he was concerned, it was he who was the one who was suffering and she, predictably, the one to blame for it. He continued: "And if this is what you have done in the moments in which you said you loved me for all eternity what wouldn't you have done if you had detested me." Such suffering, however, served a useful rhetorical purpose—it provided a yardstick by which to measure the extent to which he loved her: "I know that all this is in recompense for how much I loved you." Felipe's next letter, sent a few days later, returned to the same theme, complicated by the fact that she had yet to respond to his earlier missive: "Today I've just understood that everything you swore to me and said to me has been a passing illusion that perhaps now no longer even exist in your memory." He continued: "In these moments I don't know what to say to you I'm suffering too much and I can't say anything to you about it." Despite the despairing tone of the letter, he offered a small gift, if she were willing to accept it. All she need do was let him know.

Referring to herself as a poor wretch (*desgraciada*) in her reply, Guadalupe stressed her increasingly desperate straits, as her continuing illness made it impossible for her to go to work, and also that she was unworthy of his attention. The intimation in the letter is that, should he be so disposed, she would accept financial support. Although he did send ten pesos for her in care of the person delivering his reply, Felipe again blamed her for her own difficulties: "If you had done and said the truth [*la realidad*] you wouldn't be suffering what you're suffering." He continued: "If your love were true you wouldn't be suffering nor making suffer the man who loves you." As far as he was concerned, whether she intended to remain where she was or go out to work, it was her choice. Meanwhile, if she ever did find the will (voluntad, a concept to which I will return), he told her, she knew that he was always at her service.

In the correspondence submitted to judicial authorities, Guadalupe gets the last word. Her final letter, dated 21 September, the most expansive of all the letters comprising her correspondence, reflects the influence of her mother as well as her own frank assessment of her increasingly narrow options. Thanking Felipe for his willingness to help (*buena disposición*), she informed him that she had little choice but to return to her mother given that she lacked even the most minimum of resources to get by (*corto diario*). Her mother, upset with her, had removed her from where Felipe had taken her and brought her before judicial authorities. Reassuring Felipe that she wasn't to blame for this, Guadalupe stressed her need to comply with her mother (*ser consecuente con eya en todo*) because, as she put it, "even though late I really understand what I've done and as a result I see that I am obliged to work." Nor did her mother allow her to accept Felipe's money—she did not want her daughter to be obligated to him in any way. Thanking him repeatedly, Guadalupe closed, perhaps the relationship as well as the correspondence, by saying that was really it, that that was all there was to say.

We peer over Guadalupe's shoulder at a particularly charged moment in her young life. As the promise and excitement of embracing a future with her novio foundered on the hard rocks of getting by from day to day, she soon discovered that, in the exchange of the initiation of sexual relations and domestic duties for the provision of the diario, she had gotten much less than she had bargained for. What comes across most clearly in her letters is her vulnerability. In this, she is like many of the young women encountered in the judicial archive, both those possessing some letter-writing and reading skills and those trusting in a verbal promise of marriage. But Guadalupe did write, and her letters express most directly the lack of options available to her, a lack confronted by so many of these women, hemmed in as they are by economic hardship, youth, gender restrictions, and patriarchal prerogatives as exercised by both novios and the heads of their households. Even once she had returned to her mother's home, she faced a life of domestic labor for others, a theme stressed in almost every one of her letters to Felipe.

Hardly love letters, these are desperate pleas for sustenance and support crafted, however tenuously, within the confines of the forms of a courting correspondence. All, for example, are dated and set out the location of both the writer and recipient. Each, as well, begins by identifying the recipient by full name as well as by a more personal form of address, most often "never forgotten" (*nunca olvidado*) but also including "my dear and friend" and "dear." Each closes with the set phrase "*es cuanto le dice*" (that's all there is to say to you) followed by SS, short for "Seguro Servidor" (your faithful servant) and Guadalupe's standard closing flourish, the capitalized initials of her full name "GAT." Only one letter contains an additional personal expression of care, "receive the affection of your SS" followed by the full name in signature. In contrast to Felipe's letters, which contain a full range of the romantic vocabulary, from suffering, illusion, will, heart, and eternity to love and guilt, those written by Guadalupe stress work (*trabajo*), daily sustenance (diario), and money if also good will (buena disposición) and her own wretchedness. Love, it seems, was an emotional luxury in which only Felipe could afford to indulge. Or, having made the ultimate statement about her own feelings toward the relationship by leaving her household to join him, perhaps she felt the need, through stressing the vocabulary of work and need, rather than love, to remind him of what his part of the bargain ought to have entailed.

"No me gusta cubrirme con el velo de la hipocrasía" (I don't want to hide behind the veil of hypocrisy)

If, for Guadalupe, writing was a difficult if necessary means of scripting both a courting relationship and the role she as well as her novio were supposed to play in it, other of her contemporaries displayed much greater ease with the genre of the love letter and the language of romantic love. Writing near the end of a decade of violence associated with the outbreak of the Mexican Revolution in Chihuahua, Enriqueta, a teen only slightly older than Guadalupe and also resident in a small mining town in the district, that of Villa Escobedo, represents the other end of the spectrum of those women composing letters to their lovers. Like Guadalupe, Enriqueta was being raised by a single parent, in this instance her father, who describes himself as a widower who dedicated himself to working as an operario in the local mines. While I treat Enriqueta's writing in much greater detail in the final section of the book, I introduce her letters at this point to establish a feel for the forms or conventions of the letter-writing genre through seeking similarities and differences among some of its most divergent practitioners. My goal is not to judge or rank their relative merits. It seems to me that there is little to be gained by attempting to establish one correspondent as in some way superior relative to the other in some form, either in composition or command of the genre of the written love letter. It is, rather, to establish the range of possible engagements with the written word.

In one important respect, juxtaposing Enriqueta's letters with those written by Guadalupe is misleading rather than illustrative. The two sets of letters are not strictly comparable given that one deals with the courtship proper and the other, as you have seen, treats the difficult period after Guadalupe's abduction by her suitor. Yet in many ways they are of a piece—whereas Guadalupe uses the language of work to remind her novio of the expectations and exchanges that characterize a promise of marriage, Enriqueta deploys the language of romantic love to demonstrate and elicit ever-increasing commitment to that courting relationship, even as she does so within boundaries that she herself is adamant about defining and delimiting. Similarly, both women find in love letters the means of constituting or bringing about the very thing being discussed, their courtship. As much as they are rhetorical and symbolic, love letters are performative; that is, they produce or conjure the courtship being written about while serving as proof of its very existence. Likewise, both women mark the end of their courting relationships by asking for the return of their love letters, in Guadalupe's case to destroy them and with them, it seems, all traces of the relationship, and, in the case of Enriqueta, as an exclamation point to an ending for which she felt her novio was uniquely to blame. Clearly, for both women, courtship meant writing love letters, irrespective of the degree of facility each brought to the task.

Before such courtships could be concluded, however, they had to begin and, in the case of Enriqueta, we have access to the entire courtship correspondence, some thirty-one letters in total, sent between her and Pedro, her novio, a twenty-three-year-old mine worker who initiated the epistolary exchange.[65] In some ways, the missives that form this correspondence are less marked as letters than those exchanged between Guadalupe and Felipe. They bear no dates or addresses, identifying neither the place of writing nor the destination of their intended recipient. Although the evidence is sketchy, my sense is that, as both lived in the small community of Villa Escobedo, their letters were exchanged personally or through intermediaries, although no actual face-to-face encounters are ever mentioned in them. Rather than physical, the distance they are meant to traverse is, firstly, emotional, and, secondly, and perhaps more importantly, that vast expanse between the fear of being deceived on the one hand and the desire to believe in the sincerity of the other's pledges of love on the other, a chasm that, although ultimately somewhat narrowed by the many letters that might be exchanged, only a leap of faith could actually take one across. The world they conjure as they are composed and then read is an intensely personal and private one, almost uniquely concerned with the expression of sentiment, of the depths of their feelings for the other as well as the doubts that their love would be reciprocated. Love, passion, reassurance, trust, suffering, sincerity in matters of the heart, eternity, desperation—these were the terms through which they structured their correspondence as well as their relationship.

Taking the chance initially to reveal such personal, intimate feelings as these could only be accomplished through language conventions that endeavored to envelop such feelings, along with the writer as well as the addressee, in a mantle of respectability. Given that men initiated the correspondence, and thus courtship, I begin with Pedro. Only the constant presence of "Usted"—repeated some seven times in the brief note in which he first revealed his feelings to Enriqueta—seemed capable of mitigating the offense to the young woman's dignity that such an introductory letter had the potential to inflict. The letter that Lino M., an agricultural laborer living near one of the mining towns where Pedro had worked, hoped would initiate his courtship of fourteen-year-old Soledad a few years later, in 1925, was very similar to that written by Pedro, as you will see in the third section of this book, where I discuss "passion" in greater depth. Such introductory letters enabled men to reveal their feelings to their prospective novias while explaining what had compelled them to take such a drastic step. For both men, it had been a terrible and vehement passion in their hearts that had prompted them to write. For yet another suitor, writing in 1893, it was love, rather than passion, that had compelled him to take up pen and paper.

Regardless of what had motivated them, passion or love, all three men shared the sense that, in writing such a letter, they might be straying beyond the bounds of propriety. Drawing from a common language of formal politeness, a rhetorical way of acknowledging that they considered the woman to be decent, respectable, and honorable, they used that distance between the woman's presumed moral qualities and the liberties they themselves dared

to take with them by the mere fact of writing as the very measure of the
extent of the feelings—whether passion, love, or suffering—that compelled
them to do so. In any event, turning over their fate to the young woman
they addressed, they could only await word, in written form hopefully, as
to whether or not their feelings would be reciprocated.

Despite Pedro's profession of passion, Enriqueta, the object of his affection, needed more convincing. "Having received your esteemed and loving
letter," she responded, "with this letter I answer it in which I will speak
to you with the candidness that always characterizes me. If you really do
love me with a true and pure love, my heart will reciprocate it, but before
anything else I want you to swear to me that yours is a sincere love, not
one for passing the time reassure me of this and the feelings of your heart
will be reciprocated." In this brief note, Enriqueta emphasizes the personal
qualities of candidness, truth, and sincerity, matching those of frankness,
honesty, and truthfulness claimed by Pedro as his own characteristics in his
initial letter. Also hinted at, even in this initial exchange, is the existence
of a common vocabulary of sentiment, including an emphasis on passion,
suffering, and an excess or overflowing of emotion, that both could draw
upon, although in unique, perhaps particularly gendered, ways. Indeed,
for Carlos Monsiváis, who has written on the golden age of the letter as a
genre, a period he dates from the eighteenth into the first half of the twentieth century, such excessively sentimentalized, even corny prose (*cursi*, as
he refers to it), was particularly the hallmark of female correspondents.
Not only did it offer women a means of exercising their imaginations and
an apprenticeship in public language in the face of what he refers to as
the de facto abolition of their rights and the lack of alternative forms of
expression, apart from religious discourse, so characteristic of this time, it
also provided a means of self-invention, of plotting oneself at the center
of a narrative, one that privileged the ideal, even utopian, in place of the
mundane circumstances and obligations of daily existence.[66]

The correspondence of Pedro and Enriqueta is certainly steeped in a
rhetoric of sentimentality that signals such a shift towards the poetic. Words
are "daughters" of a "pure and sincere love," "love" a "star that lights up my
nights of darkness" and "calms my hours of sadness," while "life without

you" would be both a "desert" and an "ocean of sadness and longing" (both metaphors in the same letter, of course). In a similar vein, "the dawn of each day" brings "terrible suffering" to an "impassioned heart," a heart "captured by a furious and true love" that "drenched" it in "pleasures of sweet love and tenderness," a love, by the way, that only celestial metaphors seemed up to the task of expressing: "Just as the Sun and the Moon and the rest of the heavenly bodies move, so does my love grow for you." Yet rather than being limited to women, this is a rhetoric that, at least in the case of this courting couple, both correspondents seem equally adept at deploying. Whereas the first descriptive sentence in this paragraph is composed of quotes taken from letters written by Enriqueta, the second draws from the writing of Pedro.

Both correspondents were similarly on the same page when it came to the nature of the space that their correspondence was meant to inscribe. Apart from Enriqueta referring to a recent sickness that had kept her from writing and from Pedro finding in the gossip of her friends confirmation of his most deeply held doubts, neither, before the breakup at any rate, found in their daily activities the inspiration for the content of their missives. A world composed totally of the written expression of feelings took shape, one that grew and deepened through accretion as subsequent letters arrived, not only by means of making reference to the previous letter that had been received but also through imploring the other writer to be more resolute in their commitment and the expression of it as they themselves labored to do and demonstrate likewise. The expressions each uses capture this sense of apartness, this space of the ideal couple—for Pedro, it was a "cocoon of happiness of caring emotions and true and dear love," for Enriqueta, an entire "world of love" contained in her bosom. Rather than cramped quarters, however, the world of the imaginary couple was a capacious place, one that opened, in their case at least, onto an immense interiority, accessed only by means of reflection and introspection. Whereas Pedro only hints at the mutual need to plumb such interiority through writing when he mentions the number of drafts of one letter that he has thrown away before being satisfied with the version he finally sent, Enriqueta is articulate and explicit about the locus of writing and emotion: "Enveloped my soul in dreamy happiness and fixing hour by hour my thought on your memories, now at this moment in which I am only thinking of you, in the present lines I devote my words leaving engraved in this letter the affectionate tenderness that my heart sends to yours."

This is not to say that the writing of these novios was unmarked by difference. Although Enriqueta does mention passion in one of her letters, as part of an acrostic poem she composes out of Pedro's name, and describes as "fiery" or "passionate" (con fuego, as she puts it) the manner in which she has expressed her commitment to their love, she does not come close to comparing to Pedro either in the extent to which she uses the term or in the particular meanings she invokes with it. As was evident in the letter with which Pedro initiated the correspondence, it was passion that had driven him to write. This same self-appended descriptor appears numerous times in most of the letters that follow. Referring to himself as "your passionate Pedro" and "your passionate one," Pedro experiences passion as "vehement," "furious," and "inflaming," something that had "wounded" his heart and made him "crazy" with love for her. "Inflamed with passion," he is literally a prisoner to love, "enslaved" by its immensity, "suffering" for it, being "possessed" in a way he hadn't before experienced. More than just a trope, part of the language of sentimentality existing only in the world of the ideal couple that was being written into existence in the space of the love letters, passion here is synonymous with loss of will, of reason even, a force independent of his rational control. By contrast, the closest Enriqueta comes to such a usage of "passion" is when, in a moment of doubting Pedro's love, "passionate" screams burst forth from her lips before she can reassure herself that he truly does love her. Even here, however, for Enriqueta, passion forms but one part of a broader language of sentimentality designed to elicit ever-greater degrees of commitment from Pedro. For her it is never the obsession that seems capable of motivating Pedro to act on his rhetoric, rendering it with a lethal literality.

If the self-enclosed ideal couple is a world that Enriqueta must be drawn into, through persuasion and insistence, one entered reluctantly in the face of experience and popular wisdom that suggest that such a destination is either fleeting or illusory and that passage to it might be fraught with danger, it is also one that she can help write into existence along with her own place in it. Enriqueta's prose charts her transformation from doubter to believer. After all, "there are things in life," she told Pedro early on in their exchange of letters, "that change the flower of hope into profound oblivion." "I used to think," she continued in another letter later, "in life I would only find treachery; you convinced me that your love was immense and pure and now I am happy." Once arrived at her destination, Enriqueta finds in the language of sentimental love and the couple a means of representing herself. Much like the character Cecilia in *Los bandidos de Río Frío*, she posits herself as every bit Pedro's equal, not only through her command of the written word but also in her ability to wield the conventions and tropes of romantic love as well as in her capacity to act as a strong and principled individual determined to obtain her own personal happiness. Although her options in life were no doubt constrained by the circumstances of gender, class, and happenstance, Enriqueta nevertheless found in love letters a means of expressing an absolute equality of desire with her novio, one in which the characteristics of truthfulness and honesty in matters of the heart underwrote confidence in her own forthrightness and ability to make decisions about how she wanted to live her own her life. Her prose stands as testimony to her strength of character, premised upon relentless interrogation of her own feelings and care in expressing them, and the expectation that the other would be equally forthright and honest: "I love you," she told Pedro, "but, however, as you say to me on my part I repeat it to you: if you don't have the will to be with me tell me in order to kill with one blow my illusion." As you will see shortly, such claims of truthfulness in matters of the heart might be essential if at times insufficient insurance on a woman's life in case something went drastically wrong.

> "*Es necesario que la carta represente dignamente nuestra persona.*"
> (*The letter must represent our person in a dignified manner.*)

The rhetoric of truthfulness, one pole in the binary of honesty/deception that framed matters of the heart, the mutual constitution of the intimate world of the ideal couple, and the shared use of a common language of sentiment to bring about that world can all be described as characteristics of the love letter that mark it as a genre of writing. As such, love letters made certain demands on those choosing to employ them, positioning both writer and recipient, for example, in a limited number of ways. Carlos Monsiváis, for his part, describes the addressee of a love letter as "obligatorily cruel," a humorous and insightful means of capturing the ways in which the expression of doubt and the need to compel the other to make ever-greater commitments to the relationship necessarily call into being an imagined reader who seems to possess precisely that quality or characteristic.[67] Certainly, the quotation from one of Enriqueta's letters I used in the preceding paragraph casts both its writer and recipient in profound ways—her as open and honest in revealing her feelings and him as having the potential to bring her happiness to an end with his decision. The common rhetoric of suffering, deployed by both, also positioned writer and recipient in similar ways. It is Monsiváis's argument, in fact, that the extreme codification of the love letter as a genre up to the first half of the twentieth century was both a response to, as it helped make up for, the lack of writing abilities of those sending them.[68]

Perhaps this high degree of codification was what made it possible for a group of women of humble circumstances, residents of a small mining town in the neighboring state of Durango, to compose a love letter convincing enough to be submitted to judicial authorities in Parral, where many of the principals had moved, as proof of a written promise of marriage. Having loaned Matilde, her sixteen-year-old daughter, out to sew for Petra J., a woman she described as her patron or protector, a mother learned that José María Z., a thirty-six-year-old miner, had propositioned Matilde and then had sexual relations with her. Although, when questioned by judicial authorities, the miner agreed that a sexual relation had taken place, he argued that it had been consensual and that no promises of any kind had been made. According to the daughter, it had also been Petra who had subsequently given her a letter, saying that it had been sent to her by J. M. Z., a claim that he roundly denied. While admitting that he had sent a note by messenger to the young girl's mother and acknowledging his "hand and letter" on that occasion, he testified that the same could not be said for the love letter he had been shown. Pointing to the handwriting as evidence he had not penned it, he revealed an understanding of authorship that framed it as personal, in which an individual is defined, at least to a certain extent, by the uniqueness of their written script (unique handwriting being the mark of an individual and of authorship). Letters, however, as I have argued throughout this section, could just as easily be composed by committee as by an individual, leaving handwriting merely as the trace of the person with that particular aptitude in a collective process, like Liberato's amanuensis, rather than identifying the author, the one whose feelings or thoughts were being conveyed. In this particular instance, however, if we are to believe J. M. Z., neither he nor anyone helping him seems to have been involved in the composition of the letter, which reads as follows:

> Dear Señorita,
> From the same moment in which divine heaven saw fit to allow me to meet you there awoke in my heart this sublime and inexplicable feeling that is called love and it not being possible for me to restrain myself I am taking the liberty to make this declaration to you and my only hope is that you will kindly accept my request because I love you and it would be my pleasure to have you return my feelings and he remains in hope of your answer he who only desires to be happy at your side.
> You know who.[69]

What seems so striking to me about this letter is its generic nature. Without either date or return address, it is not unlike many of the other love letters already considered in this section. In many ways, in fact, it is a typical first letter from a male to a potential novia, with the formal "Usted" form used three times in such a brief message (along with other formal forms indicating respect). The reason offered as compelling enough to justify such an intrusion, such a violation of the forms of everyday discourse, what its writer refers to as the "inexplicable feeling that is called love," serves as a rhetorical strategy that both defines the extent or strength of feelings as reciprocal to the degree that such norms of politeness are being trespassed while, simultaneously, claiming decent and honorable status for both the letter writer and its recipient. Staples of the love letter genre are also present, such as the idea of fate bringing the couple together, for example, expressed in the form of divine intervention; the declaration of love and the hope it will be reciprocated; and some of the tropes of romantic rhetoric including the heart, sentiment, the sublime, love, desire, and happiness. The salutation and closing are typical (Dear Señorita/You know who) if unremarkable, as is the rest of the letter, so devoid of any reference to any characteristics or qualities of the actual woman being addressed. It is as if the form of the letter itself is sufficient to accomplish what the women who wrote it (if they did write it) had intended, that is, to convince judicial authorities of the existence of a courting relationship, if not precisely of a written promise of marriage. As in so many of these cases, the end of the story is, unfortunately, not known, as, within three or four days of beginning the judicial procedure, Matilde's mother, as was her right, formally desisted from pursuing further legal action, citing the difficulties it imposed on her to appear so frequently before judicial authorities and the desire that she and her daughter be left in peace.

Despite professing to be humble and in the situation of a poor woman, Matilde's mother, perhaps with Petra's help, demonstrated her ability to deploy the forms of the lettered city to her own ends. Yet, it still remains to be determined how these forms had been agreed to and passed along. To some extent, the codification of the rules for writing letters formed part of a broader process, the attempt to regulate behavior and manners that, through the course of the eighteenth and nineteenth centuries, served increasingly as a means of distinguishing between, on the one hand, those pertaining to "decent" and "civilized" society and, on the other hand, those who did not. In the second half of the nineteenth century, this meant a growing concern with etiquette, a preoccupation that was codified and disseminated, in Mexico as in much of Latin America, by means of the *Compendio del manual de urbanidad y buenas maneras de Manuel Antonio Carreño*, first published during that period and subsequently republished numerous times since then up to the present.[70] Carreño's manual, as it has come to be known, was divided into two parts, the first concerned with the moral duties of man, a religiously inspired view of the world in which man's duties to God provided a foundation for men's roles as ideal fathers, husbands, and useful citizens, and the second with etiquette, which began with personal cleanliness and hygiene and then led outward from concern with behavior in the home to rules for proper behavior outside the home, then in society, and finally to the proper application of epistolary etiquette.

Regarded as nothing other than "conversations in written form," letters were the extension or reflection of the ideal person that the manual intended to bring into being through instruction in proper etiquette. Emphasis on the need for there to be a correspondence between the spoken and the written in the manual facilitated commensurability or legibility in a way that privileged the spoken as the original and the written as its copy while it spoke the truth about the success of the disciplinary project itself. Speaker and writer are one in such a way that the letter, in both its language as well as its material circumstances, is, as the quote with which we began this section states, a "worthy representative of our person." Here form becomes the content: handwriting must be neat and well formed (elegant even), the signature clear and legible, the paper of the proper quality, the date, addressee, place, salutation, indentations, and margins all properly formatted, and the letter closed and sealed with a "certain taste and delicacy," all the while maintaining, most certainly, appropriate social divisions and gradations of respect. Moreover, the arrival of a letter established a kind of reciprocity, a claim on the person receiving it: it is "exceedingly uncivil," the authors of the manual concluded, not to answer a letter in an opportune fashion or to reply with a mere message. After all, proper form called for proper form, making the letter into a kind of pass required for entrance into the club of civil and mannered society, if one not composed of equals.[71]

Carreño's manual had little to say, however, about either the love letter specifically or the language of sentimentality that came to characterize it, that is, the ways in which the formal requirements of the genre became codified or how this codification then called into being specific kinds of writers and addressees while nudging them into predetermined subject positions. To accomplish these ends, a spate of publications picked up where Carreño's manual left off, intending by means of setting out models for the writing of many different kinds of letters to advance the moralizing and "civilizing" project as they codified and standardized the means of measuring whether or not it had been attained. Monsiváis mentions, for example, the proliferation of books setting out specifications for many different kinds of letters, including those dispensing advice, offering condolences, and sending congratulations, thanks, and complaints as well as model responses for all of these. Among these were manuals of model love letters, especially one entitled *Cartas de amor*, from which he includes in his own book a number of exemplary letters by "Zelma." Rhetorically inscribing the same sentimental anatomy as many of those sending and receiving love letters in Porfirian Chihuahua, one in which the most important organs of sentiment were the heart, soul, and eyes (the subject of the next section), Zelma's letters and others like it offered, according to Monsiváis, not only a model of *cursilería* (schmaltz) but also an important strategy of internal persuasion, a means of plotting one's own inclusion within the increasingly defined and standardized stories of the sentimental romantic narrative.[72]

Even more important than Zelma in disseminating models of letter writing, especially among the popular classes and middling groups, was Antonio Vanegas Arroyo, whose booklets and broadsheets, including but not limited to collections of drafts of love letters, were hawked in the streets of many Mexican cities, beginning in the 1880s, as well as within the pages of *Los bandidos*. Enduring in popularity, these small and inexpensive booklets are still available in newsstands and on the streets—I myself bought one about ten years ago, *Cartas amorosas y felicitaciones*,[73] on a doorstep in Oaxaca City on the way to the Central de Abastos, the main market, from an itinerant bookseller. These booklets brought together advice for the lovelorn, homilies designed to provide both humorous commentary on and ammunition for the battle between the sexes, and a series of drafts of letters and responses to them grouped around specific phases in a courting relationship, including initially declaring one's love, introducing oneself to the parents, asking for clarification, sending a portrait or a token of love, and ending the relationship. The scenarios presented in them teased out for readers, as well as those listening to them as they were shouted out by those selling them or read aloud, diverse points of view on everything from courtship to gender, family, and respectability, among other things.

Popular groups, those buying these publications, saw themselves reflected in this rich universe of ideas that constituted the imaginary of Vanegas Arroyo while, at the same time, they found there models for behavior and attitudes they could try out. It could not have been otherwise, concludes Elisa Speckman, as, if the world constructed by Vanegas Arroyo had been too far removed from popular courtship and romantic practices, these booklets would not have found a market.[74]

Certainly, among the many collections of love letters published by the Vanegas Arroyo print shop, turns of phrase, rhetorical constructions, ideals, and images can be located that resonate with those found in the love letters from the judicial archives, especially the writing of Enriqueta and Pedro. One version of a model love letter dealing with the first written protestation of love from the novio (a stage the manuals almost all began with and offered letters for), much like the initial letters from both Pedro and Lino discussed above, finds in passion the explanation for the daring to write: "However it is not in my power to dominate the passion that consumes me and I have resolved to say to you that I adore you blindly."[75] As in the actual letters above, only through the frequent use of the formal "Usted" can the writer of the model letter assure the recipient of her respectability as well as his own. Likewise, just as in Enriqueta and Pedro's correspondence, both the model letter from the man and the response to it from the prospective novia stress frankness in matters of the heart. Just like Enriqueta, fictitious novias needed assurance that the love being offered was sincere, while, like Pedro, erstwhile novios offered to prove their love, so as to dispel the doubts of the other, in any way she should desire.[76] Differences between the letters located in the judicial archive in northern Mexico and some of the model letters are also apparent: one that comes immediately to mind, for example, is that most of the model letters and responses gathered in one published collection end by anticipating a face-to-face meeting between the novios, one in which to continue in person the conversation begun on paper, a great difference from the introspective world being constructed through writing by Enriqueta and Pedro, and one perhaps designed as much for readers of these manuals who, by means of this promised tryst, are invited to imagine or perhaps even dream of and desire the eventual union of the couple.

Rather than continue comparing actual love letters with those published in the manuals of Vanegas Arroyo, it seems even more useful to elaborate on the characteristics or qualities of the presumed or ideal reader that the manuals themselves construct or call into being. Doing so makes it possible to suggest some of the ways in which those composing letters in northern Mexico may or may not have recognized themselves in such texts and whether or not viewing them as models for popular letter writing is the best way to understand to whom they might have been directed or the nature of their appeal. To begin with, it is important to note that the manuals envisioned male and female readers, addressing themselves to both. Nearly half of the letters in many of the manuals are written from the perspective of women writers (leaving aside for the moment whether or not women contributed to the writing of the booklets); at least half of the homilies regarded female readers as the targets of their advice. While pithy platitudes like "Don't try to love a coquette, as you'll never have a cent," were clearly aimed or sympathized with a male readership, an equal number were, like the following, directed at women readers: "Never tell your novio how much you love him, or you'll see yourself eclipsed by other women."[77] Likewise, the maxims or adages found on the back cover of another collection of love letters, one of its advertised features, addressed women as their presumed audience: "Women, don't be too jealous, as continuous reproach, instead of attracting the man, pushes him away killing love completely."[78] Occasionally, the editors embedded such maxims within the body of the model letters, including those supposedly written by women, making the letters didactic as well as exemplary: "Above all young gentleman," warns one model letter writer to her prospective novio, "think carefully about it as the graces of youth pass quickly and only the qualities of the heart last for a lifetime."[79]

Cartas amorosas, colección no. 1 closed with a discussion of the whims of women on its back cover, a privileged location for encouraging casual browsing. Here, however, rather than a female readership, the collection invoked an imaginary space of presumed masculine solidarity in the face of the foibles of the female sex. Among women's supposed caprices were those of disobeying parental authority to sneak off to meet novios, using

attending mass as a pretext for leaving home only to skip out for a romantic date, deception and the betrayal of promises, and accepting truth as
lies and lies as the truth, all stated, of course, in the form of truisms like
the following: "If several suitors are introduced to a women, she'll always
choose the worst one." A sense of "wouldn't you just know it" permeates the
language of the writing guide, constructing long-suffering and bewildered
male readers that one can almost imagine shaking their heads or nodding
in agreement at their collective plight. The inevitable conclusion was as
obvious as it was sexist: "I have here the reason that the world is such a
tangled web or topsy-turvy place."[80]

The enumeration of women's whims went beyond presuming a masculine readership built on the basis of common sentiment; it also invoked a
discourse that informs or structures many of the letters as well as adages
and the other kinds of writing these collections comprise—that of develop-
mentalism or the developmentalist ethic, so premised upon moral reform
and associated with new middling groups in Porfirian society. Women's
caprices, in addition to those already mentioned, for example, also included
choosing a rich man, even if vice-ridden, for a husband, while looking
down upon honest, hard-working suitors simply because they were poor;
thinking that love would overcome laziness; and losing her beauty, no
matter how attractive she might be, through being a flirt or a tease. As in
the letter above in which the (supposed) young woman writing contrasts
the fleetingness of physical beauty with the enduring qualities of the heart,
developmentalist virtues, highly gendered, were also reiterated in adages:
"Youth and physical beauty do not last. The woman must not trust solely
in her beauty to dominate the man; her moral goodness should be greater
than her physical merits." Men, also, needed instruction in the developmentalist ethic: "The suitor who is accustomed to the vice of drink doesn't
arrive at the end of the journey, he ends up exhausted in the middle of the
trip." Similarly, in model letters, editors often used the contrast between
the monetary value of goods and their symbolic properties, especially their
abilities to convey the sentiments of will and caring, to highlight the need
to privilege feeling over material wealth.[81]

As much as those adhering to the developmentalist ethic advocated moral reform as a means of self- and class-identification, especially as figured through the eradication of the evil trinity of vice—drinking, gambling, and prostitution—and the reinforcement of dominant constructions of gender to help secure these categories, they also found in respectability one of their most overriding preoccupations. If nothing else, the Vanegas Arroyo editors framed the collections of love letters within the confines of the respectable. To begin with, the only possible framework within which love can be located in these collections is that of marriage.[82] As an illustration of this, some of the collections move directly from letters dealing with the first declaration of love to those offering models for the novio to ask the woman's parents for her hand in marriage. Others include in the initial declaration of love from the man his request to introduce himself to the woman's parents, with her permission, in order to assure them of the "pure sentiments" he intended offering their daughter. In responding to the man's request in this instance, the woman also stressed the extent to which her parents cared for her interests and thus would want to meet the potential husband who might assure them of the bright prospects for their daughter's future. By contrast, in another collection, editors portrayed such parental interest as a problem for the couple, as rumors of a courting relationship had caused the woman's mother to increase her vigilance, to the point of spying, according to the young woman, making it difficult for her to exchange letters with her novio. Even here, however, readers found themselves in the midst of a drama that, rather than signaling the breakdown of family control rehearsed familiar scenarios and intergenerational tensions that seemed to confirm the generalizations about gender, especially those concerning women, around which many of the adages and homilies turned.

This is not to say, however, that editors of such collections of letters and advice imagined women as having no voice in the choice of a spouse or in other matters concerning romantic love. Model letters meant to be from fathers in response to men writing to ask for a daughter's hand in marriage stressed women's will (voluntad) as first and foremost, if not necessarily definitive, to agreeing to such a proposal.[83] After all, families, while respectable, were also envisioned as modern; that is, they were envisioned as formed on the basis of mutual feelings of romantic love rather than through economic necessity or family duty. Editors also scripted women as able to act in defense of their own honor. Believing herself the victim of her novio's gossip, another common theme in the letters in the collections, a certain "Lugarda" lambasted her novio (no longer regarding him as the gentleman she had supposed him to be) for slandering her, supposedly boasting to his friends that he had gained her favors. Given that she had "no other fortune than my honorableness," such statements, she complained, profoundly damaged her.[84]

Other women, rather than apportioning blame over the loss of their honor, turned to their novios to help salvage it. Under the category of "Asking for Clarification," Vanegas Arroyo editors drafted a fictitious exchange of letters between novios, the impact of which on readers can only be imagined. Explaining in writing to Encarnación, his novia, that another individual had introduced himself to him, claiming to have Encarnación's letters, a lock of her hair, and other *prendas* (gifts, symbols, tokens, or mementos exchanged as part of a courting relationship) from her, and thus the right to her affections, Pablo, fearing for his "eternal disgrace," nonetheless professed his unending love and implored her to be frank in her response to him. Ever so grateful, Encarnación admitted her previous relationship, the result, she stressed, of the insanity of youth, and one that had ended five years previously. Once over, she explained, the former novio had refused to return her letters and the rest of her possessions. "As I couldn't take them back by force," she explained, trading on dominant constructions of women's weakness, "in spite of myself I had to leave them in his possession." She asked Pablo to retrieve them and do with them what seemed, to him, to be right. Pablo, inviting the former novio to a meeting, and now with the letters and gifts in his possession, read out loud Encarnación's explanatory letter to him, adding his own insults that the cowardly former novio suffered in silence until driven from the room in shame. Encarnación's final letter in the mini-drama thanks Pablo for returning to her, at long last, this compromising packet from her past. Although a moral tale about the loathsome character of the former novio and the honorable and steadfast nature of Pablo, the scenario offers, nonetheless, a compelling reason why novios were so interested in having their letters and gifts returned.[85] In a world of gossip, such as that sketched out both in the collections and in the letters encountered in the judicial archives, such evidence might offer incomparable proof of, at least, the feigned nature of one's love if not, as in the context of many of the relationships I have discussed, the existence of prior sexual relations in exchange for a written promise of marriage. In another sense, the fictitious exchange highlights the ability of love letters to serve not only as proof of a relationship but as a means to stake a claim to the affections of the other, almost like demarcating a territory, as if the imaginary novio assumed he possessed Encarnación as long as he maintained in his possession her surrogate, the letters she had sent him.

Indeed, like the scenario sketched out in the imaginary letters exchanged between Pablo and Encarnación, a number of the sets of supposedly model correspondence, rather than encourage emulation, can only have been designed to shock or amuse readers (or both). This was especially the case with those letters dealing with the breakup of the couple, letters that may have served as models, but only for those wishing to learn how to compose their own death wishes. When Pancho wrote to end his relationship with Lola, for example, he did begin by trading on many of the common accusations around which romantic correspondence revolved—the feigned nature of the other's love and how he had been deceived. Her love, he felt, she really saved for some other "Don Fulano." After his initial salvo, Pancho's prose quickly deteriorated into personal insult: "Many people had already told me about the perverse and dark treachery that you were playing on me; at the beginning, it seemed unseemly to believe that you were like all the rest of the women but now I'm convinced that in truth you are the worst of them all." Not wanting to be two-timed, he ended the relationship, returning the "trinkets" (bagatelas) she had given him as tokens of a courting relationship. Not to be outdone, Lola replied in kind: "It is well known that you are so greedy and stingy like all of your type . . . that when as if by some miracle you people give someone a cigarette, you soon return to charge them for the ashes." So poor were his gifts, she continued, that they were forgettable—she asked him to remind her what they even were so she could return them. If she had replaced him for another, she wrote, she had done well, because it was for a "real" man (hombre de veras). Finding

time, amazingly, for one more dig in such a brief note, Lola made it a good
one: "Don't bother me again with your nonsense (*tonteras*)."[86]

In a similar vein, it is likewise difficult to imagine some of the advice
on offer, especially that found on the all-important back covers of these
collections, as actually being meant to be followed. An article entitled
"Useful Advice to Women to Make Someone Love Them" is a case in
point.[87] In this section, editors purported to offer women tried and true
secret techniques passed down through the ages to capture the object of
one's affections. The activities described—involving hairs, body fluids, and
food preparation—invoke many of the practices linked to ensorcelling
drawn from Inquisition records of colonial New Spain as discussed by
Ruth Behár and others.[88] Such columns do seem to give readers access to
a living, if hidden, world of love magic premised upon oral traditions still
being practiced in the early twentieth century and even much later, for
that matter. I myself have seen desiccated hummingbird corpses for sale
in popular markets along with love powders and other paraphernalia of
popular romance. In a recipe for romance from one back cover, entitled
"The Apple of Love," the woman was meant to enter an orchard at sun-
down, pick the ripest and least blemished apple, write her name as well as
that of the one she desired in blood on pieces of paper and then enclose
them, after removing the heart of the apple, in its middle, along with his
and her hairs and another paper with the magic word "Scheva" written
on it, also in blood. The two halves of the apple would then be rejoined,
dried in an oven, and secretly located beneath the pillow of the man she
desired. Perhaps the most surprising aspect of the advice offered in this
instance was its gender heterodoxy: this marvelous secret, promised the
editors, would produce the same effects if carried out by a man, allowing
him to obtain the love of the woman he desired.[89]

While in the recipe for the "Apple of Love," the magic ingredients were
pretty much at hand, such was not the case for the concoctions that then
followed. Designed to accomplish somewhat similar ends—the steadfast-
ness of love instead of its attraction—these relied, variously, on the marrow
from the left foot of a wolf, grey amber, the marrow from the spine of a
wolf, the hair from the eyes of a wolf, all designed to be mixed, worn,

applied as a pomade, or some combination thereof in order to keep one's partner faithful.[90] In some ways, the inclusion of these "folk" practices, longstanding in some cases, perhaps even fanciful in others, in collections of letters that enacted the various stages in a courting relationship within a framework that stressed respectability, honor, parental involvement, woman's will, marriage, and the written word seems somewhat incongruous. Perhaps it does mark the letter-writing manuals as liminal, or hybrid, bringing together as they do the world of folk remedies and popular romantic practices with that of print culture that included female as well as male readers and emphasized personal choice as the basis for the formation of modern couples. As such, the texts might be a perfect reflection of their readership, some with recently acquired habits of reading, others listening in on the conversation from the margins, and many ensconced, whether comfortably or otherwise, in both the world of print and of prophecy, of writing and of wolf marrow.

Or perhaps another interpretation is possible. What seems particularly striking about the Vanegas Arroyo manuals is that, in addition to being organized around important phases in a courting relationship, thus anchoring them within a particular temporal and narrative trajectory, that initiated by first meeting and culminating in either marriage or breakup, all the letters are also grouped into scenarios. Rather than being designed as form letters that can be utilized by prospective writers/novios at the various phases of courtship as need be, these multi-letter exchanges or conversations in epistolary form craft mini-dramas in order to drop the reader into highly emotionally charged situations—the return of letters sent to a previous novio, discussions of honor or gossip, the expression of desire and the hope that it would be reciprocated, bitter breakups, all delivering an emotional kick—in much the same way as the press, discussed above, used narratives of real life to stimulate reader interest and reaction. In place of sensational journalism concerned with murder-suicides and crimes of passion, however, what the love letter manuals offer up are glimpses of skirmishes in the battle between the sexes, firmly anchored not only in the rhetoric of respectability and marriage but also in stereotypes, especially about women's whims and weaknesses, as expressed not only in the letters but also in the sayings and advice sections. While the letters and adages presume both male and female readers and writers, it seems like much of the writing itself nevertheless trades on or assumes a particularly masculine bias. What the press found in the lingering of victims and the temporal vicissitudes of investigations and explanations, grounded as they were in ongoing time ("stay tuned . . ."), the mini-dramas in the manuals almost always promised actual meetings between the novios at a later date to accomplish this sense of anticipation, of ongoing and unresolved action. Both brought into being publics hanging on further details, always pending, whether delivered in the next edition, the next manual, or imagined in their own minds. At other places in the manuals, especially those dealing with break-ups, the letters are meant to provoke surprise or even astonishment, the sharp-witted tongues of the writers measuring the extent to which such prose would not be acceptable. Perhaps the wisdom of the ages presented on the back covers, that delving into love magic, served a similar purpose: to allow readers to measure through their own reaction the extent to which they had distanced themselves from such practices.

"Yo con mi mano escribí" (In my own hand I wrote)

Señorita, bien comprendo	Señorita, how well I know
que no merezco su amor;	That of your love I'm not worthy
por ser pobre y mi color	My color and poverty
considero que la ofendo;	Must offend you;
pero yo ¿qué culpa tengo	But who could blame me
de quererla tanto así?	For loving you so?
Y desde el día que la vi	From the day I first saw you
en usted vivo pensando;	Of you I live thinking;
la carta que le mando	The letter that I'm sending you
yo con mi mano escribí.[91]	In my own hand I wrote.

It seems only appropriate to move from folk remedies offering those desperate and in love some hope of attaining their hearts' desires to the copla, a genre of folkloric poetry, also much dedicated to the anguish and ecstasy of romantic love, an example of which introduces this final part of the

present section.[92] While interest in forms of popular lyric poetry in particular and folklore in general emerged in conjunction with the Mexican
Revolution, or even slightly before as part of the project of gathering forms
of oral culture discussed by Rama, it was in the decade of the 1950s that a
group of investigators at the Centro de Estudios Lingüísticos y Literarios
at El Colegio de México began collecting and organizing literary folklore.
They did so according to a number of criteria, mostly having to do with
subject and the person speaking (first person or third person), resulting
in the publication of a five-volume collection of coplas beginning in 1975
entitled *Cancionero folklórico de México* under the direction of Margit Frenk
Alatorre.[93] Of the literally thousands of coplas (defined for the purposes
of the collection as non-narrative verse, that is, as poetry in which stanzas
stand on their own, in distinction to the corrido and other forms of verse
in which events are recounted through a series of stanzas related to each
other) that compose the multi-volume work, more than half of all the lyric
poetry the El Colegio group amassed—gathered in two full volumes, the
first and second, and part of the third, and numbering almost six thousand
coplas—is preoccupied, in one manner or another, with the theme of love.

Such an embarrassment of riches in and of itself seems sufficient to suggest
the need for care in putting such material to use. My concern here is not to
exhaust the possible themes covered by such an extensive collection of verse
but rather to explore the relationship between the poetics of the coplas
and the poetics of the love letters, in effect to use the coplas to reflect upon
and suggest additional interpretive possibilities for the romantic and other
sentiments expressed in letters in prose form. It is also necessary to admit
at this point that I located no coplas in any of the archives I consulted as
part of the research carried out in Chihuahua, or elsewhere in Mexico for
that matter. Moreover, the copla being a genre characterized by a constant
process of recreation, those gathered in the 1950s, 1960s, and 1970s, that
is, those found in *Cancionero folklórico de México*, may be considerably
different from those of an earlier period or may have been specific to the
region in which they had been collected. Regardless of all these caveats, the
specific, individual, and everyday experiences that form the subject matter
of many of the coplas, everything from passion to honor, understandings

of masculinities, raptos, proofs of love, written promises of marriage, the exchange of photographic portraits, the fear of being discovered, the need to make money in order to get married, tensions between the generations, and the alchemy through which the body and the letter slide into and become one the other, seem to echo between the genres of the copla and the letter. If not blurring their boundaries, these echoes offer, at the least, confirmation of the centrality of themes common to both and, at best, through a kind of sympathetic resonance, add additional and differently nuanced readings of statements and sentiments not immediately apparent within the specific setting or generic conventions of the love letter form. Indeed, at times it has seemed that, had there been no love letters available as a means of contextualizing and historicizing romantic love, coplas might have done just as well.

As is hinted at by the verse that introduced this section, in which a male narrator of relatively humble social origins stresses his own mastery of the written word, even if in song or saying, coplas might best be approached not as a privileged repository of some sort of traditional, oral popular culture but as, at certain times at least, a profound engagement between the oral and particular types of literacies, especially the love letter. Indeed, one of the strengths of Frenk's approach as set out in the prologue to the coplas collection is the rejection of what she refers to as the "false conception" of folkloric poetry as a purely oral form; instead, she stresses the interpenetration of written and oral cultures as well as the continuous exchanges taking place across class and social boundaries that helped enrich and shape the genre. Coplas, then, may have a great deal to tell us about the relationship of writing to romantic love. In fact, the principle for selecting verses that compose an entire section of the first volume of the collection is that they are all concerned with writing love letters. Much as Carlos Monsiváis argues when discussing the relationship of the romantic song, especially the bolero, to the epistolary genre, sayings and verse such as the coplas also helped sustain the romantic vocabulary and understandings of sentimentality expressed in the letter (and vice versa I imagine).[94]

Mimicking some of the qualities of the written word, the copla that introduces this section can be regarded as a particular kind or class of letter, one that a male suitor would send to a prospective novia or intended. It is full of polite and formal language, like "señorita" and "Ud," and the author apologizes for daring to write, the extent of his indiscretion being equal to the depths of the feelings of love that drove him to do such a thing. This copla, then, is a letter in oral form, a letter meant to be sung out loud. That the two genres might even be interchangeable is, at times, played with in coplas, as in the following copla that serves as another introductory or first letter from the male suitor, even though, again, it is being delivered in oral form. Instead of writing a love letter, the copla refers, playfully, to the writing of a *décima*, or poem, that serves the same purpose as a letter; that is, it hopes to initiate a courting relationship:

Si tú me quieres a mí	If you love me
Contéstame por favor	Answer me please
Esta décima de amor	This ten-line poem of love
Que yo para tí escribí	That I wrote for you[95]

While both this copla and the earlier one that introduced this part of the section are a particular and recognizable form of writing that can be located within the broader category of courtship literacy—that of the first or introductory letter—the initial copla is remarkable for a number of other reasons as well. To begin with, the male narrator mentions his poverty and "race," characteristics only occasionally remarked upon in this genre, as well as how those factors created inequalities of class and, perhaps, of station between the writer (or singer) and his intended. The narrator's love is inappropriate, even forbidden, by virtue of these social rules, he seems to be saying, a claim that also serves to highlight the extent of his love, as only someone truly in love could even hope to transcend such social chasms. The differences in social status also serve to draw attention to another quality the writer/singer possesses: his command of the written word. In fact, the narrator is adamant that, despite the fact that his class and "race" may lead many to assume that he lacked the ability to read and write, he himself composed the letter/copla with his own hand.

The need to make authorship clear, to claim it for oneself as the narrator does, suggests that it might be entirely common, at least among certain social strata, to send letters composed by others. As I have indicated, authorship in the late nineteenth and early twentieth centuries, in many parts of the country, was often accomplished by a group rather than by an individual. It would not have been unusual, for example, to have someone else, or even a number of people, cooperate in order to write a letter, for another to read it to one's intended, and for another to take down a response. Alternatively, scribes, still found at the entrances of many public markets in many parts of Mexico, might be employed to accomplish the task of writing a letter. The following copla hints at how the relationship between writing and reading within courtship literacy not only might be accomplished by bringing together a number of people with various levels of skill in writing and reading but might also be gendered, with men having more access to or command over such skills than women, although here the novia's female friend possesses skills that she herself does not:

La carta que te mandé	The letter that I sent you
Ya tendrás quien te la lea:	Now you'll have someone read it to you
Una amiga de confianza	A girlfriend you trust
Que te diga lo que sea	Who'll tell you whatever it says
Esa amiga de confianza	This girlfriend you trust
Mándame decir quién es	Let me know who she is
Para mandarle una carta	So I can send her a letter
Con las letras al revés	With the letters all backwards[96]

The final line referring to the "letters all backwards" is most likely a reference to the use of a kind of code so that, if the letter were to fall into the wrong hands, it would be difficult or impossible to decipher or understand. I myself came across a love letter written in a similar manner when working in the judicial archives in Parral, Chihuahua, a number of years ago. After a day and a half of trying to decipher a very short letter, I finally discovered, almost by accident, that if I read the letter out loud and switched the order, not of every letter, but of every syllable, actual words rather than what seemed to be random sounds appeared and the meaning of the letter became clear. Both the above copla and my own experience help show that, as much as coplas might be letters in oral form, letters could be highly oral, that is, contain many elements of speech and could also be better understood when read out loud. The use of code also illustrates that courtship might be a time of danger, with real consequences for the discovery of a relationship, for reasons you will see in the next section.

Mine was not the only experience of understanding a letter only when reading it out loud. As many letters were often read to their addressees, they must be considered as much an oral genre as coplas are a written one. Many letters, including those not in any code, were written in syllables rather than in words, and the sentences lacked punctuation, making it difficult to understand them unless reading them out loud or having someone else do so. Letters and coplas also shared many of the same expressive strategies, playing across the supposed oral/written divide. Coplas, for example, often borrowed or copied set phrases that commonly appeared in love letters, phrases such as "I'll never forget you" or, as in the following copla, deployed a variant of the familiar closing in a letter, the "you know who":

Yo no te digo mi nombre	I'm not telling you my name
Para que no corra fama;	So that it won't get around
La que te quiere, te adora y te ama	The one who wants you, adores you and loves you
Ya sabes cómo se llama	You already know their name[97]

Given that the copla might serve as a kind of surrogate letter and that the letter might be imagined, just as easily, as a surrogate copla, it is not surprising, perhaps, that both genres tell a similar story concerning the stages and characteristics found in a courting relationship, at least from a masculine point of view. Striking as one reads the collection of coplas is the prevalence of the masculine voice in romantic verse, a dominant characteristic of most coplas, according to those compiling the collection, and one that dates to the inception of courtly love poetry in the twelfth century. Although not completely absent from the collection, women's voices in the coplas are so seldom heard that one is left wondering how or even whether women may have given expression to their romantic sentiments in such verse. Those few coplas articulating a feminine voice cover no single thematic issue or perspective. At times, as in the love letter manuals, these coplas can articulate a much more reserved or cautious point of view, one in which the woman needs a great deal more convincing or proof of the sincerity of the love being offered or is figured as the person acted upon rather than acting.

Coplas, regardless of their preoccupation with the written word and despite the fact that they were as imbricated in writing as letters were in orality, while sustaining the vocabulary of love and powerful in helping compose or give expression to such feelings, were useless when it came to enforcing any legal consequences that followed from them. Perhaps coplas referenced writing in order to bask, as if by reflection, in its power, one that came by way of its role in facilitating the working of the state and its various institutions, like the judicial system. Coplas—sung out loud in order to be remembered, their repetitive verses, rhymes, and cadences circulating knowledge and commonsense understandings in such matters as love and courtship—made pointed comments, at times, on the dynamics of the courting relationship as understood by men, expressing in song its tensions, its delights, and its dangers, all the while referencing the importance and power of the written word, even if in oral form.

It was this latter factor that separated coplas from letters. Certainly, coplas, like Liberato's letters, introduced at the very beginning of this section, were meant to be delivered orally, to be spoken or sung out loud, perhaps to a group larger than the two individuals involved in the courting relationship. Performed in this manner, coplas brought into being an audience that shared, debated, laughed at, and, perhaps, lamented or longed for many of the claims of masculinity and courtship being expressed therein. Given the power of the written word, however, it is little wonder that coplas are shot through with writing, letters, and the use of written forms. Because of these characteristics, they enable the telling of a partial history of courtship, from a masculine point of view, as they often resonated with actual behavior and attitudes that still echoed years after they had ceased being common practice. Even though coplas borrowed the forms of the letter as much as the letter was often grounded in those of speech, they could never be used to compel any man to make good on his promises, as could messages delivered in writing. While differing in this respect, coplas, as much as letters, formed a part of courtship literacy, a literacy event in which men often enjoyed greater access to and command over the written word than did women and in which forms of writing, especially letters, functioned as much as material objects as they did to convey the meaning of the words themselves. Courtship was also a series of practices where masculine prerogatives, whether expressed in written or oral form, might be defended through violence and in which a man's word, whether given in writing or orally, might be worth defending with one's life.

If coplas help us understand that the lettered countryside was a place where letters might incorporate the poetics of verse and sayings just as much as verse might express letters in oral form, they also reveal the close metaphorical connection that links the letter and the body, especially the sentimental anatomy that these very letters help bring into being. The following copla, in which a letter is addressed in the familiar "tu" form and imbued with human emotion, captures as well the power of the letter to convey feelings, even touches, from writer to reader, making of the letter a kind of surrogate lover, acting in place of the absent one:

Oh, dichosa carta escrita	Oh, lucky letter in writing
Quién fuera dentro de ti	If I could only be within you
Para darle mil abrazos	To give a thousand embraces
Al angel que te ha de abrir	To the angel who will open you.[98]

These properties of the letter as a form of writing and the sentimental anatomy love letters help compose are the themes taken up in the next section.

The Body of the Letter

Bits of bodies, both physical and textual, lie strewn throughout and between the pages of the love letters lodged in the judicial archive. Letters, at times, contained actual locks of hair and photographic images, tokens of love that stand in for the absent lover. Other body parts, eyes and hearts especially, also figure prominently in these missives, powerful symbols expressing the emotional charge of the relationship while metonymically conjuring the absent lover; along with less corporeal essences like "will" and "souls," they compose the rhetorical tools of correspondents as well as the metaphorical organs of what might be called the sentimental anatomy, breathing life into the prose of love as they are composed by it. They hint at desires that authors felt compelled to broach, if euphemistically. Living bodies are also a major preoccupation of those writing, especially of those men whose letters have been submitted for the crimes considered in section 1 of this book. As much as judicial officials, these suitors were preoccupied with female virginity, the actual or implied subject of many if not most of their letters that women submitted in such legal processes, with an intact hymen serving as a symbol of a woman's overall reputation and attesting to her apparent suitability for marriage.

If the letter and the body seemed joined at the hip, each, in some way, an ideal means of calling forth the other, the reason for this may be found partly in features common to all written forms and partly in conventions more specific to the genre of letter writing. The first explanation struck me when walking through cemeteries in Xoxocotlán and Ciudad Oaxaca during Day of the Dead celebrations in 2010, when I noticed that a symbol of a book figured as a common marker on many of the headstones. The presence of the book seemed to indicate that each life, comprising original and unique chapters, having reached its conclusion, could become knowable, made legible or given meaning as history, a passage through time translated into textual form. Capturing the life of the person interred below, the book stands in for a life—any life, every life—while simultaneously enabling the weighing of its relative merits, often, as in cemeteries, in avowedly religious terms. More than merely retrospective, the metaphorical book of life also seems capable of charting one's future, of setting out one's fate in advance, of making out of the chance encounter of a lover, for example, destiny or one's perfect match. Moreover, writing itself might even be divinely mandated, designed to last for all of eternity. "Why did God write out his commandments?" one catechism prominent in Mexico in the late nineteenth century asks of its readers. The required response: to prevent men from forgetting or changing them.[1]

As for letters, they are performative as well as metaphorical, bringing into being the very subjects and relationships that they hope to generate and, similarly, with their return, marking the end of the ideal couple, the demise of relationships, and the closing of epistolary space. Like the book and the life, letters and courtship seem mutually to beckon—with the exchanges, implied reciprocity, and gift-like properties of correspondence mimicking the exchanges, reciprocity, and incitement to increasing commitment of the courting relationship itself.[2] As a form, the letter seems to document as well as anticipate the trajectory of courtship, charting its phases, revealing as well as producing what might be called an anatomy of sentiment. The various body parts and emotions I am calling the sentimental anatomy and the phases of a courting relationship, the anatomy of sentiment, are intimately related, each taking shape in relationship to the other. So too does epistolary space bring into being not only a self that writes and a recipient that reads but also an ideal couple that may be distinct from both.[3] The writing manuals that were discussed in the previous section capture one sense of this process, in their insistence that the proper form of the ideal letter served as a reflection of the proper individual that they themselves had helped to compose.

This section of the book follows from the copla with which the previous section ends, a copla that hints at, if perhaps doesn't quite capture, the power of the letter, even the magic of the letter, to deliver to its addressee not only an intended message but, in some form, the letter's sender as well. While in the case of this copla a mere wish of somehow being included within the letter is being expressed, writers of fiction in the nineteenth century had great fun in playing with this trope of the letter as surrogate body. In the play *Don Juan Tenorio*, for example, written by José Zorrillo in 1844, a work still being staged and read in various forms during contemporary Day of the Dead celebrations in many parts of Mexico, the love letter that Doña Inés, one of the main female characters, receives from Don Juan seems to conjure out of thin air the presence of her lover; not only does it burn her hand when she touches it, it also delivers a poisoned love potion or spell into her heart.[4]

Such understandings of the corporeal capabilities of the letter as a form were hardly limited to the literary realm. In letters exchanged between Refugio, a woman living in Parral, Chihuahua, and Rodrigo, her mineworker novio who had gone to work in nearby Santa Bárbara, a correspondence that, although containing only Refugio's letters, I have drawn on heavily in writing this section of the book, Refugio is adamant about the power of the page to, if not conjure the missing correspondent, then to act as a medium for delivering their touch, to make their presence manifest.[5] Although she is discussing her desire to receive a photograph as a token of their relationship, she is as concerned with the manner of its delivery as with its indexical properties—only if activated by Rodrigo's touch, she insists, would it serve as a proper symbol of their current and, hopefully, future status. As with many correspondents, Refugio closes many of her letters by insisting that Rodrigo receive her heart, a metaphor that attempts to express the extent of her love as well as to transcend the physical distance separating them; as in the body in love, the heart beats at the center of the letter, its textual surrogate.

While the epistolary body, at least in Refugio's case, seemed capable of overcoming the impediments of time and space, it was less successful at freeing itself from the constraints imposed by the discursive resources used to animate it. As the body could be composed and then put to didactic use by legal officials, nation builders, and literary writers, as well as by medical and religious authorities, as we have seen when it comes to Melchor Ocampo's heart, so too did engagement with the discourses enunciated at these locations contort the epistolary body in particular ways. Expressions of desire as well as anguish, for example, were more often framed within the spiritual than the carnal, just as the parts of the sentimental anatomy—the soul, the will (voluntad), and perhaps even the heart—seem transplanted from a body nourished on popular religiosity. The epistolary body was also meant to be seen to be believed; just as the truth of love was to be found in a set of visual relations, the body's external surfaces, it was often hoped or expected, might make apparent deeply held internal qualities or truths. So was it gendered, bearing organs and affects specific to each sex and imbuing many of those held in common, at times, with somewhat different characteristics. While this body might inhabit epistolary space, its reach extended far beyond the textual—violence policed the boundaries of many of its behaviors, making the rhetorical turns of phrase found within letters into matters of literal life and death.

Passion

> Please excuse me for troubling you but from the first moment that I had the good fortune of seeing your image my heart felt a terrible passion that devours me and being unable to stand it any longer I resolved to declare these clumsy words to you, fearing that it won't turn out in my favor if I offend you with some blunder with my words. Be so kind to excuse me for being so vain [but] you can't imagine the love that I offer you and at the same time with the hope of being reciprocated he remains your Impassioned one awaiting the resolution of his fate—please reply as you see fit.[6]

With this letter, Lino M., a seventeen-year-old agricultural laborer living near San Francisco del Oro, a mining town in the Hidalgo del Parral mining district, hoped to initiate his courtship of fourteen-year-old Soledad, who was unable to sign the testimony she gave to judicial officials in 1925. It seems only appropriate to begin the discussion of the epistolary body with passion, as it was this particular feeling that drove many suitors to take up pen and paper in the first place. What Lino's letter also illustrates is the difficulty of separating the various emotions and organs of the epistolary body for the purposes of discussion—even in this brief paragraph, along with passion, the heart, the image, and the reciprocal nature of both courtship and letter writing are all made apparent.

Despite the difficulty of considering separately its various interdependent parts, the epistolary body was more often than not brought into being through passion. Pedro, the mine worker you encountered in the previous section, writing to Enriqueta in 1919, explained his behavior in terms similar to those used by Lino. Although the love letters exchanged between Pedro and Enriqueta are not dated and are in no particular order in the archive, Pedro's letter initiating his courtship of Enriqueta and, thus, giving birth to the epistolary body, is easy to spot:

> Señorita. I count on your kindness to address to you this letter to make known to you the vehement passion that I feel within my heart, and that is impossible for me to suffer any longer, for the same reason I speak to you with frankness and without offending your dignity, I love you with the intentions of an honorable man when he addresses himself to a young woman of your qualities. Señorita, I beg of you not to think that what I dare to say to you should be feigned, that isn't such as my heart feels and I would find myself happy if you should reciprocate my love, if you should give shelter to this love that for some time has aimlessly wandered and only in you hopes to find its happiness; but how unhappy I would be if you rejected my vows with a cruel refusal of your love.[7]

Full of formal and polite language, with an "Usted" marking almost every line, the letters from both Pedro and Lino enabled each man to reveal his feelings to his prospective novia while explaining what had compelled him to take such a drastic step in the first place. Such statements formed part of a rhetoric of formal politeness, a way of acknowledging that they considered the woman to be decent and respectable; this language also enabled suitors to demonstrate that they realized they were treading near or even outside the bounds of propriety, while offering an explanation for their behavior as well as a measure of the depths of their feelings—only the most vehement passion could have made them do such a thing.

Passion wasn't necessarily for everyone, however, even as a means for explaining why one had dared to initiate a romantic correspondence. When José María, a thirty-six-year-old miner working in Parral, found himself accused of initiating sexual relations with sixteen-year-old Matilde, for example, the following love letter was submitted to judicial officials in hopes of framing their encounter within the context of a courting relationship meant to lead to marriage:

> Esteemed Señorita, From the same moment that divine heaven deigned to grant me license to meet you, there awoke in my heart that sublime and inexplicable sentiment that is called love and being impossible for me to do without it, I am taking the liberty of making this declaration to you and I only hope that kindly you might accept my request because I love you, and it will be very gratifying for me to be reciprocated [in this feeling] by you, and I remain in hope of your answer, he who only desires to be happy at your side. You know whom.[8]

Rather than passion, it had been love, "sublime and inexplicable" and perhaps also at first sight, that had driven José María to act as well as, supposedly, to write. Such was not the case, however, as "you know whom" turned out not to be José María at all, he testifying, convincingly, that he did not recognize the words in the letter or the hand in which it had been written, a statement that provides yet another sense of the power of the letter to extend the touch of the author, to deliver both message and composer to its recipient. Given the discussion of Liberato's correspondence in the previous section of the book, it should come as no surprise that the authorship of many of the love letters in the archive might be murky, composed, as many of them were, by friends, family, or in some collective manner, in short, through the use of intermediaries of some sort. However, in this instance, rather than written on behalf of an erstwhile suitor, this love letter was an outright forgery, composed with no knowledge of "you know whom," written, as it had been, to cover up yet another crime, the making available of a sixteen-year-old woman to a stranger for the purposes of paid sex. Seeking to avoid the legal consequences of procuring, the women who had arranged this assignation now sought, by means of a forged letter, to make José María solely responsible for this act, notably at the expense of Matilde, the young woman, who faced the equally bleak prospects of a tarnished reputation or an unwanted marriage to a complete stranger (or both), feared outcomes she described directly to judicial authorities.[9]

Nor was the concern with what might be called the danger of the letter, that it might be forged, fall into the wrong hands, or, perhaps, be used against one as evidence, limited to this particular instance. Lino, for example, was adamant that Soledad should return his letters to him, not believing for a moment that she had burned them as she stated. Although Lino's concern was that Soledad not use what he had given her to go around and make a fool out of him, his letters may, in actuality, have provoked even more dire consequences—they appear as evidence in a judicial inquiry into Lino's death at the hands of Soledad's brother. Another suitor refused to believe that a letter he had received had been written by his novia. Confused by the letter's subject matter and the fact that the date attached to it was prior to events being discussed in it, as well as by its contents in general, Felipe doubted it had been composed by Guadalupe's hand. In his reply, Felipe, either suspicious by nature or having had experience in such matters, asked Guadalupe to include in all subsequent messages a password that they had already agreed upon, "for greater security."[10]

Rather than exclude from consideration the letter written on José María's behalf on the basis of its status as a forgery, it is precisely this characteristic that makes it useful to the understanding of the generic conventions of the love letter form. In all three letters discussed here in which the writer hopes to initiate a courting relationship, the heart, whether compelled by love or passion, serves as the locus of love; to be reciprocated in their feelings is the desire; happiness is the end goal. Given the relatively small size of the total sample of love letters available; the selective nature of the correspondence given that only certain letters, those proving a written promise of marriage, were submitted to judicial authorities; and the relative absence of letters by women (due again to judicial imperatives), a great deal of care must be taken in drawing any stark conclusions concerning apparent gender differences in the composition of love letters. However, it does seem suggestive at least that, whereas in the love letters written by men in hopes of initiating a romantic correspondence (in both senses of the term, that is, in writing and in life) passion was given as an explanation for the writer's behavior as well as a reason to excuse it, in this letter meant to initiate a courtship, written by women pretending to be a man, it is love, sublime and inexplicable, that (supposedly) compels its writing. Although revolving around fate, the hope for reciprocity, and the desire for happiness, the opening letters at least hint at how these concepts might be imbued with distinct inflections on the basis of gender.

In fact, such a framing of desire in terms of love rather than of passion seems more consistent with the sentiments expressed in the responses women composed and sent to their suitors upon receiving such an introductory letter from their novio. Enriqueta, for example, eschewing passion, at least in her initial letter to Pedro, demands instead a sincere love (*amor sincero*), true and pure; and, while accepting the invitation to take up the dance of courtship, she nonetheless counters with some steps of her own:

> Acquainted with your esteemed and loving letter with this letter I answer it in which I will speak to you with the candidness that always characterizes me. If you really love me with a true and pure love my heart will reciprocate it, but before anything I desire that you should swear to me that yours is a sincere love not one for passing the time reassure me of this and the feelings of your heart will be reciprocated.[11]

Whether a love was feigned or true, as well as the personal integrity and motives of the person offering it, was among the central issues in a courting relationship, as was the process of convincing one's intended that one possessed these very characteristics. Refugio, a young woman responding to the letters of Rodrigo, her novio, framed her response in a similar way: "My love is true and not just for flattery." For both women, when it came to love, there was no middle ground, only two poles, those of truth and treachery: "I used to think that in life one would encounter only treachery; you convinced me that your love was immense and pure and now I'm happy," stated Enriqueta. Focusing on this dichotomy enabled both of these women to insist on their own truthfulness in matters of the heart while participating in the process common to courtship, that of requesting ever-greater demonstrations or proofs of love from their novios as well as responding to their novios' requests for exactly that same thing: "You say to me," writes Enriqueta to Pedro, "that it still seems that my words must be feigned. Don't think that, they are born from the depths of this heart." If the epistolary body differed according to gender regarding passion and love, it was meant not only to be identical when it came to truth and honesty but also to be coherent and transparent—outward appearance, in both men and women, was to manifest or demonstrate the traits correspondents were so insistent about claiming, traits often generated in other, more profound parts of the sentimental anatomy.

Yet, correspondents, both men and women, did subsequently return to passion as a means of expressing or giving a name to what they were feeling as courtship progressed. Although not many of his letters are found in the archive, Lino, the young agriculturalist whose initial letter introduced this section on passion, found sufficient inspiration in a song that had become popular in the early 1920s to copy out the lyrics and send them to Soledad. The song, "Un viejo amor," written by Alfonso Esparza Oteo in 1920, highlights the growing reach throughout the country of commercially popular music generated in Mexico City as well as its ability to give lovers everywhere an increasingly shared language and soundtrack through which to articulate their feelings. Reflecting on an old love, metonymically present in the form of a pair of dark eyes, the narrator laments both its loss and that the passage of time has led not to forgetting or to letting go but to saying goodbye. Observing the coldness of the eyes in the song's present, the narrator can find consolation only in memories, in having loved with passion, in knowing that the eyes had once loved him: "My misfortune, my greatest misfortune is that you no longer love me and I suffer in this world but because I loved you with passion and I have my memories I can live in peace."[12]

Other men found in passion either a common closing refrain or an uncommon measure of the extreme nature of the situation or circumstances in which they found themselves. Eleno, a tailor, Remedios, a carpenter, and

Marcos, an agriculturalist, all referred to themselves in letters as "the impassioned one" (*el apasionado*) and used the phrase either as a conventional means of ending a letter or, if in the body of the letter, as a shorthanded manner of assuring their intended of the depths of their feelings. As used by Liberato and especially by Pedro, however, the term "passion" took on very different connotations, heralding the potentially dangerous and disruptive force of the feeling. For Liberato, in fact, it was passion that had forced him to resort to the written word, so difficult was it for him to gather his thoughts and express them verbally when under its sway: "My heart attacked by the most violent passion and not being able to clear my mind it seemed advisable to me to send to you my reasons by means of these brief lines stating to you the following."[13] For Pedro, passion was unbearable, debilitating even, something one suffered: "You can't imagine what this poor heart has suffered for your love and because I can't find any way to dissipate my passion I find myself constantly with my mind drunk on your love that only with death will you be forgotten to me."[14]

Just as for Liberato, the act of writing, especially to one's novia, served Pedro as the antidote to passion. "If you only knew what immense tranquility your passionate Pedro finds when turning to write to you with such growing and sweet love." Nor was Enriqueta, his novia, inured to passion's pull, although this developed subsequently, not at the beginning of their correspondence. "Do you know what my Pedro?" Enriqueta wrote, "that there are moments in which I live in panic. When it seems to me that you don't love me as you say, that another woman has robbed me of your love but all these thoughts are born from the same love that I feel for you, right? Then passionate screams are torn from my soul that, just as they reach my lips, I remember that you love me and then only then with calm do I turn once again to see the image of you that I adore, the single light that brightens my life."

That passion had the potential to be disruptive was not lost on those residing in the lettered city, who saw in the romantic couple a key site for the shaping of selves through the inscription of values and sentiments, including, but not limited to, those of gender, ethnicity, and national belonging. Ignacio Manuel Altamirano, for one, a statesman like Ocampo and a novelist, found in the dichotomy pitting good love, or romantic love, against bad love, often characterized as passion, a powerful and productive ordering device through which to bring the nation and properly instructed citizens into existence. In his novel *El Zarco (Episodes of Mexican Life in 1861–1863)*, written in the 1880s and finally published in 1901, Altamirano uses romantic love as the means of dividing the world into two opposing categories: "good," that is, supportive of family, order, morality, and country, premised upon a kind of romantic love where individuals follow all the (official) rules, leading to a happy ending, that of conjugal bliss, and "bad," epitomized by rapto, where the woman eschews family and virtue to run off with her lover, with predictably (at least in the novel) passionate and tragic and (perhaps not so predictably) anti-national consequences.[15]

Not content with stopping there, Altamirano finds in this binary a powerful means of creating and reinforcing a series of other dichotomies, some, but not all, premised upon race and gender. Manuela, the woman who leaves with her raptor, is white, aristocratic, haughty, and avaricious; she is juxtaposed with the morena, humble, self-sacrificing, and self-abnegating Pilar. El Zarco, the main character, is ostentatious, extravagantly decked out, savage, cowardly, and a vice-ridden bandit, a glaring contrast with the honorable, hard-working, ennobled-though-work, lacking-in-ostentation (as well as silver) Nicolas, a true self-made man. White and blue-eyed, the characteristic that gives the main character his name, El Zarco also signals Altamirano's preoccupation with the look, with visual markers of status, with contrasting superficial appearances against true substance, much like the concern of the love letter writers with the readability of the epistolary body, where outward appearances are meant to be commensurate with inner qualities and characteristics. In short, for Altamirano, El Zarco the bandit was a shell of a man compared to wheat-colored Nicolas who, although an Indian, as Altamirano remarks, was not "a servile and abject Indian, but a mannered man . . . aware of his power and his worth."[16]

It is in the treatment of passion where Altamirano may be of most use in helping to situate some of the discourses weaving themselves into and out of the sentimental anatomy found in the love letters. In the novel, bad love, that characterizing the relationship between El Zarco and Manuela, is savage, violent, and impassioned, a bestial sensualism based on instinct that leads to complete loss of control. "I'm crazy with passion for you; I think my heart is going to burst from the pain that your absence causes me, from the fear that the anger you're in gives me! I'm entirely yours . . . and I'll do whatever you want!" pants Manuela to El Zarco, in her "misguided state" of "frenetic passion."[17] In addition to being violently impassioned, bad love is an "*amor material*," that is, love based on things—possessions or money—with El Zarco hoping to add the young, beautiful woman from a "socially superior" class to his list of vain sensations, perhaps a step up from those acquired by possessing magnificent horses and amassing ounces of gold and jeweled riches, while Manuela was driven by the "irresistible impulses of an insatiable and domineering greed," whose face then registered all the signs of this evil passion occupying her spirit as she modeled the plundered jewelry with which El Zarco had successfully wooed her.

Contrasting with the "amor material" of El Zarco and Manuela was the spiritual or sacred love of Nicolas and Pilar. Here was an "intimate and sacred sentiment" that could open a path even in the most perverted of souls, illuminating them like a ray of sunshine illuminates even the darkest and most infected of dens. Such a love could still be all-encompassing. In a chapter entitled "An Angel," which follows one called "The Good Love," just in case readers weren't quite getting the point, Nicolas describes his reunion with Pilar after the authorities finally release him:

> And he felt her beautiful virgin arms behind his neck, and her loving heart beating together with that heart that didn't beat for anyone other than her, and he felt her tears moisten his hand and her breath bathe his face in sweet aroma. Nicolas couldn't speak. He was prisoner of an emotion that overwhelmed him and paralyzed his faculties. How could he not feel subjugated in an instant to a love so powerful? "What I feel towards you, good and beautiful child, is a holy and eternal love (*santa y eterno*). . . . Would you be my wife, and now?"[18]

Regardless of its moral superiority to passion, love was still a feeling that one might experience, at certain times at any rate, as "suffering," both in novels as in love letters. Focusing on such rhetoric as a means of understanding how love was experienced is complicated, however. Certainly, a lover's doubts, accusations, or behaviors led both men and women to don the mantle of the partner who had been done wrong, who suffered for love. Rather than intrinsic to love, as in these instances, suffering, for many writers, was something imposed by the force of external circumstances. For Refugio, for example, whose novio had left to work in another town, it was their separation that caused her to suffer. "You can't imagine how I am," she wrote to him shortly after he left, "the horrible, melancholic hours that I have had. It seems to me that your goodbye has been forever. The hours seem like years. The minutes months. I would like these fifteen days to go by in fifteen seconds so we can be with each other again happy as always." For others, it was parents who were to blame. When his father refused to give the permission necessary for eighteen-year-old Marcos to marry Marcelina, Marcos concluded that his suffering would end only if the couple overcame parental opposition to their marriage by running away together:

> Well if it's true that you love me tell me frankly and I certainly say it to you because I truly love you and I want you to tell me if you have the will to accompany me and I'm ready to take myself to wherever God should help us. . . . It's impossible to live here and I hope that you sympathize with the great deal that I've suffered for your love and let me know clearly, and receive the heart of your impassioned one who now suffers eternally, your useless S[eguro] S[ervidor] who says this to you because of the great deal that he suffers and there is no other way to have you at his side.[19]

Yet the refrain of suffering for love was also often just that—a rhetorical tool wielded by both men and women in an instrumental fashion, that is, as a means of helping them accomplish their desires. Some, like Eleno the teenage tailor, were particularly long-suffering: "I'm going to suffer alone someplace else where not even my friends will know and I'm going to keep suffering," he stated to Tula. Here, like many others, Eleno was tactical in the deployment of his own pathos. Through constant reference to suffering, Eleno expressed his disappointment at Tula's (his novia's) reluctance to leave her parental home to be with him as well as the depths of his own feelings in wanting her to do so; as importantly, he was hoping to motivate Tula to take action by manipulating her into feeling responsible for his pain. "I didn't think that you had a heart of marble to make me suffer in the way that you have," he wrote to her. "Well now you don't trust my love because you think that I'm not going to honor what I've offered you." Returning to speak of Tula's supposed heart of marble in a subsequent letter, Eleno finds in the analogy yet another example of a perceived disconnect between appearances and reality—while Tula's heart looks like all others, the good ones, as he puts it, it is not. Only by doing what he wants, he implies, can she prove otherwise: "Well it will be more suffering that my heart will have to suffer well as far as I can see everything that B. told me about you came true and for that reason [not] giving me the satisfaction I ask of you I can't marry you, that's what I'm saying to you now I don't want you to give me what I'm asking for and go back to your house if you're not coming with me."[20]

As you have already seen, Marcos, a farmer, similarly insisted that only through his novia's actions could his suffering be alleviated. Others, like Jesús, although deploying suffering in hopes of obtaining the same ends, saw in their lover's absence the source of their affliction: "I love you a great deal and it is impossible to live without you," he wrote to Maura. "You are my only thought, in you I find all my happiness, you are all that I love, if you understood what God well knows that what I want to do is fulfill [my promise] to you and that you should see that I love you and that what I want is for us to get married because I love you so much, and I suffer without you, I swear to you that you shouldn't doubt my word."[21]

In contrast, for Remedios and others like him, somewhat more resigned about things, suffering was simply what one could expect to do when in love. When confronted with the imminent departure of his novia, Remedios wrote to her: "With the most profound sadness I'm telling you that your mom told me that you all were leaving for Minas Nuevas, I don't believe that you consented to leave, I know what three words are worth, what three tears are worth and only if love for me doesn't exist will you leave . . . but I'm resigned to suffer, only the Eternal one can give me strength."[22] In a similar manner, although after the fact, Felipe, a thirty-six-year-old mine worker whose young novia had just left him to return to the house of her mother (as you read about in the previous section), found suffering to be the price one paid for having loved: "If you hadn't shown such loathsomeness you wouldn't have to suffer and if now and in the future you suffer don't complain to me and I'm telling you that I'm suffering and upset and it's only because of you. . . . I'm ready to suffer I know that it's all in recompense for having loved you so much."[23]

Finally, for a select few, suffering was almost aesthetically pleasing, the pain of its existence serving as the very measure of the pleasure or extent of one's love. Here, again, Enriqueta serves as our guide: "With the same happiness as always I answer your letter and I forgive your words with which, at times, you make me suffer through bitter periods, but it is beautiful to suffer for the one you adore, so much more when you love someone as I love you."[24]

Accusations of provoking suffering, then, could be a strategy for eliciting greater commitment to the courting relationship, another way of setting a test by which, should she accept it as such and agree to provide a proof of her love, a woman could demonstrate that she believed and trusted her novio's word. Suffering could also attest to the depth of one's love. Passion, as well, could be suffered as a compulsion that drove one to act as it left one unable to think. Both love and passion were distinct yet related, beyond one's control yet amenable to relief if only the other should act in accordance with one's wishes, available to be harnessed to moral and nationalist ends, and experienced as suffering, if in distinct ways. In short, there were many different ways to write the epistolary body into being through suffering. Yet, if the epistolary body begins to emerge through these discussions of love and passion, it is a body that, while insisting on its own transparency and legibility, is nevertheless difficult to see clearly, shrouding itself, as it often does, in the means of obtaining its own desires.

If suffering was an immediate consequence of being in love, personal happiness, expressed by means of the future tense as potential or a promise, was the goal that one day might be attained. As with suffering, there were a number of different ways that happiness could be envisioned. In the most altruistic of correspondents, or, perhaps, the most manipulative, the wish was for the eventual happiness of the person being courted. When Feliciana wrote to end her relationship with Joaquín, stating that she could not accede to his wishes to begin sexual relations, he replied, first, that he doubted her word as to her physical state, that is, whether she was a virgin, and, second, that he held her solely responsible if the couple lost all that she had desired. He then wished her all the best: "God willing that you find an honorable man like you want as my most ardent desires are to see you happy in this world."[25] Although information is lacking as to details, that the case ended up before judicial officials attests, perhaps, to her change of heart. Other writers, perhaps the most self-centered, envisioned their own happiness, although at the side of the one they loved. For most correspondents, however, the future happiness of the couple itself served as the ultimate goal. "What I want is that we should get married and be happy," stated Ysidro to María Anastasia, as did José to María.[26]

While the constant reiteration of the importance of personal happiness to couple formation attests to the centrality of romantic love, rather than duty, as the motivation for marriage, and the couple, rather than the extended family, as the social unit most deserving of it, happiness was no unmitigated ideal. Much like suffering, it was often wielded as a means of eliciting a greater degree of commitment to the relationship or to convince a reluctant novia to do one's bidding: "I anxiously repeat to you once again my intentions," wrote Ysmael, a twenty-two-year-old mineworker, to Atanasia. "I don't want anything other than your decision so that we can be happy and enjoy life with liberty, nor am I promising you this world and the other because I can't know the future, if the Creator watches over us it will be our happiness."[27] Here, the decision being hinted at was to agree to begin sexual relations in exchange for a promise of marriage, a decision that, in Ysmael's opinion at any rate, rather than breaking the rules, might even be divinely blessed. Another suitor was even more explicit: "Given that you should give me the proof of love that I ask of you I can give you what you need when the time that I've promised you is up, so that we can be happy, the two of us."[28] By contrast, few writers seem as generous as Refugio, who began each letter by wishing her absent novio much happiness and perfect health in the present rather than in some anticipated future once he has complied with her desires. One is tempted to offer a gendered reading of the relative deployment of happiness, so striking is the contrast in the letters written by men and women; however, both the availability of only a small number of letters written by women and the fact that Refugio begins almost every letter she writes to Rodrigo in this way, marking it as a convention of writing, a formulaic introduction to a letter, make such a reading difficult to prove.

Hymens

If passion compelled the epistolary body into being, it was the hymen that would eventually become, in much of the correspondence, the main focus of attention, epistolary and otherwise. As in *El Zarco*, where outward appearances are meant to reveal and be commensurate with inner qualities, for novios, the truth of the woman's inner character was laid bare in the state of her hymen. This assumption they shared not only with novelists and, as you saw in section 1, judicial officials but also with local medical authorities charged with confirming the claimed loss of virginity in cases of estupro. Acting as if evidence of a woman's state was both registered on her body and apparent to an "expert," medical examiners carried significant weight in determining the outcome of judicial proceedings. In this, however, local doctors were at odds with those at the national level. In his work, *El himen en México*, published in 1885 by the Secretaría de Fomento, Francisco A. Flores, while recognizing the significance of virginity to a courting relationship and the role of medico-legal experts in judicial proceedings in determining its state, nevertheless acknowledged the limits of both medical expertise and the body's presumed legibility. The expert will not always encounter signs of an altered membrane, Flores states, and must, in their expert opinion, say so directly without additional speculation; in such cases, he continued, it was up to judicial officials to discover the rest of the story.[29]

In addition to stressing the importance of his findings to making accurate medical determinations in legal cases concerned with estupro, Flores's more pressing preoccupation, taking up the greater part of his study, is with the forms of hymen regularly found in Mexico. In doing so, Flores reveals that his greater concern was less with the "truth" of the body than with its ability to bear the characteristics of national identity, which, supposedly, it could be made to yield upon closer examination. His main conclusion was to determine that the forms of the hymen in Mexico were annular, labial, and semi-lunar and horseshoe-shaped, with the final form meriting a place in Mexican medical classification. Just as the hymen might yield characteristics of national identity and a "national" body, it might also provide an opportunity, as Flores's work illustrates, through which to carry out scientific research in an avowedly nationalistic register.[30]

Although the term "hymen" never appears in the letters submitted to judicial authorities, the state of this membrane was the implied subject of almost all of the letters men wrote to their novias, usually in only the barest of euphemistic terms. Almost all novios would eventually express an interest in obtaining what they referred to as a *"prueba de amor,"* that is, a "proof of love," a term that, though sufficiently hazy, could mean little else when interpreted in the context of courtships that ended up in judicial proceedings of the kind I have been considering.

In this regard, the letters of Eleno, a nineteen-year-old tailor from Parral, to Tula, his eighteen-year-old novia, are particularly instructive. While perhaps more insistent than most in being provided with such a bona fide proof of his novia's status or state (Eleno was nothing if not direct and succinct), his letters are more of a piece with letters from other novios than the exception. "I implore you," he wrote her, "if you can give me a proof of your true love, send word to me if you can or not . . . during the time period that I told you before I cover your honor." Sooner or later, and usually sooner, all six letters written by Eleno (he himself acknowledged that the letters were in his handwriting) and then turned over to judicial authorities by Tula took up the terms of their exchange. Even if some reading between the lines is necessary, the implications of Eleno's prose are fairly clear: "Tula, this is with the end of saying to you that if it is the case that you should be disposed for us to do what we have said when you go out on some errand you should send me word to rent one of those rooms in the Cerro alleyway." "My dear Tula," another letter begins, "With great pleasure I answer your letter in which you say to me that you're not able to give me the proof of love—I want you to tell me why you can't give me what I've asked you for or perhaps you don't have confidence that I'll do what I say to you within the promised time period." Eleno was not anything if not dogged and, when promises of happiness in the future didn't seem to be working, he issued an ultimatum: "That's why I now say to you I don't want you to give me what I've asked you for and go back to your house or else leave with me to make a life, good or bad, that depends on the will of God, if you want to go with me it has to be right now."[31]

Such examples of requests for "proofs of love" could be multiplied as most of the relationships they help chart (perhaps unsurprisingly, given that the letters have been located as part of judicial processes having to do, in large part, with the crimes of rapto and estupro) twist and turn around the terms of this exchange or interchange between men and women over sexuality and marriage. Going even beyond Eleno, a few other men spelled out their promises simply and directly, leading the reader out of the realm of love letters and into that of what seems more like the history of contractual commitment or legal obligation. It is difficult even to regard the note written by Ismael to Atanacia as a "letter" or as a declaration of love, as the entire missive reads as follows: "In Hidalgo del Parral, 28 October 1890. Whereby I draw up these lines to the Señorita Anatacia N. I give her my word that I'll marry her as soon as I get the money and so I sign. 28 October 1890. Yours, Ismael M."[32] The same can be said about the note from José to Libradita, dating from 1903, although in his note José manages to combine desire and legal commitment: "Libradita: This letter is the last in which I swear to you and obligate myself to marry you if you accept my desire this very same day today I'll wait for you at the time you decide and I hope no one will know what is going on. I swear to you that as soon as what I desire happens we'll get married and we'll be happy as I've already told you. Libradita today I wait for you to do the right thing. Yours, J.Y."[33] José's letter, especially, reveals the multiple registers that the epistolary body might operate in simultaneously. In these messages, a legal or juridical body is made manifest, finding in the form of the letter, especially the signature, the means of extending the presence of the author and his authority into the legal realm as well as the sentimental one.

I return in due course to the terms of the interchange or exchange that are being proposed in these messages. But first I consider another possible framing: given the insistence on the desire to initiate sexual relations that predominate in them, rather than love letters, is it more accurate to regard them as letters of seduction? Certainly, the note composed by Rodolfo, a twenty-five-year-old business clerk, to a married woman he had caught a glimpse of in a store seems to fall into such a category. On a small square of pink paper, he had written simply: "My dear woman: If you are really willing, tell me if I can see you some time. Answer me on the back." Although her seemingly positive response there enticed Rodolfo into her home at a time when her husband was supposedly away, the beating Rodolfo received when he arrived, prompting a criminal investigation, suggests either a trap to teach him a lesson or an unanticipated change in the husband's schedule.[34]

There were also times, I must admit, as I sat reading some of these letters and the testimony that often framed them, when I found myself wondering about the motives of some of the men appearing there, especially those whose knowledge of the law and ability to manipulate the written word seemed, at least in part, to enable them to be very persuasive in convincing women to agree to sexual relations with them while leaving them unencumbered either by the delights of marriage or the deprivations of incarceration. Such behavior could be devastating to the woman involved. Feliciana, whose case was discussed briefly in section 1, when pushed into the initiation of sexual relations by the insinuations of her novio that she must have something to hide, ended up under doctor's care for "commotions" in her nervous system, a kind of "madness" brought on by her novio's failure to follow through with his promise of marriage.[35] As you have already seen in that section, judicial archives document the many attempts by young women and their families to pressure men into following through on such promises or to recompense them for not doing so. Novelists, likewise, found in women's perils during courtship a compelling subject matter that was avidly sought after by readers and that could be put to didactic ends.[36] These and other texts served as warnings to women, demonstrations of the consequences of yielding to temptation as well as a confirmation of their perceived tendency to do so.

Yet regardless of the broad spectrum of behavior and motives that might characterize relationships and men's actions, it seems unsatisfactory, and for a number of reasons, to insist too forcefully on distinguishing between letters of love and letters of seduction. (Nor am I particularly interested in defining and categorizing genres of letters into which to sort the missives found in these cases.) Certainly, the letters written by novios that are available in the archives almost inevitably turn to convincing each one's novia to accede to the initiation of sexual relations in exchange for a promise of marriage at some future date. Yet, as much as seduction, this was the stuff of love, at least the kind that was meant to result in marriage. As you will see shortly, such an exchange or agreement was one of many implied or anticipated in these letters, of which letters in their own right formed a part. These exchanges, an integral aspect of courtship, were asked for directly and regularly subjected to an emotional accounting, the bottom line of which revolved around the woman acceding to the beginning of sexual relations in exchange for a promise of marriage in the future. It is in this sense that the contents of the letters, dealing with reciprocity and exchanges that are characterized by increasingly serious consequences in order to elicit ever-greater commitment to the courting relationship, seem to mirror the formal requirement of corresponding, where the sending of a letter implied, as if with a gift, a claim on another person, at least for a response.[37]

Perhaps it would be even more accurate to remove the letters written by men proposing such an exchange to their novias from the realm of desire altogether. After all, as much as they are concerned with love and seduction, these letters are even more preoccupied with masculinity, with obtaining visible proof of the virginity of the woman who was in effect auditioning—that is, being asked to demonstrate her suitability as future wife material—and also, at the same time, with asserting and sustaining a definition of maleness premised upon the control of the sexuality of women. The epistolary body emerging in these letters is highly gendered, where men ask directly in writing for proofs of love and concern themselves with the symbolic properties of the hymen while women avoid the subject altogether. Just as in verbal testimony, where women distance themselves from their own desires, in the few letters written by women that are available the woman either asks her novio not to speak about such matters or takes advantage of the euphemistic haze surrounding such requests in order to obfuscate. Although only Refugio's side of the correspondence is available, it is clear from her responses that Rodrigo had been pressing her in a number of his letters as to the possibility of receiving a "proof of love" from her. Rather than dismiss the matter outright, Refugio responds, "Regarding that which you say to me that it is necessary that I should give you a proof, well as long as what you want doesn't offend honor I don't have limits on what I'll do as I believe you would do the same with me." As for Enriqueta, not only did she adamantly deny Pedro's request for such a gesture, she asked that he never return again to the subject in subsequent letters. Moreover, the actual letter in which Pedro makes such a request is not available, the only letter, it seems, that is missing from the overall body of their correspondence. My guess is that Enriqueta destroyed it, thus eliminating such a blemish from the epistolary body that their correspondence was writing into being.

If the man's preoccupation was with the state of the woman's hymen, the woman's was with determining the trustworthiness of the man as well as the sincerity of the commitments being made. In fact, for both men and women, signs, abundant and apparent, seemed everywhere and at all times to indicate just how feckless or feigned love might be. When a novia failed to respond with sufficient enthusiasm to being greeted in a social setting or when she used formal language instead of more caring, familiar tones, what was a suitor supposed to think? Similarly, women rushed to judgment when their novios were slow to visit, when they used pretexts like work or sick parents to avoid seeing them, when gifts were not reciprocated, or when they blew out of proportion gossip that was probably misreported anyways. Responses, sometimes accusatory, almost always seeking reassurance, were quickly forthcoming: "Your love has turned on me"; "it's not the same as you used to profess"; "I'm desperate to know if you have the same disposition as before"; "I know you don't love me anymore"; "perhaps it is that you don't love me"; and on and on. More than merely seeking reassurance, however, these and similar phrases were the means by which progressively greater degrees of commitment to the relationship were demanded and secured. Such statements, always strategic, seized on and, at times, even fabricated a perceived slight in order to test the other's commitment while pushing toward the point in time when it would be difficult to turn back or terminate the relationship.

As much as the woman's physical state, then, it was the woman's belief in the man's word that was being verified with a "proof of love." If you look again at the brief messages written by Ismael and José, the notes that read like legal promises, you will see how clearly they stress obligation, the fulfillment of one's promises, the giving of one's word, swearing to uphold one's commitments, that is, the language of male honor. Rather than having language distinct from that in the letters more recognizable as love letters, they express precisely the same concerns, as terms like "I swear" (*juro*), "I carry out" (*cumplo*), "to obligate oneself" (*obligarse*), and "my word" (*mi palabra*) figure centrally in the male discourse of love and courtship in the longer letters as well. Love letters, then, are a site at which a negotiation or exchange is taking place. I have used the terms "interchange" and "exchange" at times in this section in an attempt to capture this give and take, choosing to avoid terms like "transaction" or "bargain" as metaphors too associated with buying and selling, with the marketplace. Suitors, however, did not hesitate to spell out some of the expectations of these interchanges in economic turns, with men offering, for example, to bring home the daily wage to fund the household in exchange for cooking and other household duties. These economic arrangements form only one subset of the many exchanges or interchanges characterizing love letters. In fact, love letters themselves were one important "currency" (if you will allow me that metaphor) used to calculate the balance sheet of courtship, as was the language employed in them; glances, conversations, secret meetings, and gifts, especially (as you will see) one's photographic portrait, were other units of exchange and negotiation.

For all its significance as the very definition of commitment and trust in a courting relationship, the exchange of a "proof of love" for a promise to "cover" the woman's honor was, in fact, although the ultimate proof, merely the logical culmination of a series of such transactions, each with progressively higher stakes, that characterized courtship. As the degree of commitment increased, so too did the personal stakes of those invested in the process, although these differed by gender. For men, fear of being deceived or toyed with, expressed in the powerful rhetoric of betrayal and deception (*burlado, engañado*) and in a concern for one's self-respect and dignity, was paramount. For women, fear of having their reputation destroyed predominated. In fact, for both men and women, it was the public perception of one's reputation that counted most. Knowing what was at stake helps give a sense of the degree of trust and commitment that women were demonstrating when they agreed to provide their novios with a "proof of love."

Voluntad

You have already heard a number of times from Refugio, a young woman living in Parral in the early years of the twentieth century, most recently when, pressed for a "proof of love" by Rodrigo, her novio who had gone off to work in the mines of nearby Santa Bárbara, she agreed to do anything he asked as long as it did not offend her honor. Earlier in this section, you saw how, despite desperately suffering Rodrigo's absence, she wished him much happiness and perfect health at the beginning of each of her letters to him and asked, as well, that he receive her heart at the end of each of them. In total, thirteen of Refugio's letters to Rodrigo, dated between November 1904 and March 1905, have been located in the archive; in Rodrigo's hand there is nothing, in glaring contrast to most of the correspondence lodged in cases there, largely written by men.[38] About him, we know only about what Refugio chooses to respond to in his letters, how she reacts to certain things that he has said, the way in which she frames their relationship, and how she attempts, within the constraints of her own abilities, personality, circumstances, and the broader conventions of gender, to elicit from him greater commitment to their relationship. And in this, no part of the sentimental anatomy is more central to Refugio than voluntad (will), an inner quality or conviction that each and every one of her letters demonstrates on her part and demands on his.

To define what Refugio means by "voluntad" and to understand the ways in which she mobilizes and deploys the term, it is first necessary to sketch out some of the contours of the epistolary space that she brings into being with her correspondence. About her family and the tenor of life in her home Refugio's letters reveal almost nothing, other than the fact that family relationships weigh particularly heavily on her. Household chores, especially ironing, make it difficult for her to attend dances, while the presence near the doorway of some of the other women living in the home, who are not even named or identified in any way in any of her letters, leads her to abandon plans to sneak out to meet Rodrigo and him to tease her about it in a subsequent letter. As for her father, whom she describes as "the lost one," so difficult does he make life for her ("only God and I know how much I suffer," she tells Rodrigo) that she makes plans to leave Parral for Chihuahua or even El Paso, Texas, again leading to teasing from Rodrigo and a spat with him over his response to her plight.[39] The broader context within which Refugio takes up the pen, then, is one of unhappiness and suffering, both at Rodrigo's departure and at her lot in life in her home, of which one can only assume Rodrigo was already well enough informed.

As much as Refugio's letters are unconcerned with the details of family and everyday life, they are relentless in their focus on her relationships with friends and with Rodrigo, from whom she attempts to entice expressions of love, clarity, and commitment to their relationship, seemingly to little avail. And while actual family relationships serve as little other than a background upon which Refugio can paint her current anguish in more defined strokes and from a more ample emotional palette, metaphors of family nonetheless provide her with a unique means of capturing the degree of trust or emotional closeness that she was experiencing. When Rodrigo expressed his embarrassment, for example, that she was showing his letters to her friend Quica, Refugio was quick to reassure him, telling him that he shouldn't worry about anything, as she not only trusted Quica "as a friend" but also considered her "almost" as a sister. Reiterating her trust in Quica a number of times in a brief letter, Refugio asked Rodrigo to extend to her the same confidence. The category "friend" blurred into those of both family and potential family relationships, capturing the trustworthiness that was meant, ideally, to characterize all these realms, including that of *noviazgo*. When Rodrigo, feeling hard done by, complained in another letter that he seemed to be the "last" of Refugio's friends, she asserted, to the contrary, that he was the friend she most "esteemed." "Where in the world did you get the idea," she asked him subsequently, "that I would value a female friend more than the only angel of my dreams?" While, here, Refugio distinguished between the love she felt for a friend and her love for Rodrigo, her letters highlight that her emotional world was one that she peopled with female friends with whom she shared her innermost feelings, with male friends who kept her posted about Rodrigo, and, at the center of it, with Rodrigo himself, who seemed to imbue the category of friend with its emotional content as he transcended it. So firmly did this cohort of friends anchor Refugio's emotional life that when Rodrigo failed to return from Santa Bárbara when he said he finally would, Refugio, who had orchestrated a warm welcome for him, was adamant that not only had she been deceived and offended by being stood up but so had "all" of the "humble" women who had gathered to mark such a special occasion. It was the last letter that she would write or at least the last letter that made its way into the archive.

If family was suffered but not discussed and friendship formed the substance of many of her letters, it was her feelings for Rodrigo that dominated the epistolary space Refugio brought into being with her letters. And these feelings she gave expression to through a series of interrelated binaries, all of which required, in the end, a demonstration of *voluntad* to resolve, either on his part or hers. Perhaps it is not surprising, given that it is Rodrigo's departure that prompts the initiation of their correspondence in the first place, that remembering and forgetting provides one dominant axis around which Refugio's letters revolve. Certainly, Refugio was convinced that absence would lead to forgetting, so much so that she made a pact with him even before he left: "I'm not going to fail in my promise to you," she states in the first letter she writes to him, "even if you are away for ten years I won't forget you." Given Rodrigo's failure to write back in a manner she considered timely and his seeming reluctance to make return visits, by the second letter she is closing her correspondence with phrases such as "your forgotten one," a common way for her to refer to herself in almost all subsequent letters. So preoccupied is she with the idea that out of sight did indeed mean out of mind that she envisions moving away not only as absence but as a new kind of space, the "realm of the forgotten," to which Rodrigo will even further banish her should she make good on her promise to go.

Yet, as with all the binaries she deploys in her writing, that of remembering/forgetting also enabled Refugio to position both herself and Rodrigo in specific ways, with a particular goal in mind, that of convincing Rodrigo to commit to their relationship. When Rodrigo announced in what must have been his first letter to her that, instead of coming home in two weeks as he had planned, he would not be returning for two months, Refugio was beside herself, wondering out loud whether, concomitantly with her being forgotten, someone in Santa Bárbara had quickly taken her place. "It seems you already have someone preventing you coming," she insinuated, "and that's why you say to me that two months is so little time." She continued in the next letter, "And receive the heart of your forgotten one that you already don't remember nor do you have the clothes to come and see her but for the one in Santa Bárbara, sure." For Refugio, the framing of their relationship within the binary of remembering/forgetting allowed her to position herself as the faithful one, committed to her promises and their relationship, while attempting to convince Rodrigo to demonstrate his commitment by, in essence, doing her bidding.

As is apparent in Refugio's accusation, the binary of remembering/forgetting quickly shaded into another set of opposing terms that structured her correspondence—those of true love versus hypocrisy or appearances. "Even if you were away for ten years don't believe I would forget you," you've already heard Refugio state to Rodrigo; in the next phrase, she continues, "because my love is true and not just flattery." And, in an irony of sorts, given that Rodrigo, if we are to take Refugio at her word, lacked the will to return home regularly and even to answer her letters in a timely fashion, it was nonetheless Rodrigo who requested that Refugio demonstrate her commitment to their relationship, about which much of his correspondence was seemingly concerned. When pressed by Rodrigo to offer a proof of her loyalty to him, an only slightly veiled attempt to compel her to begin sexual relations, she turned the accusation back on him while asserting the veracity of her own feelings: "Rodrigo—you say to me that you may be in doubt about my love you doubt it because I haven't given you proof of my loyalty you know that I have never had limits toward you and I have given proof of my loyalty I don't know what reason caused you to doubt my love in this matter I should be more likely to doubt your love than you mine because how am I to know if you already have another girlfriend because you are so far away who is going to know?" Subsequent letters returned to the same dynamic, both in terms of Rodrigo's demands and Refugio's reframing of the discussion. In these instances, as in many others, some reading between the lines is involved as far as Rodrigo's intentions are concerned, as only Refugio's letters are available. "Well Rodrigo," Refugio responded, "it really surprises me that you should make those remarks about me saying that it seems to you that I don't love you—well I haven't given you any reason to think that I don't esteem you—you know that at all times there has existed a true affection for you."

In fact, for Refugio, the binary of truth versus appearance seemed all-encompassing, extending well beyond defining love to characterizing writing and even will. The pace at which he answered her letters having slowed only a few months after his leaving, Refugio wondered out loud, "Before, you used to answer them [my letters] which is what I desire, tell me why there has been this change, since then what you show me are pure appearances." Likewise, as with will itself, appearance or hypocrisy provided the opposite pole to truth: "Rodrigo—I'm not giving you the portrait now because I don't have it but I intend to get a portrait made of myself in the next 8 days—well you have to choose—a handkerchief, a ring, and/or a kiss—whatever you want in order to prove to you that I have true will for you (*voluntad verdadera*) and not hypocrisy."

If, in this last instance, will could be either true or hypocritical, all other binaries seemingly could be resolved, at least for Refugio, through the exercise or demonstration of voluntad, an act of which both men and women were equally capable. "Don't think it was because of lack of will," she wrote to Rodrigo in her first letter to him, explaining that she hadn't gone to the train station to see him off because she hadn't had the courage to see him leave his home. The delay in his reception of her second letter was not due to her lack of will either but because the post office was closing as she arrived and she didn't trust sufficiently to leave her letter in the mailbox there until it reopened. "As far as will goes," she assured him, "I have lots to spare."[40] Similarly, as you have already seen above, rather than lack of will it had been the presence of members of her household in the doorway of her home that had kept her from meeting Rodrigo. "Don't believe I haven't answered you for lack of will or for lack of time," she began yet another letter, "it was nothing other than to give you time so that you could pour your heart out and have time to answer me because you don't even have time to write me about what's going on."

Refugio's sarcasm is only slightly muted in her statement that she was giving Rodrigo time to "pour his heart out" to her. What was really at issue was Rodrigo's seeming lack of will, something that he made all too apparent to her by, among other things, taking so long to respond to her letters: "I thought that in the eight days that you have had to answer my humble letter that you would have had fifteen minutes free to put down a few words, when you find a little will [voluntad] then, yes, you'll be able to answer my crappy letters [mis mugres de cartas] as quickly as you get them." "As far as I can see," she concluded, "my letters serve only to bother you because I understand the little will [poca voluntad] that exists in you regarding me." Likewise, when Rodrigo postponed visiting her, extending his expected absence from fifteen days to two months and made excuses for not coming, Refugio, finding sarcasm not up to the task of shaming Rodrigo into doing what she wanted him to do, opted for lecturing instead: "In truth, that you don't have clothes, or time or, in the end, will, it is more will that is the main thing lacking because the person who does more is he who wants to rather than he who is able to because he who is able to doesn't do them because he doesn't want to, while he who wants to soon overcomes all difficulties that present themselves to him even though it might be at the cost of some sacrifice, but make your will known." In the final letter she wrote to him, angered and offended at his failure to return to attend a small gathering she was having to welcome him home, in short exasperated with him, she delivered an ultimatum: "Well Rodrigo if now you don't have the voluntad to be in a relationship with me well then I won't continue it with you, I don't want things to be forced nor can I obligate anyone or demand willfulness [*voluntades*], if a shred of caring doesn't exist now you need to talk to me frankly—why would you want to live with repugnance with someone you don't love."

It is in the mutual expression of voluntad, then, where, ultimately, Refugio located all matters of the heart. So centrally did mutual voluntad organize her feelings and how she expressed them in her letters that, for her, love might best be defined as an exchange of voluntad between equals. Such notions of equality or mutuality permeate Refugio's correspondence, spilling over from voluntad into other areas of her relationship with Rodrigo. When Rodrigo turned to the subject that most preoccupied male correspondents, and around which, given Refugio's responses, most of his letters seemed to turn, she commented directly on the need for reciprocity or equality in the provision of a "proof of love," or at least pointed out its inherent unfairness should she accede to his demands: "I answer your very esteemed letter where you say to me with respect to the 'proof of love' [*prueba de cariño*] ... I don't know what came over me upon reading your letter, an e nor mous sentiment but at the same time I was thinking that you've never demonstrated to me a similar thing." She similarly turned the tables on him in another message, although with regard to the same request: "Regarding what you say to me about giving you a proof well as long as what you want doesn't offend honor I don't have limits on what I'll do as I believe that you would do the same with me." In yet another she states directly her guiding assumption about the need for reciprocity in courtship and in love: "I'm going to grant you what you want so that sometime when I say something to you in the same way you'll grant it to me."

Despite understanding love as reciprocal or as a mutual exchange of will, Refugio, in her correspondence, simultaneously reveals how the ideal of equality of voluntad clashed with the meager resources at her disposal to make such equality a reality.[41] Sarcasm and scolding, as noted above, were two of the strategies that composed her written rhetoric of persuasion. Others, with equal effect (that is, without much effect at all), included attempting to provoke responses through anger or jealousy, appeals to religion, and even invoking Rodrigo's mother, pleading with him on the grounds of what he most esteemed—which she believed to be his mother—not to refer to himself (as he must have done in one letter he wrote to her) with what she regarded as the horrible name of "*desdichado*" (wretched one). Such a name was part of his already-mentioned strategy for eliciting from her the beginning of sexual relations, implying, as it did, that she had betrayed him for another, a charge she rejected categorically: "Not even force could make me do it you know that I have never done it never mind with any other person because two beings who have been born to love each other never ever offend each other in any manner because the least glance seems a grave offence."

Perhaps the dominant tone that Refugio adopts, however, is that of resignation, if tinged with self-pity. A woe-is-me sensibility pervades the letters, seeming to signal her almost complete powerlessness in getting Rodrigo to reciprocate her feelings by making manifest his will. "But you do what you want and I'll do what widows do," she finally tells him in one of her letters, sarcasm, pleading, scolding, and even reason having failed to move him, "I leave everything to God." "If it suits you, answer me quickly," she ended the next letter. "If not, do whatever you want." Finally, in a veritable throwing up of the hands metaphorically: "It doesn't matter, never mind, God's will be done thus it will be fine with me."

Refugio's resignation, as well as the contradiction inherent between the assumption of equality that was meant to structure a relationship and her lack of ability to achieve such equality in her own, seems to extend to the means of expressing emotion, that is, to the written form itself. Almost without fail, Refugio is self-effacing, commenting on the poor quality of her writing, even to the point of expressing her frustration with the very form of the letter: "I don't like to fight by means of papers—I would much prefer your presence because in that way I could better say it to you and answer you with my own mouth [boca] and not with that of pen and paper." While you have already seen female letter writers deploy the trope of the trembling hand (which Refugio also adopts), to that she adds those of the "humbleness" of her page, the "messiness" of her letters (*mis mugres de cartas*), how poorly written they are, and a plea that the quality of her writing be forgiven. Refugio adopts a number of gendered conventions of writing, bowing down to Rodrigo in a kind of formulaic kowtowing, acknowledging, in this manner, the man as the initiator of the courtship correspondence, and the one supposedly more at home in the rules, practices, and procedures associated with the power of the written word.

Yet it is also striking that Refugio, concomitant with her supposed, if self-professed, deficiencies in her command of the written word and her deference, nonetheless simultaneously and relentlessly incites Rodrigo to respond in that format. "Answer quickly," she ends a letter sent early in their correspondence, which gives way in a letter a little later on to "Answer me as quickly as you can" and then finally, given Rodrigo's seeming nonchalance when it came to replying, "Answer as quickly as you can if it suits you." Certainly, such messages were strategic, part of Refugio's rhetoric of persuasion designed to provoke a response (and, perhaps, a letter). Writing about writing also enabled her to portray herself as hard done by, the injured party in a relationship that didn't measure up to the expectations of reciprocity that were supposed to structure it. "For you to write to me is a bother," she concluded in one letter; "fifteen days to answer," she exclaimed in another. "It must be boring for you to write so much." Is it that you don't have time to write, she wondered out loud, or, she wrote (implying that Rodrigo had replaced her with someone else, that is, with another novia nearer his heart as well as much closer at hand), is it that she in Santa Bárbara, the town where Rodrigo was working, "is receiving written answers morning, noon, and night and me every fifteen days." No doubt, demands that Rodrigo write to her were motivated by all these things—jealousy, sarcasm, insecurity, a sense of being hurt and forgotten. But they also attest to the expectation of reciprocity, even equality, in the exchange of correspondence as well as in constructing epistolary space itself. As much as will and writing, love was understood as reciprocal, a feeling that was experienced mutually and constituted in a similar manner, in which writing and will each served as demonstrations of the other as well as the means of composing that feeling. It was a desire to demonstrate her own will, as well as her conclusion that Rodrigo lacked that very same thing, that led her to stand up to him in her final letter, reject his version of events, state the truth as she saw it, and, it seems, draw to a close both the epistolary space and the relationship they had, ultimately, failed to write into being together.

Nor was Refugio alone in linking love and will; other novias and novios expressed much the same sentiment in very similar terms. Angry at Jesús María, his novia, or trying to convince her to become more committed to their relationship (or, likely, both), Remedios, a novio writing more than a decade earlier, expressed himself in a way that hints at the same understanding of will as Refugio had, or at least at a similar strategic use of the concept: "I well understand the little love that you have for me, you've been here a long time now and you haven't been by not even to say hello, at the very least you must have been able to have gone to the house of your *comadre* but the great affection that you have for me is clear because for me your excuses aren't worth much, because if you really had willpower [voluntad] as at other times nothing in you could have prevented it."[42] And similarly, writing more than a decade after Refugio stopped writing to Rodrigo, Enriqueta, whom you will hear more about shortly, lived up to her self-proclaimed reputation for candidness by evoking voluntad. Thinking that Pedro, her novio, was looking for a pretext to end their relationship, a fairly common reaction to the trials lovers set for themselves and each other in print, Enriqueta anguished: "I love you but regardless of that as you yourself say to me, for my part I repeat to you: if you don't have will [voluntad] for me tell me in order to kill in one blow my hopes and dreams [*ilusión*]." As is apparent in these instances and in the case of Refugio, no single word seems to capture the nuances in the meaning of "voluntad," a concept that brought together desire and affection with notions of willpower and agency, a means of expressing the degree to which a person really wanted something.

The agency implied by the term "voluntad" stands out even more given that many of those deploying the concept contrasted it with the (what must have seemed to them) overwhelming force of circumstances to which one might, at times, fall victim. When Remedios's parents, for example, refused to let him remain in Parral to court Jesús María, he pleaded with her to understand: "With a sadness I've never before felt in my poor heart

I send you these brief lines so you won't think that I'm doing this of my own will [voluntad] and you should go and forget me." Yet another young suitor, Jesús, needing parental permission to marry, also framed parental refusal to consent to his choice of Maura as his bride-to-be in terms of will or voluntad: "Last night I spoke with my father and he told me that he didn't want me to get married for any reason whatsoever, that I should do whatever should suit me, that he would not give his consent [voluntad], which means that I can't even figure out what to do to fulfill that which I've promised you."[43] Used in this sense, the very definition of what it meant to become an adult was the ability to act on one's will or voluntad: "Even though you were saying that in my house they don't want you well that's not true, you're not right and even if it were that way I'm very independent from them and as for my will [voluntad] nobody tells me what to do," asserted José to his novia in 1912.[44]

As you also saw in the discussion of Refugio's correspondence, demands for proof of love (prueba de amor) and will (voluntad) could be intimately, even inextricably, joined. If to act on one's will was to make a claim to adulthood, leaving one's parental home with one's intended was often the ultimate expression of voluntad. And although Refugio declined to do so, offering a proof of love, that is, the beginning of sexual relations, could be seen as the ultimate expression of a woman's will to make a commitment to the relationship. Marcos, for example, faced with no other options given the intransigence of both sets of parents in refusing to agree to their marriage, attempted to convince Marcelina to leave her home to be with him: "Well if it's true that you love me tell it to me frankly, I certainly declared it to you because truly I love you and I want you to tell me if you have will [voluntad] to accompany me, I'm prepared to take myself to wherever God should help us."[45] Another suitor in a similar predicament made much the same plea:

> Because you already know that I really love you and that my love is yours, it's just that if you shouldn't love me tell me now, now I know that you'll be offended by what I'm going to say to you but it's necessary for you to see that I have voluntad for you and that I'm not deceiving you,

if by chance I hadn't had voluntad for you or didn't want you, I would have found some excuse to lose you, but no, what I want is for us to be together so that you can see for yourself, don't come if you don't want to, do what suits you.[46]

In struggles between parents and children that marked a coming of age, then, as when proving one's commitment to a suitor, will or voluntad served as a way of expressing agency, both of one's self and of others, as well as the means by which such agency was exercised.

Although being asked to demonstrate will was a powerful call to action for both novios and novias, proving it might mean decidedly different things for men and women. What women were demonstrating, then, when they left the household, often having agreed to the initiation of sexual relations at the hands of their suitors, was not only their voluntad or degree of commitment toward the relationship but also their commitment to the man's word, their trust that the man would carry through on his promise of marriage. Will and trust went together, the former being the ultimate proof of the latter and the latter being centrally concerned with having one's word believed and being accepted as someone who could be counted on to fulfill his word, that is, his promises. As men and women negotiated the gap between word and deed, seeking to elicit increasing degrees of mutual commitment, men's word became precisely what was at issue. To insist on receiving a "proof of love," therefore—and here I revisit some of the discussion that took place earlier, in the subsection on the hymen—was, certainly, designed to ascertain whether the women was a virgin but also to confirm that she perceived the man to be one who would keep his word.

For many men, women's willingness to demonstrate their will or voluntad served as judgment, a measure of their own masculinity in the eyes of their novias. Some were explicit in conceptualizing being male as an ability to keep their word, to back it up with actions, if necessary, to make their word "mean" something (*hacer valer su palabra*). Jesús, for example, searching for a way to express the degree of his commitment to Maura, captured what was at stake for him: "Don't think that it's because of will [voluntad] nor of money because I've got extra of everything, money and will, for you, if you want to see things as they really are I'm ready to give you whatever proof [prueba] you should want and however you should want it." Jesús's words are almost like fighting words—"whenever you want, wherever you want, in whatever way you want"—that is, those exchanged between men. They illustrate that men, just as did women, needed to be prepared to offer proof of love, helping to place Refugio's earlier statement that Rodrigo had never offered her such a thing in a different light, one much less far-fetched and more concerned, it might be speculated, with Rodrigo's ability to back up his words with action. As for Jesús, he continued, rhetorically, to beat his manly chest: "I'm not deceiving you, if you want me to show through my actions that my word is worth something tell me."[47]

Such assertions on the part of novios are captured in a series of key words found in letters written by men as was discussed briefly above. The constant reiteration of verbs like "*engañar*" (to deceive, mislead, lie to), "*confiar*" (to trust), and "*cumplir*" (to fulfill or carry out, as in a promise) and nouns like "*confianza*" (trust, confidence, reliability) attest to men's preoccupation with backing up their word with action and with being accepted as men who could be counted on to do so. And, for some men, their novias's lack of voluntad must have felt like a questioning of their masculinity. You have already read Eleno's words in which he complains that his novia has a "heart of marble" to make him suffer so much. Yet Eleno was equally preoccupied with what his novia's refusal to leave her home said about him: "Well, now that I see the lack of will that you have, I think that you're doing it because you don't trust me . . . well seeing that you don't have trust in my love because you think I won't fulfill what I've offered you."[48] Perhaps Jesús was speaking not only for himself but for Eleno and others when he stated how far he, for one, was willing to go to fulfill his word, to offer a proof of his love: "Now you see that I'm speaking the truth to you, never will I deceive you, my life, believe me in all that I say, know that I will fulfill all my promises to you even though it might be at the cost of my life so that you should see that my love is true. To deceive you is impossible because I just can't, for you even though I might lose everything, even my life, but if that will convince you that I loved you and that I love you . . ."[49]

Certainly, it might very well be, as with the rhetoric around suffering and happiness discussed earlier, that such promises made by men were strategic or instrumental; that is, they were designed with one goal in mind—that of persuading novias to do what their suitors were asking of them. No doubt this is true, to a greater or lesser extent, depending on the particular case. Yet men's statements about acting to back up their words, convenient lines yes, could also be much more than that: they were powerful assertions of masculine identity encompassing notions of self-respect and concern with the public perception of one's standing in the community as well as intended to protect male prerogatives, especially when it came to the treatment of women. Men's insistence on trust, word, and promises in these letters, often the way that men defined voluntad or responded to its perceived absence, helps make sense of a number of things, ranging from the seemingly excessive preoccupation of some men with what seem like small personal slights to a general male concern with credibility to the descriptions some men offered of the extent they were prepared to go to assert the worth of their words. Such statements may also help establish a framework for teasing out the kind of power that women could wield with their words in these letters. Rather than being acted upon, passive recipients of male agency within courtship, women might be able to deploy such rhetoric to their own ends, convincing men with their words to increase their investment in a given relationship and to act on that growing commitment by offering a proof of their love, that is, by removing their novias from the households of uncooperative parents in order to start life, one in which they might exercise their own voluntad.

So powerful could these words be and so heavily did the understandings of masculinity they called forth weigh on the minds of some men that, at times, there was no need for novias even to say anything. Take for instance the sentence that Jesús writes to Maura in which he anticipates what she will say to him as a result of, given his father's refusal to grant permission to marry, his inability to do so: "I already know that you will say I'm not a man." The brevity of his statement belies the far-reaching implications contained in it. In the first place, it underscores the fact that, as you have seen, one of the essential components of masculinity was the ability to back up one's word, to make it worth something. Moreover, when combined with the endless repetition of reassurances that he was not deceiving her, his words help show that it was a commonly held assumption that men could or often did do precisely that. The statement also helps show that assumptions about masculinity and male behavior more generally were not only shared by men and women but that women might hold men to such standards, spur them to act by questioning their ability to do so, and make it more generally known, through face-to-face conversations or other letters perhaps, that they were not living up to these expectations.

Another novio was so sensitive to the fear, perhaps self-generated, that he might be perceived as someone who could not back up his words—that is, that he could not demonstrate his will in this way—that he rehearsed all the stereotypes about men in the late nineteenth century, especially those dealing with working- or lower-class masculinities. In an impressive performance of proactive ventriloquism, Remedios imagined, in writing, what his novia might have to say to him: "Esteemed Jesús María," he began, "Look, if you loved me it wouldn't have been impossible, but as you don't love me, you don't believe a thing I say to you, you're right, I'm a lazy lay-about who hasn't found anything to do to occupy his time; I live through deceiving you and I can figure out how to feign what doesn't exist; you don't believe what I tell you because now I'm a lost soul who can't figure out to do anything other than to kill time and I'm only playing with you, the oaths I've made to you I've made falsely because as I'm of the lower classes [*soy del pueblo*] I have nothing and I believe that with that I'm seducing you to be unhappy, and as you know that these are my intentions, you're right to look out for your own good because in the heart of a bandit not a wholesome thought exists, everything is disgrace or misfortune."[50] Few characters in didactic novels of the same time period that I have already discussed, like those in *Bandidos de Río Frío* or *El Zarco*, are as effective as Remedios at succinctly expressing some of the main preoccupations of middle-class reformers and writers towards lower-class men. To their descriptions of such men as lazy, vice-ridden, not inured to time and work discipline, and in need of moral reform (all references in Remedios's state-ment), Remedios himself adds that lower-class men might also be regarded as treacherous and deceitful in their treatment of women. That he attributes such thoughts to his novia hints at both the reach of what might be called this developmentalist discourse and its role in shaping not only expectations and values but also the tactics of courtship.[51] His diatribe also helps illustrate that voluntad, in addition to constituting love through its mutual profession, reverberated through the epistolary body, giving shape to its expression in highly gendered terms.

Eyes, Hearts, and Souls

P   Passion fervidly embraces my soul
E   Enclosed, it lives in this heart
D   Divine eyes of my beloved darling
R   Remove from my soul this agony
O   Oh so proud of loving you my love

V   Voice, trembling I feel your lilt
I   Illuminating my dark existence
LL   Call me yours; joined at last the two of us
A   Ending this agony in my soul[52]

Just as Refugio's letters help flesh out voluntad as one of the main faculties of the sentimental anatomy, Enriqueta's, utilized earlier in this section in the discussion of both passion and suffering, place at its center a beating heart and an understanding of love, for which it stood, sustained in the visual relation. The close connection between eyes and heart is evident even in the brief acrostic with which this part begins, one Enriqueta wrote to Pedro, her novio, in a letter to him; the reasons I discuss eyes and hearts together follow largely, but not exclusively, from Enriqueta's usage and will, hopefully, become clearer as the section progresses. Before that, however, a more formal introduction of Enriqueta and a brief discussion of the epistolary space that she and Pedro (whose letters are also available) brought into being through their correspondence is merited. Indeed, their letters form an important basis for the discussion not only of eyes and hearts but also of souls, another major component of the epistolary body, one that Enriqueta works into the first line of the acrostic that begins this section.

As in the case of Refugio, not much is known about Enriqueta, or about Pedro, for that matter. From the brief description of her in the judicial archive we know that she was a young woman, still a teenager, between the age of sixteen and eighteen, and that he, described as an operario or mine worker, someone who usually worked for a wage, was twenty-three. Both lived in the small mining town of Villa Escobedo, not too far from Parral or Santa Bárbara, places that have already been mentioned, all in Hidalgo District in the state of Chihuahua. Their romance of some five months took place in 1919, set against the backdrop of a decade of revolutionary violence in Mexico, difficult years in Chihuahua. None of these matters, however, are discussed in the fourteen letters she composed or the seventeen written by Pedro, nor is anything else other than the emotions they felt and their expressions of them.[53] Although friends are mentioned in passing by Pedro (as the source of something he has been told), they are not named in any of the letters nor are there hints of any larger family contexts or how they might have been experienced, although it seems reasonable to assume, from what others said to judicial authorities, that Enriqueta continued to live at home with her father and at least one sibling, an older sister. In contrast to the case of Refugio and Rodrigo, their correspondence was not occasioned by the need for Pedro to move in order to find work; rather, concerned almost exclusively with affect, it seems to have been employed as a means of bringing into being an emotional and intimate life, a task for which letters, for this couple, seemed particularly suited. And although I can't know for certain, I have become convinced from the brief hints in the letters, as when Pedro swoons at the idea of having in his hand something Enriqueta had written with hers, that they had composed the letters themselves, an accomplishment that would only have been possible with a certain level of formal education. In fact, when I was presenting a paper based on these particular letters to a group from the law school in Oaxaca, Mexico, the dean of that institution was so struck by Enriqueta's letters (as am I) that he assumed a high school education or its equivalent would have been required to have been able to write them.[54]

The epistolary space that Pedro and Enriqueta compose is saturated in affect. Featuring the use of highly sentimental language and preoccupied with feelings, these love letters are closer to those that Carlos Monsiváis describes as excessively sentimental, even cursi (over the top), meant not to be taken at face value but read through a particular lens, that intended to bring into being the ideal couple in an idealized world removed from the difficulties of family life and everyday chores or *quehaceres*.[55] To do so, both letter writers draw on eyes, hearts, and souls, seeing in them the metaphorical organs of the sentimental anatomy. Yet as much as they are concerned with breathing life into the sentimental anatomy, their letters also track an anatomy of sentiment, the trajectory of a courtship, both through the words and metaphors used in their writing and in and of themselves as material and symbolic objects. I have already suggested that the love letters that you have been reading about could convey meanings in a number of registers—through the words written in them; through their ability to stand in for the absent writer, to deliver their touch, feelings, or, ideally, the writer themselves to the other; and through their status as symbols, as objects that signified a courting relationship as well as such things as love, promises, and, as you have seen in the discussion of will, mutuality and reciprocity. Eyes, hearts, and souls figured in all these registers simultaneously, composing feeling through their literal meanings as well as in their capacity as metaphors both for the manner in which courtship was meant to progress as well as in expressing the relationship between letter and body.

As has become increasingly apparent over the course of this section, in courtship, the need to convince a novio or novia to trust in the love being offered became more compelling as the courtship progressed, just as the means chosen to do so likewise escalated in meaning and in consequence. In the early stages of courtship there appears, as expressed in many of the letters, a certain coyness in some of the asides, purposely made to seem carelessly asserted, that were intended to elicit reassuring responses from suitors. Enriqueta, for example, so notable for her candidness and for the straightforward manner in which she clearly established the boundaries of expected behavior within courtship, nevertheless employs this convention in one of her early letters to Pedro: "If you will always love me with the sweetest expression that you state in writing I would consider myself happy, well sometimes I don't know, because it seems to me that the love that you say that you profess to me is not true. Dissipate this doubt that envelopes my soul and I will live happily." You have also seen that often the ultimate proof of love was for the woman to accede to the initiation of sexual relations in exchange for a promise to cover her honor, that is, marry her, at a later date, verifying, in this way, not only her virginity but also her acceptance of the man's ability to make his word worth something.

Between coyness and copulation, the ends bookmarking the courting process, were prendas, a term that, like voluntad, could take on many meanings depending on context but which can for the purposes of beginning this discussion be understood as gifts, symbols, tokens, or mementos exchanged as part of a courting relationship. Enriqueta hints at both the representational as well as emotional punch the term could carry in the third line of the acrostic she wrote above, the one beginning with "D," in which she metonymically conjures Pedro by reference to his "divine eyes." Here, as she uses it in the phrase *"mi prenda amada"* (my beloved darling), the word "prenda" can only refer to Pedro himself, the person she deeply loves. Oscillating between heralding the loved one themselves and embodying them symbolically, prendas could take many forms. For some suitors, a lock of hair, a ring, or even a kiss would do. For others, religious imagery or a rosary served the same purposes, as could a handkerchief embroidered with the initials of one's love. As you will see, photographs were a particularly important kind of prenda, as were love letters themselves. To say that love letters could serve as prendas is to emphasize the "magic" of the letter over its content, that is, over the meaning of the words found in it.[56] In fact, the arrival of a letter from a man had serious implications that both parties understood if seldom spelled out. Letters could be, and sometimes, were, returned unopened and unread, indicating that the woman's feelings did not correspond with those of her prospective suitor. When a son in the household in which fifteen-year-old Luz performed domestic labor tried to give her a love letter, for example, she refused to accept it and said nothing about it either to him or to his mother, the head of the household.[57] As you have also read, returning love letters was the most compelling evidence that a courtship had indeed come to an end. It is in this sense, then, that prendas, in this case letters but also more generally, served to herald the desired future as well as to recall, in a successful courtship, the history of its coming to pass.

After daring to declare their love and then finding their feelings reciprocated, perhaps by the acceptance of a letter, suitors typically protested ever more loudly that the love they offered was indeed true while, at the same time, becoming more insistent in demanding proof of sincerity and commitment from their correspondent. Constant written assurance, essential but somehow never quite sufficient, was soon accompanied by requests for more tangible proof that would better demonstrate the true extent of the commitment of the object of their affection. Referred to variously as "proofs of affection" (prueba de cariño), "proofs of loyalty" (*prueba de su lealtad*), and even "incomparable proofs," prendas became the physical manifestations of the truth of one's love. Both men and women in courting relationships were explicit when it came to setting out the role that prendas were designed to serve—they were lifelines that might rescue lovers from the depths of their doubts. Enriqueta's response to Pedro in writing upon her receipt of a prenda from him confirms that reassurance followed: "I don't doubt now Pedro," she wrote, "that love that I have understood in your words and in your eyes and much more today now that I have an incomparable proof—your photograph—in the saddest hours of your absence it will calm the anguish of my soul, dissipate the doubts that momentarily assault me and if as today Pedro you are a caring lover and know to reward your abnegation with a life of tenderness and love, think of me as I am devoting my youthful thoughts to you." Similarly, for Refugio, giving a prenda and even allowing Rodrigo to choose its particular form, resolved the dichotomy between true and false will in her favor: "Rodrigo," she wrote, "as for the portrait I'm not sending it to you now because I don't have it but I intend to get my portrait taken within the next eight days. Well, you have to choose: a handkerchief, a ring . . . even a kiss. Whatever you should most want to prove to you that I have true will and not one with hypocrisy." Just as the truth of voluntad might be confirmed for Refugio, for Enriqueta, the truth of love was made apparent with the arrival of a prenda.

The reciprocal nature of courtship, so apparent in the concern with voluntad, can also be glimpsed in the giving and receiving of prendas. Rather than just waiting for one to arrive or sending one on their own initiative, novios, both men and women, might ask directly for their suitor to send such a token. Pedro, for example, hoped out loud that, some day, Enriqueta might provide him with a prenda, in this case a lock of her hair: "I would like to have a token of yours in my possession," he wrote. "Tell me if one day I'll be able to get one or not." Refugio directly asked Rodrigo to send his portrait—"Yo quiero su retrato," she wrote—but not before establishing a precedent in a previous letter, that of agreeing to provide him with something if he would agree to do the same when asked to in the future. With this request Refugio was, in effect, creating a ledger of sorts, by which means the accounts of their courtship might be balanced or made equal. In the case of another courting couple, Tula and Eleno, when Tula refused to provide him with the final proof of her love, Eleno cited the disparity in the number of prendas that had been exchanged to that point in their courtship. Disputing her accounting and even the very terms by which the ledger of their courtship had been reckoned, Eleno proclaimed: "Well, I'm ready to give you everything you ask me for if you accept that which I'm saying to you, in regard to what you say to me that you have already given me three things and I haven't given you even one what more do you want me to give you or by chance do you want me to rip out my heart to give to you, I'm capable of giving you soul, life and heart."[58] Potent symbols, prendas seemed able to make tangible the metaphorical organs responsible for love, either by standing in for them or, as in Eleno's case, by bypassing their representative capacity and becoming the actual organs themselves, "given" to the other as part of what happens when one falls in love.

Prendas, each one another step up the aisle toward the wedding altar, were not sought out frivolously. In fact, doing so might be regarded as a kind of test designed to probe the extent of commitment as well as to elicit ever-greater degrees of it. Pedro, for one, asked Enriqueta whether, some day, she might provide him with a token to attest to the truth of her commitment: "Enriqueta," he implored, "you will think me inopportune for having asked you for a lock of your hair so I can be more satisfied as to your love. Even though I don't believe it is feigned, I would like to have a prenda of yours in my power." Of course, asking for a prenda also chanced refusal, leaving suitors to draw what seemed, to them, the obvious conclusion. When Carlota, for example, declined to gift him her photograph after he asked her to do so, Jesús was beside himself: "And as I see that you refuse to give me your photograph, what am I supposed to think! That there is no will, true? You'd think the same if I refused to give you something . . . everything feigned nothing true, how ignorant I was, I believed my love to be reciprocated from the beginning and it was just the opposite."[59] Conversely, once asked for and delivered, prendas signaled the triumph of certainty over doubt, both for the donor as well as the recipient. "Enriqueta," wrote Pedro when he gave her his photograph, "to dispel doubt I now make you a present of my photograph that I believe with this proof of affection [prueba de cariño] you will no longer doubt, even for a moment, the sincere love that I have professed and you will live in tranquility and give me life."

Although it was not directly mentioned in any of the love letters, it may have been the case that photographic portraits served as particularly suitable prendas not only because they offered an image of the novio or novia and could, therefore, evoke his or her memory and presence but also because they emphasized the very act of looking. "I can't be without seeing you," implored Enriqueta to Pedro, giving expression to one way in which looking might be central to love. "Happiness returns to me the instant that I once again contemplate your idolized image; that I see portrayed in your eyes a love that is mine." The visual apprehension of one's suitor, that is, of them directly as well as of their image, made of photos more than met the eye; they reveal the assumption that, for many, love could be captured in the visual relation, just as could, many assumed, such qualities as criminality or "deviance" or even "race."[60] Pedro's photo arrived in Enriqueta's hands in 1919 and you may remember from Refugio's letters that she also mentioned the use of a photographic portrait as a prenda; in fact, the relationship between Refugio and Rodrigo was the first one in which a photographic portrait is mentioned, dating the earliest use of such images as prendas found in the judicial archives utilized for this research to 1904, although, as the correspondence is only partial in most of the courtships discussed, others may also have exchanged such images at an earlier date. Additional courting couples that mention the use of photographs as prendas included Jesús and Maura in 1909 and Jesús and Carlota in 1912. In the case of the lone image that serves as a prenda located in the judicial archive itself, dating from just after the turn of the century, the head of a novio is portrayed in an oval, of a size that reminds one of a school photo suitable for a wallet or to be included in a letter. It seems no coincidence that some of the first images of criminality are also encountered in the judicial archive in Parral at precisely this time, just after the turn of the century, in which thumbnail portraits of the heads of criminals are arranged in a kind of collage formed into the shape of a tree. The grouping of many small images of "criminals" onto a single page seems to offer both a means of quick identification and a sense that the entire universe of criminality in Parral at this time can be taken in with a single glance. Apart from the uses the state made of photographs, the kinds of self-fashioning seen in images taken in other parts of Mexico at this time, including other mining areas like Guanajuato, were not encountered in the archives, nor were images in which one's novio was worn as a brooch or cameo, turning the body into a backdrop or mobile gallery for the public display of the image of one's other, close to the heart of course.[61]

In the case of the use of photographic images as prendas, Enriqueta is especially articulate in setting out her understanding of visuality and its relationship to writing: "My heart drunk with happiness can't find the words to explain to you the sweet emotions that my soul feels on looking over the lines of your kind letters, being those and your serene look the things that rob my eyes of sleep and my soul of tranquility. Tell me one more time that your love is mine alone; tell me that your eyes only look upon me with such tenderness, it is pleasing to my eyes to see it written by your hand, for the heart of the woman who loves you there isn't a greater pleasure than to contemplate your eyes, to see portrayed in them the love that your heart feels for me." Pedro was equally adamant about the centrality of looking or beholding to romantic love: "Receive this heart dead," he wrote to Enriqueta, "so that with your loving looks you might resuscitate it." More than images, mementos, or representations, photographs as prendas were premised upon the assumption that the eyes provided a direct conduit to the heart, thus offering the means of accessing the truth found there or even truth itself. Heart, eyes, hand, soul, these, the metaphorical organs of the romantic body, found their sustenance in images and words, the lifeblood of the sentimental anatomy of love. And, if the sentimental anatomy embodying these organs along with various degrees of will, suffering, and happiness was mostly torso, the photographic image of one's novio or novia might be thought of as providing a face or head for this epistolary body, thus offering both a means of expressing and a conduit for reading the body's desires.

As is apparent in Enriqueta's writing, letters might serve as ideal prendas for many of the same reasons as could photographic portraits. To begin with, they allowed for the same kind of visual apprehension of one's novio or novia as did photographs, only, in this case, rather than of their eyes, it was of their writing, another visual representation of the true feelings located in the heart. "Everything that I say to you in my letters," explains Pedro to Enriqueta, "is dictated by my heart." In fact, a kind of parallel or metaphorical affinity existed between visuality, or looking, and writing: both served as a means of communicating or expressing the sincerity or truth of love as both led directly to or from the heart, the locus of love. "I'm yours," Enriqueta assures Pedro in one of her letters, "and no one will succeed in tearing your image from my heart, only the implacable hand of death." For another novio, writing was the next best thing to being there: "Well, in the end, you know what you're doing," wrote Teofilo to fifteen-year-old Ramona, "because it's impossible for me to put you within my breast for you to read my thoughts, well, in the end you know what you're doing."[62]

Just as the image of one's novio or novia could be impressed upon the heart by means of the look, these same feelings, expressed in writing, could be impressed upon the page. Enriqueta is particularly cognizant of the alchemy of writing, of its power to transform the truth of the heart into words, to represent the image of love in writing: "I would like only to see you," she wrote in one letter to Pedro, "to be able to explain to you what is going on in this heart that is yours alone but I'm not doing it verbally now because I'm not brave enough, I will leave engraved on this paper all the impressions that my soul feels for you." And, in another letter: "My soul enveloped in happiness and fixing my thoughts hour by hour on your memory [*recuerdos*, keepsakes or mementos], today at this moment in which I'm only thinking of you, in the present lines I offer [*dedicar*] my words leaving inscribed [*gravado*] in this letter the tenderness that my heart sends to yours." Only once such feelings had been expressed in writing, specifically in love letters, did they become available for visual appropriation: "It is gratifying to my eyes to see it written in your hand," she wrote to Pedro. In the constant circulation between heart, eyes, hand, and soul, pleasure derived not only from the words themselves but from the ability of letters to conjure up the missing partner, to deliver their touch, their true feelings and, in an act of transubstantiation, to make manifest on the page what was imprinted on the heart.

Ideal as prendas, then, love letters seemed nevertheless to exceed the bounds of what was encompassed by that very category. As you have seen, letters, as physical entities, marked a phase in a person's life, their arrival signaling the beginning of courtship and the return of all letters that had been exchanged punctuating its end. During their courtship, Enriqueta described the love letters she sent to Pedro as recuerdos (keepsakes, mementos), by which means the absent partner could be recalled and contemplated. Mobilized in this way, love letters serve as symbols or tokens. Both Pedro and Enriqueta understood love letters to be privileged forms of expressing and communicating deeply held emotional truths, that is, windows opening onto the heart that, through the parallel relationship between looking and writing—the heart and the page—enabled the truth of one's love to be determined, expressed, and apprehended. Much more than gifts, symbols, or tokens, love letters were essential to their love, bringing into being the very feelings that were being expressed. Heart and page, page and heart, each not only made manifest what was to be found in the other but dictated those very sentiments.

Much like the letters written by Refugio, perhaps even more so, those exchanged by Pedro and Enriqueta were singularly unconcerned with conveying information about their daily lives in any of its many aspects. In their letters, the two disavow the humdrum world of everyday concerns to create an intensely emotional space of intimacy, exchange, and mutual self-reflection. In this utopian or idealized space, time was not calibrated exclusively in minutes, hours, and days, but could take on mythic and, at times, apocalyptic, proportion, as when they stressed that the narrative that they were together composing would not be concluded until death, or, even more strongly put, would not be concluded at all but would last through all eternity. Here, a certain kind of future was being written into existence while, in other places, a personal and private history was being narrated, one in which the letters were meant to be preserved for posterity in order to document the feelings that each had for the other at the particular point in time in which each had been written. A complicated sense of time emerges from their letters: each letter became a chapter in the emotional history of their relationship, creating a past for it while establishing the course for the future trajectory of their lives together. In addition, the letters as objects served as physical evidence that their courtship was progressing toward its inevitable climax, that is, towards marriage.

As for the future, two senses of future time shared the duties of enabling these novios to imagine their love and what would become of it. The first, what I refer to as "mundane time," flowed from the dynamic that structured courtship, a dynamic where, as you have seen, each needed to convince the other of the truth of their love in an escalating series of proofs. "If your love is pure and true," wrote Enriqueta, "my heart will reciprocate." And, in another letter: "If your love is honorable I will reciprocate your feelings." Pedro expressed a similar sense of mundane future time when, writing about the possibility of obtaining a prenda, he asked specifically for a lock of Enriqueta's hair: "Tell me if some day I'll be able to acquire it or not." And, once again drawing from Enriqueta: "Dissipate this doubt that envelopes my soul and I will live happily." And Pedro: "If it's as you say, I will be very happy with your love." Constructed in this manner, the future tense offers the promise of ever-greater commitment while setting the terms for its realization; it becomes the measure of how the anatomy of sentiment is progressing. Ultimately, it would be used to articulate one's hopes and aspirations for the outcome of courtship, which, as Pedro confessed to Enriqueta, were for him to be at her side.

At some point in courtship, mundane time slipped into what might be called "ethereal time," the second sense of future time that novios, at points, shifted into, perhaps once they became convinced that the other's love was not feigned or as a means of assuring the other of the extent of one's own commitment to the relationship. When Enriqueta states, "If you will always love me with the sweetest expression as is in your writing I would consider myself happy," you can see the slip to ethereal time starting to take place. "Always love," or "never forget," staples of romantic discourse, confirmed the shift, which was soon followed by the pledging of one's love at least until the end of mortal time: "I'm yours," confesses Enriqueta, "and no one will be able to tear your image from my heart, only the implacable hand of death." Or in another letter she wrote: "No one will be able to wrench you from your Enriqueta, I will live through you and for you. Tell me the same and I will be happy." And, finally, one's love might be so powerful as even to elude death's perhaps not-so-implacable hand: "I love you and this love that I feel for you will be eternal."

As for Pedro, rather than distinct categories, mundane and ethereal notions of future time seem so intertwined as to be well-nigh indistinguishable. He certainly had no difficulty using the mundane future to try to elicit ever-increasing degrees of commitment from Enriqueta; nor was his use of "always" and "never" much different from the way in which she employs its ethereal variant, as when he writes: "We must always form a happy sphere of noble emotions of true and caring love," and "Never will I forget you." Yet, time in his love letters is often marked and measured in mundane and ethereal terms simultaneously, an indication of how he experienced and understood love itself. And here, religious and even celestial analogies were central in helping him express not only the enduring quality of their love but its magnitude, ensuring, at the same time, that such powerful passions would be perceived as pure, even graced with the presence of the divine. Referring to Enriqueta with her nickname, Trigueñita, Pedro captures, with his prose, this sense of the time of love: "Trigueñita, just as the Sun, the Moon and the rest of the stars move across the heavens, so moves my love growing for you, just as you assure me that you are mine, be as assured of my love as of your own existence and that I am only yours."

As you might imagine, wrapping one's love in a mantle of religious analogy, even purity, was important, perhaps even essential, given the overriding
preoccupation with the carnal when striking the bargain that was meant
to lead to marriage, an exchange, as you have seen, in which the woman
traded proof of her virginity for the man's word, his promise to cover her
honor and marry her at a later date. Pedro's language exudes passion and
desire, yet his hope, he seems to suggest, is for spiritual, rather than carnal,
union: "Inflamed with immensity the unbearable pleasures that you profess
to me with your faithful and loving eulogies," he writes, "Enriqueta, mine
for you are like those of the angels when they offer a prayer of adoration
to the eternal Creator." When he broaches the subject of what Enriqueta
takes to be a request for a "prueba de amor," the use of language is again
euphemistic, subject to some interpretation, with his use of the ethereal
future contributing, perhaps purposely, to a lack of clarity in the exact
meaning of his request: "Enriqueta, it still appears to me that they [your
words] must be feigned even though you speak warmly to me that yours
is a true love, but I desire satisfaction and I'll have it when our love should
truly be one alone because still up to now it seems that we are independent
and when we should be united you and I then you will see your adorer in
the most happy tranquility and eternal virtue."

Enriqueta, on the other hand, had little trouble understanding what
he was getting at: "With the same love as always I answer your letter,"
she responded. "You say to me that still it seems that my words must be
feigned. Don't think that, they are born from the deepest part of this heart.
At the same time I say to you that never will I consent to what you desire
because you know that this is for me an offense. Never again pronounce
those words because if you do I'll never answer another one of your letters. Not for this will I stop loving you because my heart is yours alone."
Despondent at Enriqueta's response, Pedro interpreted it as evidence of
her lack of honesty in matters of the heart: "How much you think of me
that I should find myself with my heart broken into a thousand pieces
because you say to me that never will you answer me because I explained
to you that my ambitions are to be at your side, for as much as you say to
me that you are mine and that you'll never forget me. Enriqueta, I believe

that you know what you are saying and you won't be able to deceive me because I've never feigned love to anyone and much less to you, the only owner of all the love of your passionate Pedro."

Choosing to take offense rather than to explain himself, Pedro does nonetheless offer evidence elsewhere in his correspondence that makes it plausible to suggest that union was, for him, conceptualized in spiritual as much as physical terms. And the union that Pedro was (perhaps) after was of hearts and souls, two of the most important organs of the sentimental anatomy, both of which suggested that love could mean implicating the spiritual or even the divine. Sharing with Enriqueta the metaphorical association of the heart and the letter, in which love was engraved on the heart the same way as words on the pages of a letter, Pedro, nevertheless, went further, including soul as well as heart in most of his reflections on love: "If you knew what immense tranquility your passionate Pedro has received writing to you once again with such a growing and sweet love it is true that I was suffering frightening desperation when I didn't know what was happening to you but now I am entirely happy and I know that I won't forget you even for an instant because never will you be effaced from the heart of your Pedro, you are intertwined with the soul that is dying for you." In another letter, heart and soul are again the twin loci of love: "If your heart feels great happiness when receiving one of my letters that which mine receives on seeing one of yours is incomparable, because I believe that no impassioned man should have felt for his loved one that which I feel for you, you are the sustenance and the consolation of the soul that you have imprisoned through your loving praises of energy with such powerful love that I don't believe that there has ever existed another that can compete with the one that I have for my dear Enriqueta." In yet another letter, the sense of intertwining or intermixing, of blending and coming together, again predominates, not only as the main means of expressing what is meant by love but also as an important way of stressing its chaste, even spiritual quality: "And I am the man that in my loved one I expect my heart to find itself immensely intertwined in the most ardent and pure love."

Nor was Pedro alone in endowing the sentimental anatomy with a soul or in drawing from popular religiosity to give form to the epistolary body.

Liberato, the campesino you read about in a previous section, also used the term "soul" in much the same way as Pedro; already being married, Liberato forged a marriage certificate to convince María to leave her home in order to form with him, as he put it, nothing other than a "single soul" [*un alma no más*].[63] You have also already read how Eleno was prepared to give "soul, life, and heart" to Tula, his novia, in exchange for the "prueba de Amor." Attempts to capture the extent of one's love, references to the soul also invoked, if indirectly, the ethereal future, even a sense of the eternal. None of the letter writers discussed the soul in any further detail, nor did they feel it necessary to explain what they meant when they used the term, either preferring the ambiguity they wielded with its use, one in which the spiritual might or might not imply the carnal, taking it for granted that the term would be understood by their co-correspondent, or both. There is a source, however, in which one writer is explicit about the soul and its afterlife. Much earlier, in the 1860s, Luciano Gallardo, who wrote a multi-volume diary of his courtship of Carlota Gil in the city of Guadalajara, gives a sense of how "soul" was understood, at least by him and his novia.[64] When Carlota's mother died near the beginning of their courtship, Luciano's novia was understandably upset, as was Luciano. Rather than disappearing from the narrative of their courtship, however, the dearly departed mother comes to structure it, as the couple makes a pilgrimage to her grave every month, on the date of her death, to leave a wreath; meanwhile, the mother herself not only blessed the couple and their union on her deathbed but seems, even after death, to be looking out for them from on high, a being with an active and ongoing presence that they acknowledge, appeal to, and, it seems, attempt to appease. In fact, the powerful influence of the mother, not only prior to but also after her death, seems to have been somewhat of a trope, as another dying mother, this time a fictitious one, not only blesses the love of Nicolas and Pilar in *El Zarco*, the novel discussed earlier, but, in fact, with that blessing, places that love within the realm of the sacred or spiritual.[65] Nor is she absent from the love letters considered here, although mostly in her flesh-and-blood incarnation, serving as the most sacred object that novios and novias can think of to swear on, a touchstone for the truth of their pronouncements about love and hinting at her power to do something about it, perhaps even after her death. "Promise me on that which you esteem most dearly in life, which I believe is your mother," begs Refugio of Rodrigo, "that you won't again refer to yourself as wretched." Another finds comfort when his novia swears on the blood of her mother that she has been faithful to him.

If the language of love and the language of faith found a meeting point in the soul, so too might religious understandings of the eternal and constructions of the times of love borrow from and help define each other. Invoking God's name was both simple and complex, serving any number of purposes. To begin with, religious references were a part of popular parlance, and the letters abound with phrases that hedge in human agency with reference to the will of God, if only not to tempt fate. Leaving things in God's hands was to acknowledge the limits of human power while, and in a manner that only appears contradictory, simultaneously highlighting the extent of one's own individual efforts. When Marcos states, for example, that he would only go back on his word if God should cut short his footsteps, that is, end his life, it is not a statement of resignation in the face of the Almighty but of the fact that nothing in this world can stop him from keeping his promises. Joaquín makes much the same category of statement to Feliciana some years later when he tells her that only if God takes away his life will he not honor his word and fail to come back to her. (Marcos does as well.) These statements, then, seem much more a measure of male agency rather than of impotence in the face of a higher power; other novios, as well, preferred to act in the here and now and leave the future up to God. "I'm not promising you this world and the next," stated Ismael to Atanacia, "because I don't know what the future holds for us, if the Creator protects us, it will be our happiness."[66] Eleno develops much the same idea when he asks Tula to come with him "to have a life good or bad, but that depends on the will of God." "God willing," writes Joaquín to Feliciana, "we will see each to enjoy our love once again."[67] Finally, while the will of God might work in mysterious ways, deploying His name did not—doing so enabled writers to give emphasis to their statements; like the mother, dead or alive, God's name lent any claim an aura of the sacred, and a heightened relationship to truth and honesty. "If only you knew what God so well knows," stated Jesús in one of his letters, implying that his explanations as to why he was unable to marry were not to be questioned but rather that they should be accepted at face value. Likewise, when Liberato writes, "If only the Eternal One had not allowed me to get married so that I could do so now with you," his ruing takes on added weight and significance. One can only wonder what Carlota made of Jesús's statement: "But God is great and I trust in Him like I trust in you."[68] One way to read Jesús's comment is through the lens of metaphor, to see a relationship being established between one's love for God and one's love for another. Just as Pedro's passions were like those of angels for their God, Jesús's trust in his novia was of the highest order.

As the soul helped imbue the epistolary body with a hint of the sacred, a language steeped in faith lent itself to the forging of metaphorical affinities between love of God and love of another, while, simultaneously, heralding a conception of time that went beyond the bounds of that measured in mortal terms. For the most part, the links are subtle and can be established only by taking context into account. To plead with "the Eternal One" to give him strength, as does Remedios, is one thing, but then to read Felipe's anguish over Guadalupe, in which he laments that she "promised to love him until the end of time" and that, as a result of the failure of their relationship, he would "suffer eternally," is, through association and the constant reiteration of such phrases, not only to get a sense of his suffering, to have a measure of it, but to get a sense as well of how the time of love and the time of the sacred might help provide the measure of each other.[69]

Perhaps it is this same process of reiteration that in addition to the references to God's will and other aspects of religiosity makes it possible to locate the plots or narratives of many of the courtships you have been reading about in these love letters within a context broadly informed by popular religiosity. After all, what could be more generically religious than a narrative about overcoming suffering and hardship through the exercise of will ultimately to triumph in love, a state that might just as easily refer to the sacred as the profane? This reading becomes even more persuasive once the continued importance of such texts as the catechism of Padre Ripalda, one of the most disseminated works of its kind in the Spanish-speaking world of the colonial period, are taken into account. Not only did this catechism continue to form an important part of the literature of moral uplift in late nineteenth-century Mexico, it also linked the two concepts that, I have been arguing, were central categories in the love letters, specifically identifying will (voluntad) as one of the three faculties of the soul (alma).[70] And perhaps, to speculate even further, what more appropriate model might there be for corresponding with a distant, or not so distant, Other than the relationship between self and God, undertaken through prayer and petition, and implicating many of the same organs as the sentimental anatomy?[71]

Ultimately, however, such slippage between the language of the sacred and the language of the profane might have been the only means for many novios to approach the subject of desire, especially with novias of "high moral qualities," as Pedro describes Enriqueta. Approaching desire in metaphorical terms, in a kind of a code, offered a means of broaching the subject of sexual desire while maintaining the ability to claim one's innocence or rectitude while doing so. The implication of Pedro's expressed desire to be with Enriqueta, clothed even as it may have been in the language of love on a higher plane, in religious metaphors, was, as you have seen, certainly clear enough to her. But, just for good measure, in case the implications of speaking in code meant that she had missed the message, Pedro's "soul" could be quite corporeal in some of its incarnations: "Enriqueta, because of your love I have suffered and I am suffering and I offer to take you in my arms and clutch you against my soul and it will be receiving the kisses of your sweet and enchanting mouth."

Death

death: "*la novia fiel*" (the faithful novia)[72]

Just as invoking the name of God might enable novios to express the magnitude of their feelings, so could deploying the rhetoric of death. You have already read how Enriqueta regarded the "implacable hand of death," at least rhetorically, as the only force capable of tearing Pedro's image from her heart; you should also know that, like his novia, Pedro found in death a powerful trope for measuring the extent and intensity of his love: "Enriqueta, if I'm not yours I won't be anyone's and it will be easier to lose my life, I prefer that to losing you." Pedro's use of such references was more than in passing—rather, for him, death was a much reiterated refrain: "Even at death's door my desires will not be forgotten," he states in another letter. And in yet another: "Only in death will you be forgotten to me." Nor is this pair of lovers unique in this regard. In their correspondence with each of their novias, Eleno and Jesús draw on death in this manner, as do others. "And I ask God that he allow me to have you at my side," wrote Marcos to Marcelina, for example, "because this is the way I intend it and I would consider myself the happiest person in the Universe because without you at my side I wouldn't even want to be on the earth."[73] So powerful was death in the figurative language of love—as a means to express the strength of feelings, the sense that no earthly force could change the way one felt about their loved one, and to emphasize the idea that love was permanent rather than in passing—that it was not uncommon to end love letters by summoning it yet one more time. "Yours until the tomb" and "He who loves you until death," closings in a number of the love letters, strive to reiterate in the most compelling of terms the extent of one's love. Yet, they do more than that: they also frame the entire letter, and perhaps love itself, within the idiom of death.

Nor was the idiom of death limited, in its figurative usage, to measuring the intensity of one's love. For some men, death, or, more specifically, stating one's willingness to die or give up their life for love, epitomized the most conclusive prueba de amor they could possibly provide, the apex within the hierarchy of proof discussed earlier, that began with letters and continued with photos, rosaries, and locks of hairs, culminating in the initiation of sexual relations in exchange for a man's word in the form of a promise of marriage, backed up by the willingness to risk one's life to make those words count for something. When, for example, Jesús wrote to Maura at a critical point in their courtship, after his father's refusal to grant permission for Jesús to marry made it impossible for him to fulfill the promises he had given her, death's presence, while open to interpretation, seems to linger on its figurative meaning, providing him with a compelling means of reassuring Maura of the extent of his love; yet at the same time, death seems to escape from these figurative constraints to become something that was not always beyond one's control: "To deceive you is impossible," he wrote, "because I can't, for you even though I might lose everything, even my life, but if it convinces you that I loved you and that I still love you, if you don't want to do what I'm saying to you, then who knows what will become of me and of you." If Jesús's use of death in this statement is open to interpretation, later in the letter he is much more specific about how death, specifically his own, might serve as the ultimate prenda: "I love you," he assured Maura. "You should never mistrust me, I'm ready even to give you my life to prove to you that my love is solely for you."[74]

In addition to serving as a proof or a prenda, giving one's life might also be construed as the ultimate expression of voluntad, that essential component of the sentimental anatomy that was, as you have already seen, so central a part of the epistolary body Refugio brought into being with her prose. To illustrate how being willing to die might serve as evidence of one's will, I return to Pedro, as he relentlessly pushes such sentiments to their final conclusion. Near the end of their courtship, despondent at what has come to pass, he writes to Enriqueta: "I can't make you love me, but what I do know is that because I love you it is going to cost me my life, [and] I lose it with all my will."

Pedro's preoccupation with death, tragically, it turns out, was more than merely a rhetorical strategy—a lethal literality lurked within the hitherto figurative references to death that so marked the rhetoric of his love. When he failed to live up to a promise he had made to her, that of giving up drinking, Enriqueta ended the relationship. Frustrated at the insecurities that his drinking engendered and driven to despair at the need to reassure him that she did indeed love him each time he did so, she had set limits on what she was prepared to accept in their relationship: "You swore to me," she wrote to him, "not to do it [drink alcohol] again anticipating that if you did it one more time that until that day our relations would last and for that reason everything is over between us and you will see that only you are to blame." In the last line that Enriqueta wrote to Pedro, she asked whether he would be so kind as to bring her all the letters she had sent to him, a sure sign that the courtship was indeed at an end. Meeting one final time to retrieve these tokens, these small pieces of themselves, each from the other, Pedro, despite insisting that he couldn't make her love him and that she should do as she pleased, shot Enriqueta to death before turning the gun on himself and taking his own life. Along with the love letters, judicial officials found on their corpses a white handkerchief embroidered with the name "Pedro" and a locket containing Enriqueta's photograph, prendas that were also being returned to those for whom they had stood.

I want to pause here, first to provide some space for you briefly to ponder what you have just read, to reflect upon Enriqueta's life, a life of which I (and thus you) have been afforded only the briefest of glimpses through the traces of herself that she has left in her letters to Pedro, yet one that has impressed itself upon me (as, I hope, it has upon you) as I have read and worked with her prose over the course of writing this book, and second to take some time to state very specifically and very carefully the nature and extent of the conclusions I feel I can draw and the observations I am willing to make based on how their particular courtship ended. In this regard, Enriqueta's murder seems to highlight the main question and preoccupation that I have wrestled over the entire length of this project: what kind of interpretive burden can the sources I have used, mostly love letters in this section, be asked to bear? Perhaps the first thing that is immediately apparent is that, despite the fact that this section of the book has focused on what I have been calling the epistolary body and the sentimental anatomy, very real and dire consequences were, at times, registered on living, breathing bodies as a result of this correspondence and the sentiments it helped compose. This is true in the beatings that women in courting relationships received from, at some times, family members in defense of masculine honor and, at others, from novios to facilitate compliance with their desires; in the deaths of men like Lino, whom you met near the beginning of this section, killed by his former novia's brother; in the loss of virginity and the physical and emotional consequences that, at times, followed for many women, as in the example of Feliciana, who, you saw, ended up under a doctor's care for "commotions" after her novio refused to follow through on his promise of marriage, or that of Guadalupe, who, having changed her mind about running away with her novio, faced a life of uncertain prospects under the control, at least in the short term, of her mother; and in the murder of a woman like Enriqueta. These consequences also took the form of the feelings and emotions that were expressed through embodied reactions, ranging from the anger Refugio must have felt when Rodrigo stood her up to the anxiousness many novios experienced when waiting for letters to the fear, or in some cases exhilaration, they must have felt at an unknown future after having left with one's correspondent (as I write this on Valentine's Day!) to love itself, given expression by the epistolary body as it helped bring such a body into existence. The epistolary body, then, seemed to exceed or transgress the page upon which it had been written, meting out and having registered upon it all the consequences that might follow from its very composition.

If the love letter and the sentimental codes and discourses that went into its writing formed a specific genre, one of high sentimentality and extreme emotion designed to distance from their daily lives the actual couple in order to bring its ideal variant into being, some negotiated the journey between the ideal and the mundane much more easily than others. Enriqueta seems to have been able to traverse this divide, proving adept at expressing herself in her correspondence in the language of love, of drawing on and defining the metaphorical organs of the sentimental anatomy and utilizing the senses of time that helped compose what love meant in early twentieth-century northern Mexico while simultaneously being able to say "no"—to in effect pull out of the romantic tailspin by recalling her own values, interests, and the limits of her willingness to suspend everyday reality. When asked to provide Pedro with the prueba de amor of agreeing to begin sexual relations with him, she declined and, as you have just read, she eventually ended the relationship because of Pedro's drinking. A woman's ability to end such a relationship must have involved a number of factors that depended on her personality and circumstances as well as the existence of other choices and possibilities, options that did not always exist for all women. Pedro, on the other hand, seemed unable or unwilling to switch between registers—from that required for writing love letters to that locating him in the mundane, from the figurative to the literal—and, perhaps, to even acknowledge that a gap separated one from the other. In the end, such a combination was lethal: for Enriqueta, just saying "no" ultimately proved fatal.

Yet, it seems less than satisfactory, to say the least, to blame Enriqueta's death on genre or on the failure to distinguish between epistolary space and the spaces comprised by the realities of everyday life—that lets Pedro off the hook all too easily. This much is certain: Pedro murdered Enriqueta before committing suicide. When it comes to contextualizing and drawing conclusions about the significance of this event, however, great care must be taken. It is certainly possible that this murder-suicide was the work of a pathological individual, that is, an exceptional act motivated by rage and mental disturbance exacerbated by the effects of alcohol. Given the evidence, it is simply not possible to know whether or not that is what happened in this case. When the outcome of this courtship is situated more broadly, within the universe of all courtships that have left an archival trace, its exceptionally tragic conclusion becomes even more apparent—even Pedro admitted in a letter to Enriqueta that not all men thought about or acted on such matters in the same way, not all men, that is, assumed that murder had to inevitably follow from the end of a courtship or from a sense of being deceived in love. Many courtships, some of which must have ended with one or both parties feeling hard done by, ran their own courses without novios ever feeling compelled to kill or parents compelled to involve the judicial system in any way. Certainly, murder-suicide was not the preordained and expected conclusion to every courtship that failed to result in marriage.

Yet neither was such a horrific scenario completely out of the ordinary. Just a few years earlier, for example, and in the same small community, José's courtship of Josefa had ended in identical fashion to that of Pedro and Enriqueta, with her murder and his suicide. As part of the investigation of their deaths, judicial authorities recorded that José's pockets had yielded, along with matches, cigarettes, and a few other such items: one sealed envelope containing a letter to his novia's mother; one unsealed envelope with a letter to his sister; a letter signed by someone not mentioned in any of the materials concerned with the investigation; a message written by yet another person; a postcard addressed to Josefa, possibly a kind of prenda or gift; an unsigned letter addressed to "Angelita"; a letter addressed to "Pepa"; a suicide note written in pencil, signed by José; and a handkerchief embroidered with his novia's initials, definitely a prenda that was being returned to its original owner.[75] As judicial officials did not find any love letters at the scene, returning them could not have served as a pretext for the couple's final meeting. Despite the absence of this particular genre of letter, the presence of so many other written documents helps illustrate that, just as the sentimental anatomy might be composed in epistolary space, so could its demise be anticipated and given meaning there. Just as writing was more than an expression of feelings but also gave rise to those very feelings that were being expressed, writing also gave shape to the meaning of death, forging out of it a didactic narrative crafted to make apparent the consequences of acting against, or failing to heed, the terms of the discourse of masculinity being composed in them.

As judicial authorities inscribed José's letters to his sister and to his novia's mother into the archival record, there is, at least from his perspective, something of an explanation of his actions. In fact, José, a twenty-one-year-old clerk (empleado) originally from Durango but resident in Parral, meant for his letters and the deaths they heralded to be read, to become known, the letters serving as manifestos in support of his aggrieved masculinity, written justification for taking his own life along with that of another as well as instructions to others as to how to interpret the meaning of such acts. Writing to his sister, perhaps on the day he killed Josefa and then took his own life, José began: "My dear sister, Don't blame anyone other than THAT woman who, as you already know, tore me from your side— oh—it seems as if it's not possible that this woman should have robbed me of my heart because for me, now, it seems I'll never love another like this." The words here are reminiscent of those Pedro used in his letters to Enriqueta when he described giving up his heart, dead, to her so that she could resuscitate it with her loving caresses. In another letter, Pedro went even further: "Trigueñita," he wrote, using the nickname he had for her, "all my affection, my love and my dreams, I have placed them all in you, the same affection that is born from my heart for you drives me to jealousy even if they [other men] should just even see you." In terms of the rhetoric of the sentimental anatomy, giving one's heart to the other, something that, once done, seemed impossible to reverse, makes of love a kind of metaphorical death with the other responsible for life support, that is, of the sentimental anatomy, at least, if not its living, breathing variant. Past the point of no return, having been persuaded to cede one's heart to the other in what was supposed to be a mutual process of incremental proofs, a novio, so the story went, might find himself unable to love again, that is, to continue living, should the courting relationship end.

Yet such an explanation, offered within the confines of the sentimental anatomy as it has already been established to this point, is not sufficient, something upon which both Pedro and José agreed. Offering additional reasons for their actions, the two men, by so doing, provide evidence attesting not only to their motives but also to the existence of yet another component of the sentimental anatomy, one responsible for pride, reputation, and ego, with which men, granted some more than others, seemed uniquely, perhaps even exclusively, endowed. José continued on in the letter to his sister: "And what's more this young woman has tried to make a fool of me and I've sworn that she'll never make a fool out of anyone ever again." He was equally adamant as to what had motivated him in the letter he wrote to his novia's mother, where he felt compelled to explain to her why he had killed her daughter: "The present letter is written solely with the end of communicating to you that you shouldn't blame me for being a wretch for having taken the life of your daughter, friend, there are friends [amigas] in life who aren't good for anything other than causing the misfortune of others. I loved Josefa a great deal but she tried to scorn me guided by the advice of Rayo. I tried many times to avoid these relations but they were never going to amount to what I was hoping for . . . don't pay any attention to this . . . I'm not explaining anything more to you because I don't have any more time. Your friend."[76]

Pedro was similarly beset by feelings of personal betrayal, of deception in the most intimate of possible terms. Such betrayal and deception, however, no matter how closely it cut to the bone, was never only personal, or, perhaps, it was simultaneously personal and public. "Trigueñita," he wrote to Enriqueta after she had ended their relationship, "what I really urge on you on the life of the one whom you most esteem is that when you love another man don't show him more than what's there as you did with me because I can't find sufficient reason for you to break off with me, for you to say to me that I alone am to blame." Here, Pedro is accusing Enriqueta of not really possessing the feelings that she has been expressing to him all along in her letters, of showing him a love that was "feigned" rather than true, returning again to the axis around which their love letters, as did those of many others, revolved. In his opinion, drinking was nothing other than a pretext she had seized upon to be rid of him. More ominously, he contextualized such deception both within and beyond the realm of the couple, becoming more explicit about what, to him, was really at stake: "What I certainly swear to you," he told her, "on what you most love is that you're not going to belittle me by taking another."

Both men, then, were preoccupied with reputation, with pride, with the fear of being perceived as foolish enough to allow themselves to be deceived by women, whose supposed coquettishness was a staple of all kinds of genres of writing, from the novel to the newspaper to the guide-books you read about in the previous section. The only novia, it seemed, whose fidelity could be counted on was the one with whom I began this discussion of murder and suicide: death herself, the faithful novia. Such a construction of death is so powerfully and avowedly a masculine one—if the only true novia were death, it seems to be suggesting, then all others, by implication, could be characterized by their potential, at the very least, for deception and betrayal. It is possible to go back and reread the love letters, letters written by many of the men, not just those of Pedro and José, through a new lens, that of male preoccupation with betrayal and its impact on reputation. Doing so creates a trajectory or a rhetorical chain, joining such things as accusations of insults; perceived slights and gossip; expressions of fears of deception, betrayal, even treason; demands for the demonstration of trust and the provision of proofs of love and honesty; and the need to swear on the blood of one's mother or on that of the person one held most dear that one's love was true in order to be convincing. The world, so it seemed, was a cold, cruel, and lonely place where all one could expect with any certainly, other than death, was that betrayal and deception were lying in wait. To trust a woman with your love was to expose yourself to grave danger, as if only by means of plumbing the depths of the precipices of potential disaster could a measure of the heights of one's love be taken. In short, daring to love was, it seemed, to court disaster.

If death was the faithful novia, the only one that could be counted upon, perhaps it is also possible to reverse what I have suggested was being implied by this statement: in addition to a commentary juxtaposing the fickleness of all women with the certainly of death, could there not also be an understanding of death as the ultimate means of imposing such fidelity, of ensuring one would not be betrayed? With this perspective, the many references to death in the love letters become revealed as thinly veiled threats rather than as mere figures of speech; they are meant to remind women of the potentially deadly consequences of deceiving men with love that was feigned. Returning to a statement like the one Jesús wrote to Maura, discussed above, "who knows what will become of me and you," which seemed, when first introduced, to be about the vagaries of fate, now appears, when read through this lens, as potentially much more sinister, a possible warning as to what might happen if she failed to go along with his plans, those of abandoning her parental home to be with him. In fact, when Enriqueta failed to grasp what he was getting at with his references to death, Pedro quickly switched from insinuation to being openly threatening: "But in the end what I'm really urging on you is that you should really pay attention to what you are doing because not all us men think the same way and tomorrow or the day after some mishap could befall you but don't be foolish."

Certainly, not all men acted like Pedro and José. Murdering one's novia was exceptional, not standard practice, the stuff of screaming newspaper headlines rather than an everyday occurrence. It might even be argued that the unusual circumstances brought about by the Mexican Revolution between 1910 and 1920, especially as experienced in northern states like Chihuahua, made violence into an accepted means of resolving not only political rivalries and divisions but also personal grievances, including those associated with the end of a courtship. After all, José murdered

Josefa in 1912 while Pedro killed Enriqueta in 1919. Yet as you read in section 2, newspapers like *El Correo de Chihuahua* reported many instances of novios murdering novias and then, at times, killing themselves, not only those that took place in Chihuahua but also similar acts of violence elsewhere in the republic and even elsewhere in the world in the decade before the outbreak of revolution. In fact, such crimes of passion were not only extensively reported; they seemed almost ideally suited to selling papers, capturing, as they did, one of the preoccupations of the times and enabling the creation not only of sensational headlines but also of a certain kind of reader, one formed by their simultaneous proximity to, as well as distance from, such events. In doing so, *El Correo* was very much like newspapers just across the border at precisely the same time; the *El Paso Morning Times*, for example, seized on every instance, not only in the United States but throughout the world, in which an African American or black man was accused of committing a crime, especially one of a sexual nature, against a white woman, transgressing, by so doing, the boundary not only sexual propriety but also that of "race" at the same time.[77]

It does not seem accidental, then, that both José and Pedro chose public venues—parks and park benches—to carry out their final acts, or, in the case of José, that a veritable flurry of correspondence made certain that the murder of a novia and his own death would be understood in a certain way, as a spectacle not only of what might befall a woman who deceived in love but also, perhaps even more centrally, of the performance of a certain kind of masculinity, one that acted at all costs in defense of reputation, pride, and whatever part of the sentimental anatomy was responsible for the sense of self-worth in the eyes of other men. No, not all men acted in this way. Yet, those who did established parameters, at the extreme end of a spectrum, and in so doing determined the ways in which behavior during courtship was to take place and how it would be interpreted. Given the spectacular nature of the murder-suicide, the many references to death in these letters seem as much thinly veiled threats as they are figures of speech. They are meant to remind women of the potentially deadly consequences of deceiving men with love that was supposedly feigned while drenching courtship and its rhetoric in masculine prerogatives of power and entitlement. For both men, killing their novias and then themselves was a public act in defense of a particular conception of a masculine self—by definition, a public demonstration of the consequences of betrayal—a warning to all women and a model to all men.

What with the murders of Enriqueta and Josefa, followed by the suicides of Pedro and José, their murderers; the popular reference to death as the only "faithful novia"; the killing of Lino at the hands of the brother of his former novia; the warnings about the potential of danger from the throes of passion; the multiple appeals to dead mothers; reiterated references to death in love letters like "Yours until the grave"; and the pledge to give one's life to prove one's love, death seems to stalk the body, epistolary and otherwise. As I have tried to argue throughout the section, this is due partly to the kinds of sources that I have had to use to try to give some form to the body of the letter, that is, criminal acts that drew the attention of judicial authorities; partly to an understanding of love that was rooted in a religious tradition in which concepts such as time and the soul were reckoned eternally as well as in days, months, and years; and partly to the discursive resources available to express and give meaning to feelings and sensations, particularly those associated with being in love, and those shaping the performances of certain understandings of gender. Recognizing, indeed, the almost complete absence in this section of those who would undoubtedly go on to live "happily ever after," I am still convinced that it is possible to learn a great deal about the expression of desire and the letter form that was, it seems fair to say, regarded as extremely important to composing and exchanging such feelings. Ultimately, you will need to be the judge of that—don't say that you haven't been warned about how partial the sources are or how tentative conclusions drawn from them might be!

Conclusion

The love letters that comprised the sources for the writing of this section, if brief and at times designed to accomplish certain ends, were, if nothing else, complex and complicated texts.[78] To begin with, the exchange of love letters attests to a certain understanding of the power of the written word and the form of the letter, the echoes of which can still be heard, if faintly and in unexpected places.[79] For many of the correspondents in northern Mexico such letters seemed capable not only of delivering the message of love but also of extending the reach of their composer, who, having touched the letter to write it, found in it the means for transmitting that touch, their feelings, their body to the object of their desire. It was as if letters were their surrogate bodies, enabling those authorizing them by means of signature, touching the page, or writing in their own distinct hand to make, in their absence, promises that could be legally enforced as well as emotional attachments, both of which could at times, as you have seen, be accomplished in the same message.

Central to this process was the bringing into being of what I have been calling the sentimental anatomy—passion, hymens, will, eyes, heart, souls, and the photographic image of the face—organs and emotions that come together to form not only the body of the letter but also the major divisions in this section of the book. Many things can be said about the sentimental anatomy and the ability of the letter to bring it to life. To begin with, a series of metaphors drew affinities or parallels between writing on a page and inscribing into a heart while visuality or seeing was regarded as essential to knowing. In these matters, Enriqueta has been a most eloquent guide. The sentimental anatomy also took form in conjunction with a sense of deepening promise and commitment that can be seen to characterize courtship, a process that I described as an anatomy of sentiment in that it took place over time; involved escalating demands, prendas, or gifts; and culminated in the provision of a "proof of love," all phases that can be identified in this correspondence. In addition, the various organs of the sentimental anatomy and the feelings that went along with them could also be instrumental; that is, they could serve as a means to an end. Suffering and happiness, for example, could be mobilized to convince someone to do what the writer wanted; passion might excuse the daring of initiating a courting correspondence and the desires that went with it; and verifying the woman's virginity was often the goal men sought before agreeing to marriage.

The body of the letter was also composed out of the discursive resources that were at hand and in conjunction with codes or rules that helped determine appropriate topics of discussion for each gender. Souls, for example, already layered in a thick veneer of previous understanding drawn from popular religiosity, could nevertheless be quite voracious in their appetites and corporal in their manifestations, enabling the broaching of the topic of sex without ever uttering that word. Will (voluntad), as well, might be situated within this definitional milieu, given its centrality as one of the attributes of the soul in popular catechisms. Yet will also emerges as a central category of courtship, one that seems to define courtship as a specific and coherent period in the lives of both young men and young women, representing an assertion of not only their choice in a relationship but also their independence from parents. For many, women included, courtship was about self-knowledge and acting on it, even in the face of grave danger and advice, both novelistic and parental, against doing so.

The body of the letter, then, was in many ways a surprisingly egalitarian one, in which love was experienced, at least ideally, as the mutual expression of voluntad, as an escalating series of reciprocal exchanges, for both men and women. This was the case despite the existence of important differences that marked the letters according to gender, especially those concerning the ability to speak directly of desire and a concern with ego or pride, the exclusive preserve of many men. When I introduced the concept of the "ideal couple" it was in an attempt to distinguish between the letter writer and the ways they represented themselves in love letters, that is, as you have seen, as truthful, for example, and not feigned in matters of the heart; however, in addition to regarding the ideal couple as an attempt to meet or match up to preconceived ideals about how lovers were meant to present themselves, women writers often composed their own identities in radically egalitarian fashion. When Refugio demands the same proofs that Rodrigo wanted from her, when she asks to be treated in the same way, when she describes love as acting on mutually expressed will, she sees in her definition of love a concomitant need for more egalitarian gender relations. Likewise, Enriqueta, while positioning herself as truthful in expressing love, manages to find the means even in her highly sentimentalized and metaphorical prose to say "no" and to demand an emotional equal as a partner, not one wracked by insecurity and in need of constant reassurance after excessive bouts of drinking.

Experiencing love or expecting to experience love as the meeting of mutual or reciprocal wills or as a shared sense of reciprocity or equality more generally might also represent the limits of the body of the letter in the most extreme cases, those in which the violent enforcement of masculine prerogatives was enacted upon actual bodies. In these instances, the quality of love letters as sites of negotiation carried out through the mutual construction of epistolary space, one often characterized by the trying out of new roles and more equal selves, yielded to a scenario in which the body itself became the text, the main focus in performances or didactic spectacles designed to instruct both women and men in the real balance of power, one that the reciprocatory and egalitarian body of the letter, especially as written into being by women, threatened to shift.

Postscript

As this book opened in a museum, one newly dedicated to Melchor Ocampo, with his heart assuming a place of prominence there as a biological and metaphorical link between the institution of San Nicolás and the person whose values, beliefs, and actions it honored, perhaps it is only fitting that the book close with a trip to another museum, this time to the Vancouver Art Gallery. I try to make a habit of visiting that institution on a more or less regular basis, although perhaps I should go more often as I always find something that stays with me and makes me think about things in ways I hadn't before. It is an exhibition I attended in 2008 that continues to resonate with and influence my thinking about many things, especially as they concern love letters, the written word, the stories people tell and the ways they do so; the invention and performance of identities; the positioning of the audience or the viewer; and most broadly, the promise and practice of history.

In "Kuba," Kutlug Ataman's prize-winning video installation that was exhibited there, forty people, mostly Kurdish, all members of a marginal community in danger of eradication located near the airport in Istanbul, Turkey, narrate their own extensive stories before the camera, each one filmed then played and replayed on separate old television sets that have been set up for viewing in front of dilapidated armchairs, as if in forty individual living rooms, yet gathered together in one large exhibition space. The museum viewer is thus confronted with a kind of communal cacophony—forty individual heads all talking at once—a white noise that is impossible to take in given that, in total, the narratives stretch to twenty-eight hours of recorded material. While that very impossibility is perhaps the point, it is still possible, nevertheless, to glimpse the community itself coming into being through these stories—both by means of the common themes and disagreements that are being narrated and in the tales of difficulties, hardships, violence, and crime—making, by means of interconnections and the cumulative weight of narration and self-invention, the entire exhibition more than the sum of its forty parts. Originally commissioned as an installation for Artangel in London, where it was shown in 2004, Kuba was exhibited in Vancouver between February and May 2008, in conjunction with Paradise, another video installation created by Ataman in which twenty-four southern Californians create a portrait of their encounter with their own, very different, region.[1]

Just to be clear, the video installation "Kuba" is not about northern Mexico or love letters or writing practices or legal systems or the sentimental anatomy at the turn of the previous century there, the subjects of the present book. In fact, the only connection "Kuba" has to Latin America may be a fanciful one. The name "Kuba" is one that residents of that community themselves have come up with, for reasons that are not quite clear to those being interviewed, some suggesting that it may refer to the country of Cuba, a place associated in the popular imagination with revolution, challenging the status quo, and other possibilities and potentialities, some of them verging on the utopic. As for the installation's political significance, while it may be a cliché to state that the personal is political, here it clearly is, as the work not only records people talking about police torture and official persecution but also features extensive accounts of violence against women, unemployment, and precarious economic conditions, none of these realities deterring the people interviewed for the piece from, concomitantly, articulating or even inventing through their stories a shared sense of belonging to the place that seems to emerge in spite of and out of all the obstacles. Ataman himself suggests that his piece might be seen as a rejoinder to other exhibitions contemporary with it, like "Turks: A Journey of a Thousand Years," showing at the Royal Academy, an exhibit that, by ending at the height of Ottoman power in 1600, celebrates all that went right in the empire without addressing, in the words of one reviewer, what subsequently "went wrong."[2]

Regardless of its distance in time and space from northern Mexico during the Porfiriato and the revolution, Kuba nonetheless offers a means of addressing, in visual, visceral, and aural form, many of the themes and questions with which I have been preoccupied in the present book. In fact, it seems to me that the work could stand as a metaphor for the writing of history more generally, especially the kind concerned with people's everyday lives and their ways of plotting themselves within its structures, exigencies, and delights. The recorded interviews, detailing the dreams, failures, difficulties, realities, hopes, and circumstances of those narrating them, when taken together, comprise an archive, one very much beyond the ability of the museumgoer/historian to do more than eavesdrop on as they move between the monitors, lingering longer here, more briefly there, carrying out, in a sense, their own editing as they slowly and tentatively discern connections and common themes linking and separating some of the various stories, out of which some bigger picture might emerge or be suggested. While each story takes place as if in an individual living room or home, relentlessly personal and individual, the grouping of forty such individual stories in a common area, visible and audible as a din as well as in the form of individual narrations, forces the viewer/listener to realize that there is a larger context that is, at least partially, a creation of these individual narratives and within which each individual narration has taken shape. Moreover, the visible presence of the camera and the use of individual television monitors foregrounds the conventions and expectations of the media itself, revealing how individuals use their stories to create roles for themselves when in front of a camera, while, at the same time, making the viewer aware of their own position as located at the receiving end of such performances. "Kuba," Ataman himself insists, is a history.[3]

It is not too much of a stretch to regard the cases pertaining to rapto and estupro, taken from legal processes located in the judicial archive in Chihuahua, and the love letters that were generated during the course of the courting relationships of a number of specific couples, the main sources utilized in this book, in a manner similar to the way one might regard these narrations in the "Kuba" exhibition. Such sources—the legal cases and letters—are the "talking heads" that tell their stories to a presumed viewer, whether judicial officials, a prospective novio or novia, or—in cases where the writers knew that such letters had the potential to serve as legal evidence under certain circumstances and, indeed, did—both simultaneously. Taken together, these narrations form an archive, a partial one, just as in the exhibition, as the historian/viewer can never read everything and is always making selections (or editing, as Ataman insists), as in the present book, for example, when I choose to focus on or ignore certain kinds of cases or concentrate on one collection of documents rather than on others, at all times overwhelmed by the volume of material that potentially might be consulted for this, as for almost any, project.

Likewise, the conventions and expectations of the media shape the stories and narrations in particular ways, only here in this book, rather than video and television monitors, the judicial system itself acts as a kind of screen—with its particular format for accepting testimony, the transposition of all answers into the third person, the specific requirements for what needed to be proven in particular legal cases and even what might serve as suitable proof—as does the genre of the letter, in which lovers invent or narrate themselves and their desired characteristics (truthfulness in matters of the heart or ability to back up one's word are examples that come to mind) as well as compose an ideal couple in this singular zone of epistolary space. It might even be argued that writing itself forms yet another kind of screen: as a discourse of power, wielded by means of the judicial system and given shape in such things as national literature; as a means of self-invention and imagination; and even perhaps as a weapon of sorts. In short, conventions, whether those associated with writing, the form of the letter, or the judicial system, invoke power. People also perform their own identities in these narratives they craft, whether in love letters or in offering judicial testimony, to achieve specific outcomes and because of varied expectations and understandings.

Accepting that sources like the testimony found in judicial proceedings and the writing found in love letters have been "mediated," in a manner similar to the way in which those narrations captured by Ataman's camera and replayed on television sets were, helps make more apparent the work of the viewer/historian. Instead of entering the archives and retrieving the nuggets of information if not of valuable metal—a metaphor that in no way captures the nature of the task at hand—the mandate of the historian, as I see it and as I believe I have tried to carry out in this book, is instead continually to ask about the nature of the interpretive burden that the sources one chooses to use can be asked to bear and the kinds or categories of conclusions that are in fact possible. Thinking about sources in this way has forced me to reflect on the ways in which the format of such things as providing testimony in judicial proceedings and the conventions and understandings that shape the letter and the written word more generally can influence the kinds of statements being made as well as their manner of expression. The types of questions that emerge, those I have tried to address here, are as much about how to work with evidence as they are about specific practices and behaviors.

If Ataman's installation offers a compelling means of apprehending the epistemological considerations that have helped determine the approach I have taken in the writing of this book, it is the love letter that serves not only as its subject matter but also as the common thread running through it, joining it together, serving as a pretext for the manner of its organization and as the means of moving the narrative along. The logic of the book has had to do, first, with setting out the circumstances through which love letters became available for consultation by the historian, as evidence within judicial procedures, the task of section 1; then, in section 2, with contextualizing or situating love letters within the broader world of writing with which they were contemporaneous, especially as it pertained to the letter form, as well as offering a discussion of the particular literacy event of courtship, one of many possible literacies, its characteristics, and how that form of literacy may have been accomplished; and finally, in section 3, with the metaphorical, symbolic, and performative aspects of love letters as well as with the constitution of a self, an ideal couple, and an epistolary body within the space of the letter. Each of these places or locations—the judicial system, the lettered countryside, and the love letter—generated a particular way of reading text, as evidence, as part of a more ample body of writing circulating in the lettered countryside, and as an expression of emotion as well as a strategy to move hearts and accomplish the formation of couples.

The different venues for contextualizing love letters also became home to a number of bodies, both metaphorical and symbolic, with real and at times fatal consequences for those of the less textual and more flesh-and-blood variety. These bodies seem to gain their substance from the words, symbols, and properties of the letters that wrote them into being then provided symbolic sustenance for their anatomies, sentimental and otherwise. In section 1, the body that emerged was that of the judicial persona, an entity recognized by and entitled to protection from the judicial system, that pillar of the lettered city. This persona was, concurrently, part of an official family, the addressee of much of the liberal legislative and judicial codes; gendered, in that these codes privileged husbands over wives, provided little in the way of actual consequences for novios committing crimes against the supposed good order of families, and sanctioned only those women whose medically demonstrated virginity qualified them for protection; and above all lettered, that is, able to wield the weapon that had brought it into being—writing—in the form of birth certificates, marriage records, and contracts like written promises of marriages, that, as official documents, compose the scrip of the state. Along with introducing the judicial persona, the section revealed how the law was inscribed onto the various bodies appearing before it, classifying and separating them; ordering them according to voices, either in the first or third person corresponding to how they were positioned in the legal process, using categories that authorities, rather than those offering testimony, determined to be relevant; imposing medical exams; and compelling the use of a highly gendered and euphemistic language for expressing what had happened, that is, if the subject could even be broached at all—some could not. Given the lack of penalties actually imposed in processes of rapto and estupro as well as the informal (or perhaps planned) use of the judicial system to buy time to work things out in other, less formal ways, perhaps it is no exaggeration to locate power not in the ability (in these cases, at least) to punish or incarcerate but rather in its didactic capacities, separating, ordering, and identifying bodies according to legal criteria and ranking them in their abilities to wield the scrip of the state.

One body that took shape in section 2 was that of the presumed or ideal reader, an entity that the various forms of writing that increasingly characterized life after the late nineteenth century imagined into being in text. In the novel *Los bandidos de Río Frío*, Payno offers a complex engagement between the oral and the written, with all its characters from the most humble to the most aristocratic learning to read and write, if they did not already know how to do so, able to deflate many of the pretenses of the lettered city even as they saw themselves reflected in and produced by the texts of their times—the judicial expedientes, the novels, the newspapers, the letters, the secret notes, the recipe books, the robbery inventories—that are littered throughout its pages. Newspapers as well, reporting in a sensational manner on crimes of passion and suicide, often accomplishing the illusion of being "at the scene" through the use of correspondents whose submissions came in the form of a kind of a letter and through the inclusion of actual documents like suicide notes and love letters within newspaper columns, evoked shared sentiments as well as a common lens through which to feel them. Newspapers helped bring into being not only an ideal reader joined by sensation and affect but a public that could eavesdrop, even if in print form, on such shocking events throughout the nation. Likewise, letter-writing manuals and other books of manners concerned with epistolary etiquette envisioned a direct relationship between the ideal form of the letter and that of the ideal person that they themselves were attempting to bring about. Collections of love letters aimed at a more popular audience, like those produced by Vanegas Arroyo, composed and thus helped bring about an ideal reader that could be either female or male, one that had already associated herself or himself with respectability and the manners and morals of the developmentalist ethos so prevalent a means of self-definition among the new middling groups at the time. Like novels and newspapers, popular letter-writing collections used highly sensational and emotional mini-dramas to create readers who not only were left wanting more but also shared in the feelings of, and sense of belonging to, an emerging passionate public. While Payno's novel might come closest to representing the letrado dream of universal literacy, of everyone joined by their common reading on the same page as the novel of the nation, it is also the text that has alerted us to the radical equality that the common command of writing, including of love letters, promises: the humble female character's ability to respond to the love letters of her elite suitor is a shorthand that marks her as his equal in every aspect of life.

In section 3, the epistolary body made its appearance, born in the heat of passion and sustained in its sentimental anatomy—composed of heart, eyes, souls, and wills—by the prose of those lovers who created it. The love letter—brought into being by means of a hand on paper, designed to extend a lover's touch as well as manifest what was impressed upon the heart—accomplished many tasks simultaneously: it symbolized a courting relationship, served as a metaphor for its writer, and functioned as performative text that brought about the very thing it composed, not only a relationship but a self and other as well as an ideal couple within it. Convincing as much to its sender as its recipient, the love letter conjured the epistolary body through its words as well as through its properties as a material object, a physical manifestation of an absence that its very presence created. As the properties of writing and the letter form joined to make the body of the letter a surrogate for the body of the absent lover, it was a body formed out of the discursive resources that were readily at hand. Souls, wills, and hearts all seem to be composed out of language drawn as much from the sacred as the profane, as much from the legal as the lay. Moreover, the epistolary body was one that somehow exceeded or transgressed the limits of the page, as the supposed lessons of its demise— feigned love, belittled masculinity, male pride—became inscribed on texts deemed more appropriate to such instruction, living bodies themselves.

Although the judicial persona, the ideal or imagined reader, and the epistolary body were all associated with specific forms of writing and the places of their inscription, the law, the lettered city, and the love letter, they were hardly strangers. These bodies could mesh, blend into each other, exist in multiple registers, and, occasionally, collide violently. This was due in large part to the fact that love letters could serve simultaneously as both written promises of marriage, that is, as evidence in a type of legal case having to do with the written promise to form a contract, that of matrimony, and missives designed to win hearts and form an ideal couple. Love letters contain references to legal terms and promise, at least in the case of one already-married novio, to conjure out of such terminology and the paper used to express it a state of "just-like-being-married." Love letters and the epistolary body were born out of passion, a condition that novelists and other more formal residents of the lettered city found to be potentially dangerous and destabilizing, in need of boundaries and control, a threat not only to the individuals themselves but also to the order and morals of family and even the nation. Moreover, the litany of suicides and crimes of passion in the burgeoning press seemed designed to mold out of a shared sense of horror and fascination with such sensational events an ideal reader formed into a kind of passionate public. Passion could be productive, then, a transfer point of values, feelings, discourses, and controls that linked and moved between love, letters, and the law and the bodies they brought into being.

And so could voluntad (will), a main characteristic of the judicial persona and a critical attribute of the sentimental anatomy. Not everyone, however, was entitled to exercise voluntad. Those under the age of majority, for example, no matter how moved by love, could not, at least according to the legal system, and while their parents or guardians might be granted such agency, that was never guaranteed unless they could do so in writing. Voluntad, then, was something recognizable to judicial authorities only in certain forms and only when it came bearing the passports that provided entrance to the lettered city—those birth certificates, marriage certificates, and written promises around which establishing a legal or judicial persona revolved. Meanwhile, in the struggle between genders and generations over the formation of couples, it was voluntad that was most often at issue—or, at least, a number of behaviors, conflicts, and feelings found in "voluntad" the term most appropriate for their expression. Demanded by lovers as a demonstration of both self-knowledge and an avowed choice to be with the other, seen as the very measure of adult status and independence from parental control, voluntad could be manifested in a number of different ways, some depending on gender. Whereas for women the ultimate demonstration of voluntad might be agreeing to the initiation of sexual relations in exchange for a promise of marriage, for men it might take the form of being recognized as someone who could back up their word and make it count. Voluntad, then, reverberated through the epistolary body, often in highly gendered ways with consequences that could sometimes prove deadly.

In many ways, it was the woman's hymen that served as the measure of voluntad in both judicial and epistolary bodies. Legal codes reflected the belief that the truth of crime or of behavior could be read directly on the body, especially the woman's body, giving medical officials the last word on what, supposedly, had really taken place. Despite the existence of other evidence and even in the face of women's pregnancies and men's admissions, it was the absence of supporting medical evidence that led many prosecutions for estupro to founder. Judicial officials investigating cases of rapto and estupro seemed only slightly less interested in the state of women's hymens than were novios, who found in the taking of virginity the proof they required, both of the woman's character (and thus her suitability for marriage) and of her willingness to take them at their word. The hymen, captured by lovers through the euphemism "prueba de amor," or proof of love, represented the apogee, even if implied, of a series of transactions designed to lead to ever-greater degrees of commitment in courtship in almost all the correspondence in such cases that found its way into the judicial archive. Nor were novelists and other residents of the lettered city unaware of the hymen's potential to elicit emotional reactions from the readers they were bringing into being. Although not discussed in section 2, in *Santa*, perhaps the most famous novel written during the Porfiriato, it is the main character's fall from grace at the beginning of the novel, accomplished when Santa "allows her cloak of innocence to be torn asunder," that ensures her fate in the rest of it.[4]

Yet the meanings of voluntad extended beyond the terms of an equation involving the initiation of sexual relations. Women could and did say "no," at times paying a terrible price to do so. In place of an exchange in which voluntad revolved around sexual relations and written promises, some women, like Refugio and Enriqueta, had come to locate in voluntad the very meaning of romantic love. For these women, love was either true or nothing other than appearance, real or only feigned, characteristics that extended to their use and characterization of the written word as well as to voluntad. For them, if love was an exchange of voluntad, it was meant to be a reciprocal or mutual exchange; when it came to love, the relationship was to be one between equals. Despite all the obstacles in her ability to attain it, Refugio demanded equality from Rodrigo and a radical reciprocity in the provision of any proofs of love, as long as honor was not offended. Enriqueta, as well, drew a line beyond which she was not prepared to cross, demanding an emotional equal as a partner and setting limits on his behavior. Her prose, sentimental as it may be, still provides her with the tools to construct herself as her own person, to envision the ideal couple in surprisingly egalitarian terms, and to conceptualize love as the mutual and reciprocal expression of voluntad in which it is possible to be truthful and sincere in matters of the heart and still say "no."

If writing gave a certain epistolary power to women, much of it came from the form or properties of the letter. Although the close association between letter writing and love has diminished, usurped, early on, by the immediacy of the telephone and perhaps recovered somewhat more recently in a changed form with the arrival of Facebook and text messaging, letter writing continues to be a privileged location for the composition and expression of affect. A recent study of small rural communities in the northern state of Zacatecas with a history of migration to the United States, for example, found that between 1981 and 1991 a total population of some 375 families generated an enormous amount of text, ranging from two thousand to four thousand letters per month, with women being "privileged users of written language in this social practice."[5] Like the communities studied in this book, those in more contemporary Zacatecas evinced a strong tradition of writing and reading, although not necessarily of the texts of the lettered city. In Zacatecas as in Chihuahua, as well as on the lettered mountain (the term Frank Salomon and Mercedes Niño-Murcia use to refer to Tupicocha, the highland Andean community in Huarochirí province, discussed in this book's introduction), the spread of writing to people like Liberato and the others suitors and their correspondents that people the pages of this book may have occurred outside the bounds of formal schooling and have been accomplished on a group, rather than an individual, basis.[6]

Thinking about the efficacy of letters in facilitating the composition and exchange of affect long after the time period considered in this book introduces the vexing question of change over time, the presumed métier of the historian. In this, I suppose I have proven a dismal failure (perhaps I'll be turned out of the guild!). Certainly, it seems appropriate to ponder the impact, if any, of the violent years of revolution, the writing of the Mexican Constitution of 1917, revolutionary state formation more generally, and the informal changes that generally accompany such periods of ferment on love, courtship, and the written word, some of the main topics that have been taken up in these pages. It is clearly the case, for example, that the bloodshed and violence that took place between 1910 and 1917 was also inflicted upon women and that the abduction of women and sexual violence took place under the auspices of most if not all revolutionary factions. Although the incomplete nature of the archive attests to the difficulties in continuing the operation of judicial institutions during some of the period of revolutionary violence, hints are nevertheless available that, at the very least, running away to join the revolution provided at least some, including twenty-five-year-old blacksmith Jesús H. in 1912, with both a pretext for abducting and initiating sexual relations with a young woman and a means of avoiding the wrath of fathers and judicial officials that followed.[7] As for the 1920s, given the rather consistent manner in which lovers told their stories to judicial officials and the similarity in the contents of love letters that were located dating to that decade to those records and letters found before the revolution, perhaps the change that most stands out is the first use of an automobile to carry out rapto, in this case of two female friends.[8] Again, their narratives indicate that many of the same dynamics continued to be at work in such scenarios: the use of abduction to force the hands of reluctant parents, lack of women's options, and fear of violence, both from their abductors, should they refuse to leave, and, should they return home, at the hands of male family members, who blamed them and held them responsible for these actions.

Perhaps it should not be surprising that changes in love and courtship came to the lettered countryside only after the period covered in this study. After all, a recent study of courtship in Mexican transnational families dates such change, at least in the case of two rural communities, to the most recent generation, the result of such things as the growth in the influence of mass media, education, and increased migration. According to Jennifer Hirsch, whereas women courting in the 1950s and 1960s narrated their experience of courtship in terms very reminiscent to the cases presented here, the subsequent generation of women regarded marriage as more companionate, the result of mutual affection rather than obligation, and courtship itself as more of a period in which to develop romantic ties with a potential partner than a rush to accomplish the fait accompli of a respectable marriage. Of course, the timing of such a shift to a more companionate view of marriage might be different depending on location, circumstances, and class.[9] Any history of love and courtship over the long term, then, would have to take into account the fact that while many changes were brought about by revolution, many lovers continued to narrate such intimate aspects of their lives in terms that did not seem so revolutionary at all. It would also have to take into account the fact that, in their letter writing, women of a far earlier generation than that studied by Hirsch envisioned love as more of a reciprocal or mutual exchange, at least when it came to voluntad, an essential component of it.

As for letter writing, the timing of any changes in the use and composition of letters is even more elusive to pin down. The relative paucity of such documents—mentioned in 24 of the 77 cases involving courtship and yielding some one hundred letters in all if to this number are added those love letters contained in cases of murder-suicide of courting couples from over a nearly sixty-year period dating from 1872 to 1929—makes it difficult to identify and track any changes that may be taking place. The identities and characteristics of those writing this smattering of letters, if they have indeed been written by those sending them, are difficult to know except in the most general of terms, like "worker" and "laborer," or in the case of women, through phrases like "concerned with household duties." As a result, any finer-grained conclusions concerning class or forms of masculinities and femininities seem destined to be spurious or unsupportable given the sources at hand. The periodization of this book, you will recall—a study that focuses on contextualizing the love letter within the judicial system at the local level, within a broader range of writing concerned with the letter form, and within the epistolary space lovers brought into being—has resulted from the demands in judicial processes concerned with rapto and estupro that, to be enforceable, promises of marriage be given in written form, a requirement that ended with the new penal codes that came into effect in 1929 and 1931.

What can be said about the love letters consulted for this book is that there was a great range and variety in the writing, messages, and forms that fell into that general category. Some letters, as you have seen, were written more like legally enforceable contracts or promises to marry; others combined pledges of love with formal legal commitments; others are closer to the spoken word and concerned with the mundane tasks of getting by; while still others seem far removed from the mundane realm and more at home in the specialized register of excessive sentimentalism and metaphorical prose. All seemed designed to accomplish certain ends: to make a contract, to incite or draw out commitment to the relationship, to up the ante as courtship progressed, to spell out the exchanges that were being proposed, to bring into being the very feelings that were being composed, to extend the body of the absent lover, to signify as much by their physical presence as by means of the messages they carried, to provide a space for the invention of self and ideal couple. Their great range in form and function helps point out that, when it came to love and the formation of couples, such unions could be framed, wholly or in various combinations, as an economic arrangement in which the man agreed to the provision of a diario in exchange for the woman's carrying out of domestic duties; as legal or quasi-legal entities (as in the case of Liberato); as premised upon the proving of certain attributes of femininity and masculinity considered as essential prerequisites to such unions; as an expression of gratitude for the provision of care and domestic services; as growing out of passion that could not be repressed; or as the mutual expression of reciprocal voluntad. Love itself was thus shaped by the contractual nature of the courting relationship, by the sacral charge that many of the attributes of the sentimental anatomy (heart, eyes, will, and soul) brought with them, by understandings of masculinities and femininities, by senses of mundane and ethereal time, and, at times, in utopic terms as an expression of equality and reciprocity. That some women died for these ideals attests to how far-reaching and revolutionary such understandings were thought to be.

The potential impact of such a construction of love seems enormous, perhaps even revolutionary. What might it mean, for example, if the relationship between husband and wife—the unit upon which the official family was premised and the order and inequities of which were protected in penal and other codes in such sections as "Crimes against the order of families, public morality or good customs"—was conceptualized as one of equals? How might such a reciprocal and mutual exchange of wills be reconciled with documents like the Law of Civil Matrimony, especially the epistle penned by Melchor Ocampo, a discussion of which began this book, in which men and women, rather than being considered equals, were divided on the basis of the perceived need for the strong to provide for the weak as well as by their supposedly natural attributes, which included strength and courage in the former and self-denial, beauty, compassion, shrewdness, and tenderness in the latter? Although I am not sure that Rama had women in mind when he was thinking about how newly emerging social groups over the course of the nineteenth and twentieth centuries attempted to storm the walls of the lettered city, perhaps his observation that positions of social power could only be assailed on the "two-dimensional battlefield of line and space," that is, through writing, is still as pertinent in the case of women as it is in those of the individuals he discusses.[10] In fact, Rama's metaphor of the page as battlefield seems particularly apt, given that the terrain of love was one strewn with casualties. Given women's limited opportunities to gain access to the lettered city, love letters may have represented a privileged, almost unique space, one in which to construct self, other, and couple; one in which women might compose their own "Kuba," as residents of the marginal community in Istanbul did, from which to challenge the world they inherited from Melchor Ocampo; a space from which they might imagine other worlds into being.

NOTES

Note: All court cases cited from the Archivo Judicial in Parral, Chihuahua (hereafter referred to as AJ), for which no box (caja) number is given were loose (that is, not in any box). Names have been replaced by initials in all cases cited from the Archivo Judicial.

INTRODUCTION

1. Rama, *Lettered City*, first published as *La ciudad letrada* (1984). For a discussion of the lettered city in the period after Mexican Independence, including the epoch in which Ocampo lived and its focus on the drafting of new laws and constitutions as well as on the establishment of educational systems, see pp. 41–49.
2. Ruiz, *Bosquejo biográfico*, 46. A number of websites are dedicated to Ocampo's heart and the institution that houses it.
3. Tuck, "Melchor Ocampo (1814–1861)."
4. In March 2006, Congress passed a resolution asking judges to eliminate the reading of the epistle from the marriage ceremony; see Dellios, "Women's rights activists hail end of Mexican marriage epistle," *Chicago Tribune*, 21 May 2006, consulted 17 August 2013, http://newsgroups.derkeiler.com/Archive/Soc/soc.men/2006-05/msg02167.html. See also "Entérate: ¿Cuál es la epístola de Melchor Ocampo?" *El Universal*, 7 March 2013, consulted 17 August 2013, http://www.eluniversal.com.mx/notas/908664.html.
5. Ruiz identifies the name of his estate as "Pomoca," an anagram of his name. See *Bosquejo biográfico*, 19.
6. Rama, *Lettered City*, 63–64. Rappaport and Cummins offer a slightly different critique. Arguing for the need to move beyond Rama's exclusive focus on "República de los Españoles" and letrados in their discussion of literacies in the colonial Andes, they conclude: "The lettered city transcends the strictly European, erudite, and alphabetic bounds placed on it by Rama" (Rappaport and Cummins, *Beyond the Lettered City*, 122). See chapter 3, "The Indigenous Lettered City."

7. Rama, *Lettered City*, 65; the quotation is from p. 63; the definition of "lettered city" is from p. 29.

8. Rama, *Lettered City*, 67.

9. Ong, *Orality and Literacy*, 78. On the "chirographic mentality," see p. 172. According to Ong, writing made possible "increasingly articulate introspectivity" (105), was a major factor in the development of personal privacy (130), and also led to a different conceptualization of "history" itself; in fact, it was responsible for "creating" history (172).

10. Ahearn, *Invitations to Love*, 47–48.

11. For an author concerned with an "event-centered" approach to literacy or "literacy events," see Besnier, *Literacy, Emotion and Authority*.

12. Salomon and Niño-Murcia, *Lettered Mountain*. The authors go even further than this, maintaining that, in some ways, "post-1532 Andean society constituted itself through writing" (287). They characterize their stance toward Rama as one of "loyal opposition," arguing that Rama omits to contextualize the building of the lettered city within an already "knotted countryside," that is, within an "Andean world already richly supplied with systems of inscription" (289).

13. A recognized peasant community is defined as a "self-governing corporation endowed with control of 'immemorial' communal titles to land and water" whose chief duty is to administer the intricate system of canals, terraces, and walled pastures still critical to its subsistence (Salomon and Niño-Murcia, *Lettered Mountain*, 21).

14. Salomon and Niño-Murcia, *Lettered Mountain*, 293.

15. Breckenridge, "Reasons for Writing," 145, 152. See also Breckenridge, "Love Letters and Amanuenses," 337–48. One of his main arguments in the article published in 2000 Breckenridge summarizes as follows: "Working class South Africans have constructed private lives, and individual selves, out of an unusual combination of literary affect and collaborative authorship (and reading)" (338).

16. Barber, "Introduction," in *Africa's Hidden Histories*, 3, 4.

17. Thomas, "Schoolgirl Pregnancies, Letter-Writing, and 'Modern' Persons in Late Colonial East Africa," 191.

18. In a book that has just been published, Lyons shows that such was also the case in western Europe, where, between 1860 and the 1920s, a "democratisation" of writing "took a quantum leap forward." Lyons's interest is in the "scribal culture of ordinary people," and the book explores the significance of writing for peasants, workers, and the illiterate; see Lyons, *Writing Culture*. Quotations are from pp. 3, 8, 18.

19. For a detailed study of Distrito Hidalgo in the state of Chihuahua at this time that focuses on the broader economic setting, patterns, and meanings of work as well as the struggle over the inculcation of a developmentalist ethic among this floating population, see French, *Peaceful and Working People*.

20. Kalman, *Discovering Literacy*, 48.

21. Barber, "Introduction," in Barber (ed.), *Africa's Hidden Histories*, 3, 4.
22. Giddens, *Transformation of Intimacy*, 2, 58.
23. Giddens, *Transformation of Intimacy*, 40. For Giddens on romantic love and the imagining of a mutual narrative biography and the future, see pp. 44–45.
24. "Introduction" in Padilla, Hirsch, Muñoz-Laboy, Sember, and Parker (eds.), *Love and Globalization*, xviii.
25. Hirsch, "'Love Makes a Family,'" 94. Hirsch's debt to Giddens is most clear when she states, "Marriage was a system for organizing social reproduction, not a project for personal satisfaction" (94). See also Hirsch, *Courtship after Marriage*, discussed further in this book's postscript.
26. Many of the contributors to *Cuidado con el corazón* also insist on the importance of studying the norms of romantic morality in specific regional and temporal contexts; see Blanco (ed.), *Cuidado con el corazón*.

1. THE LETTER OF THE LAW

1. Exhorto del Juez Menor de Balleza para aprehender á Jesús L.Y. procesado por el delito de rapto, 25 de mayo 1901, AJ.
2. Criminal contra Indalesio P. por rapto, Valle de Olivas, 6 de abril 1894, AJ, caja 1894V.
3. This phrase, of course, refers to the title of Davis's influential book in which she focuses on the narratives murderers constructed in their attempts to receive pardons from the monarch; see Davis, *Fiction in the Archives*. Alonso is also interested in how to approach the problem of "voice" in legal cases; see Alonso, "Love, Sex and Gossip."
4. Martínez de Castro, *Exposición de motivos del Código Penal*, 1.
5. Martínez de Castro, *Exposición de motivos del Código Penal*, 54.
6. The 1871 Penal Code was formally known as the Código penal para el Distrito Federal y territorio de la Baja California sobre delitos del fuero común y para toda la República sobre delitos contra la federación.
7. Código penal del estado libre y soberano de Chihuahua.
8. Código de procedimientos penales del estado libre y soberano de Chihuahua. Codes of criminal proceedings were also adopted at the national level in 1880 and 1894; for a discussion of these, see Speckman Guerra, *Crimen y castigo*, 30.
9. See the discussion in Clagett and Valderrama, *Revised Guide to the Law and Legal Literature of Mexico*, 175–78.
10. Lopez de Garay, "El delito de estupro," 43. See also the discussion in Martínez Roaro, *Delitos sexuales incluye delitos contra la correcta formación del menor, la libertad sexual y la moral social en lo sexual*, 212–17.
11. "*Derechos de familia*" (rights of family) are set out in Art. 775, Cap. 1, Título Sexto, "Delitos contra el órden de las familias, la moral pública, ó las buenas costumbres,"

in Código penal para el Distrito Federal y Territorio de la Baja California, sobre delitos del fuero común, y para toda la República, sobre delitos contra la Federación, 215.

12. Capítulo V, Rapto, Título VI, Delitos contra el órden de las familias, la moral pública, ó las buenas costumbres, Código Penal para el Distrito Federal y Territorio de la Baja California, sobre delitos del fuero común, y para toda la República, sobre delitos contra la Federación, 1872, 222–23.

13. Capítulo V, Rapto, Título VI, Delitos contra el orden de las familias, la moral pública, ó las buenas costumbres, Código penal del estado libre y soberano de Chihuahua, 182–84.

14. Speckman Guerra discusses the assumptions and thinking of Mexican lawmakers concerned with the drafting of nineteenth-century Mexican penal codes, including those that led to the identification of rapto and estupro as crimes that offended individuals more than society; see Speckman Guerra, *Crimen y castigo*, 31–33.

15. Capítulo III, Atentados contra el pudor, Estupro, Violación, Código Penal para el Distrito Federal, 218–21.

16. Capítulo III, Atentados al pudor, Estupro, Violación, Código Penal del estado libre y soberano de Chihuahua, 178–81.

17. By 1931, no mention of a written promise can be found and estupro had become listed as a "sexual crime"; see Capítulo I, Atentados al pudor, estupro y violación, Título Decimoquinto, Delitos sexuales, Código Penal para el Distrito y Territorios Federales de 13 de agosto de 1931, 63–64.

18. See notes 14 and 15 for page references.

19. Arrom, *Women of Mexico City, 1790–1857*, 64.

20. Martínez de Castro, *Exposición de motivos del Código Penal*, 54.

21. Speckman Guerra, *Crimen y castigo*, 43–45.

22. García Peña, *El fracaso del amor*, 31, 47–48, 55–57, 68–70, 105–6.

23. Alonso, *Thread of Blood*, 121. Vaughan also uses this term; see her "Modernizing Patriarchy."

24. For a discussion of the pragmática, see Socolow, "Acceptable Partners."

25. McCaa, "Marriageways in Mexico and Spain, 1500–1900," 20–21, 29.

26. McCaa, see note 105. For a discussion of the 1870 and 1884 Civil Codes, see Arrom, "Changes in Mexican Family Law in the Nineteenth Century."

27. In the case of the 1884 Civil Code, see "Título Quinto. Del Matrimonio. Capítulo Primero: De los requisitos necesarios para contraer matrimonio," Código Civil del Distrito Federal y Territorio de la Baja California, 1884, 329–30.

28. For a definition of "esponsales" in Spanish ("sponsales" in Latin), see Pérez Duarte y N., "Esponsales," 97. See as well the discussion of promise of marriage in Lavrin, *Sexuality and Marriage*, 4–7. For the case of Spain, see Dyer, "Seduction by Promise of Marriage": "The notion that an exchange of vows made either in private or

before lay witnesses constituted marriage persisted in some parts of Spain into the nineteenth century" (444). For a pioneering discussion of the treatment of rapto and estupro under the law, see Castañeda García, *Violación, estupro y sexualidad*.

29. Criminal contra Cruz C. por estupro, 1896, A J.

30. McCaa, "Marriageways in Mexico and Spain," 12.

31. McCaa, "Marriageways in Mexico and Spain," 30–31.

32. Criminal contra Florentino A., acusado por delito de estupro, Parral, 1891, A J.

33. Delito de rapto, Parral, 2 July 1925, A J, caja 1925J.

34. Averiguación por el delito de rapto en contra del Teofilo T., 27 de Julio de 1910, Santa Bárbara, A J. Although civil divorce was possible in Mexico after 1859, it only involved the "separation of bodies" with no possibility of remarriage. Full divorce with the possibility of remarriage became law in 1914; see García Peña, *El fracaso del amor*, 71.

35. Criminal contra Antonio M. por rapto, Parral, 7 March 1886, A J.

36. The young woman testifying was María, the novia of Liberato, whom you will read more about in section 2: Criminal contra Liberato M. por rapto y contra José J. por complicidad en dicho delito, September 26, 1894, Huejotitan, A J.

37. This is the total number of cases encountered. Not all cases had to do with courting couples, and in other cases information is incomplete. Out of the total of 97 cases having to do with rapto, estupro, and violación, 15 deal with matters not in any way related to courtship, including the sexual assault of children (aged four, five, ten, eleven, and fourteen), at times resulting in charges of violación and at others of estupro; sexual assaults by unknown men (4 cases); 1 case in which a father is accused of sexually abusing his daughter; 1 case involving the abduction of a wife; and 1 case involving control of the labor of a young woman rather than a courting relationship. I set aside these cases for the purposes of analyzing courtship as well as cases where information is simply not available, and as a result totals will vary in the discussion that follows.

38. Marcial V., al Jefe Político del Distrito Hidalgo, 1 March 1907, A J, caja 1907Ll.

39. On the composition of the labor force in Hidalgo District, see French, *Peaceful and Working People*, 35–44.

40. See the testimony of Ysmael M., an operario (mine worker) in Criminal contra Ysmael M., acusado por delito de estupro, Parral, 1891, A J.

41. Although the total number of cases in which a complainant can be identified is 70, the number of young women in these 70 cases totals seventy-four, as four pairs of sisters are involved (as in the case of the Martínez sisters).

42. Caulfield, *In Defense of Honor*, 131.

43. Both were bakers; see Averiguación con motivo de la querella presentada por el Sr. Margarito G., acusando de rapto y violación á los acusados Dolores H. y Epigmenio M., Parral, 5 December 1910, A J.

44. Criminal contra Celestino G. por el delito de estupro, 1 de septiembre de 1894, Parral, AJ.

45. Criminal promovida por Doña Casimira A. contra D. Ysauro A. por delito de estupro, principió de 22 de octubre de 1888, AJ, and Criminal contra José María Z., por estupro, Año 1893, Parral, el 30 de abril de 1893, AJ.

46. Averiguación por el delito de rapto en contra del Teofilo T., 27 de julio de 1910, Santa Bárbara, AJ; Averiguación con motivo de la querella presentada por el Sr. Margarito G., acusando de rapto y violación á los acusados Dolores H. y Epigmenio M., Parral, 5 de diciembre de 1910, AJ; Criminal contra Jesús B. por rapto, Villa Escobedo, 5 de febrero de 1912, AJ.

47. Criminal contra Francisco S. por rapto. Año 1896, AJ.

48. Criminal contra Celestino G. por el delito de estupro, 1 de septiembre de 1894, Parral, AJ.

49. Criminal contra Remedios V., por rapto. Año 1888, AJ. Here, the father states, "Que se ha perpetrado contra mi honor y fama." For another example of a man who regarded his honor as the main victim, see Criminal contra Manuel H., por rapto, Parral, 17 de febrero de 1891, AJ: "Y haciendo las pesquizas que a mi honor ultrajado correspondían" ("and carry out investigations appropriate to my insulted honor").

50. Doña Eugenia G., viuda de G. ál Juez 1 de Letras de este Distrito Judicial, Hidalgo del Parral, 18 de noviembre de 1884, AJ, states: "Y mi honor infamamente ultrajado."

51. Criminal contra Marcos G. por el delito de rapto, San Antonio del Tule, 8 de febrero de 1908, AJ.

52. Sumaria instruida contra José María y Julio B. por rapto, 1882, AJ.

53. Criminal contra José María Z., por estupro, Año 1893, Parral, 30 de abril de 1893, AJ.

54. Of the 8 cases in the judicial archive listed only as violación, 3 seem to have involved a courting relationship. The ages of the women in these three cases are given as fourteen, twelve, and eleven. Out of the total of 32 cases listed solely as estupro and the 8 of rapto and estupro, some 10 (or one-fourth of the total) do not seem to have been carried out within the context of a courting relationship. The total number of couples in courting relationships, as far as I can determine, is 77, although information such as ages is not available in all cases.

55. Of the 5 cases in the archives listed as both violación and estupro, 3 could possibly refer to courtships. There are specific statements in the judicial record in a number of these cases and in others listed only as violación that the wrong procedure had been initiated.

56. Twelve cases feature some age confusion concerning the young woman; in an additional 3 cases, the woman stated that she was not sure of her age; and in the

1 case of rapto in which a wife left her husband of forty-seven, the woman stated she did not know her age.

57. See Criminal en contra de José C. por el delito de violación. Iniciación marzo 3 de 1926, A J.

58. See the discussion in García Peña, *El fracaso del amor*, concerning the three types of divorce available in Mexico from the colonial period to the present: *eclesiástico por separación de cuerpos* up to 1859; *civil por separación de cuerpos* from 1859 to 1914; and *civil vincular o total* after 1914, p. 71. Because in the type of divorce in effect from 1859 to 1914 remarriage was not possible, five of the six men in the cases from 1882, 1888, 1894, 1905, and 1910 would not have been able legally to remarry.

59. Averiguación con motivo de la querella presentada por el Sr. Margarito G, acusando de rapto y violación á los acusados Dolores H. y Epigmenio M, Parral, 5 de diciembre de 1910, A J.

60. Of the men whose place of origin can be identified, the majority are from communities within Hidalgo District, Chihuahua; at least sixteen are from outside the state, including six from Durango, four from Jalisco, two from Nuevo León, and one each from Zacatecas, Aguascalientes, Querétaro, and San Luis Potosí. For a further discussion of occupational categories, the relationship between agricultural labor and wage labor in the mine, and the existence of a floating population during the Porfiriato and revolution in Chihuahua, see French, *Peaceful and Working People*, chapter 1, "Ways of Working."

61. In the language of the judicial proceeding, "usó de su persona" (used her person) and "hizo uso de dicha persona" (he made use of said person).

62. Delito de rapto, Parral, 20 de julio de 1925, A J, caja 1925J. Women often use the phrase "*prestarse*" to refer to "lending" or "offering" their bodies to men, as in "prestarse para que usara de su persona, se casaba con la declarante" ("offering herself so that he could make use of her person, she got married to the deponente"), in Criminal contra Remedios V., por rapto, Año 1888, A J.

63. Criminal contra Remedios V., por rapto. Año 1888, A J. Many young women framed their actions as the understandable result of such insistence and promises, in such statements as "below this same promise he abused my virginity" and "muchas insinuaciones y coerción moral" ("many insinuations and moral coercion").

64. Criminal contra José S. por el delito de estupro. Querella necesaria promovida por la Señora Refugio R., viuda de A., Parral, 11 de marzo de 1925, A J. In a case of estupro thirty-five years earlier, another woman made the same point: "Habiendo tenido distintos actos carnales, por que a cada uno de ellos hacía prender la misma promesa" ("having had several carnal acts, each time he made me the same promise"). In Criminal contra Zeferino A. por estupro, 1890, Parral, 17 de abril de 1890, A J.

65. See Criminal contra Francisco S., por rapto, año 1896, A J.

66. His statement to judicial officials reads, "Of course I used her person, that's why I conquered her" (Que como es natural hizo use de dicha persona, pues que con ese objeto la había conquistado). In Criminal por rapto. Acusado Margarito B., Parral, 2 de agosto de 1911, AJ.

67. Criminal contra Leonardo P. por estupro en la persona de María Francisca E., año 1888, AJ. In another case, a man explained the need "to try her out in order to know what her condition was" (por tantearla para saber de que carácter era); see Criminal contra Marcos G. por el delito de rapto, San Antonio del Tule, 8 de febrero de 1908, AJ.

68. Querella presentada por Feliciana E. en contra de Joaquín S., 12 de abril de 1924, Parral, AJ. Feliciana described to judicial officials the consequences of her seduction or deception in medical terms, explaining that it had caused such a "commotion in my nervous system that it produced a madness, that I have been able to recover from, thanks to the medical attention imparted by Doctor R." (Viéndome burlada de tal manera sufrí una conmoción en mi sistema nervioso que me produjo una locura.). Although this is speculation on my part, such medically verifiable symptoms of the consequences of her deception seem to provide Feliciana with another kind of proof, that of her own decencia despite her having acceded to sexual intercourse.

69. It seems reasonable to conclude that obtaining proof of the woman's virginity was a predominant concern in at least 27 of the cases of couples in a courting relationship.

70. These labels are complicated in that while most refer to a woman's sexual reputation, some, like "mujer libre," may imply independence from the control of parents or guardians. In this case, the claim is being made by the man being charged with these crimes that he did not realize that a formal "accuser" or "initiator" (as required by law) even existed. Men could also refer to their relationships with such women as "relaciones ilícitas."

71. A number of cases mention the existence of a witness to a verbal promise of marriage; see Criminal contra Cruz C. por estupro, año 1896, AJ. (In this case the witness's statement has even been entered into the judicial record.) Another mentions that the marriage promise had been made before the jefe político; see Criminal contra José Urbina por el delito de rapto, Año de 1903, AJ.

72. One woman states explicitly, for example, that the reason she refused to leave her abductor's side when the authorities arrived was that she believed that being apart from him would make him less likely to fulfill the verbal promise of marriage he had given her; see Criminal contra Estéban R. por estupro cometido en la joven Aurelia M., Año de 1885, AJ.

73. Women often used the terms "with her full consent" (con su pleno consentimiento) and "all her will" (toda su voluntad) or, less often, "voluntarily" (voluntariamente) and "she consented" (consintió) to describe their degree of volition, which was usually linked to a promise of marriage or maintenance. Men used very similar

phrases, including "with her will" (*con su voluntad*), but often modified "will" or "consent" with adjectives like "spontaneous," "entire," or "all" as a means of stressing women's free choice, often without any broader context of promises.

74. Averiguación criminal en contra de Jesús H., por rapto y estupro, Parral, 30 de octubre de 1912, AJ.

75. In fact, novio and novia, both twenty-one, saw abduction as the only way to overcome the opposition of the woman's mother who, despite the will (voluntad) of her daughter, had refused to grant permission for marriage to take place; see Criminal contra Lucas T. y Andrés S. por rapto. Año del 1882, AJ.

76. Peones reported, "Si no se la daban para casarse él se la sacaría afuera, que tenía personas de quien valerse." (If they didn't give her to him to marry, he would take her away, that he had people he could turn to.") Criminal contra Rafael M. por rapto de la joven María Rosa B., Año de 1885. Hidalgo del Parral, AJ.

77. For a discussion of the effectiveness of elopement in another context, see Martínez-Alier, "Elopement and Seduction in Nineteenth-Century Cuba."

78. "Yo como madre y aunque hechos pedazos mi corazon por la conducta de mi ingrata hija, no puedo menos que enviarle un: Dios te vendiga." M.A.V. de Q., Hidalgo del Parral á Juez de Primera Instancia de lo Penal, 19 de mayo de 1918, AJ.

79. Criminal contra Angel P. por esturpo, Valle de Zaragoza, Año de 1891, AJ. Others also mention that the complaint itself only served to make more public the dishonor of the woman; see for example the statement of the twenty-year-old woman in Criminal contra Gregorio V., por rapto, Año 1885, AJ: "Y esta queja que ha dado lugar á la averiguación, es un grave mal para ella por que será mas pública su deshonra" ("and the complaint that has given rise to this investigation, has seriously wronged her because it will make her dishonor more public"). See also Criminal contra Leonardo P. por estupro en la persona de María Francisca E., Año 1888, AJ.

80. Exhorto del Juez Menor de Balleza para aprehender á Jesús L.Y. procesado por el delito de rapto, 25 de mayo de 1901, AJ.

81. Criminal contra Eleno G. por rapto, Parral, 23 de marzo de 1893, AJ. For another case that hinged on the refusal of a mother to give permission for her eighteen-year-old son to marry, see Criminal contra Marcos G. por el delito de rapto, San Antonio del Tule, 8 de febrero de 1908, AJ.

82. See the mediating role of the man's father in Criminal en contra de Filiberto Q. por el delito de rapto de que se querelló el señor Felipe M., 11 de noviembre de 1926, AJ. See also the mediation of the abductor's father in Averiguación criminal en contra de Jesús B. por rapto de la Señorita Pomposa T., Parral, 19 de septiembre de 1913, AJ.

83. Criminal contra Merced F. por el delito de rapto perpetrado en la joven Beatriz T., Villa Escobedo, 11 de julio de 1905, AJ.

84. Querella interpuesta por la señora Marcelina Arrieta Viuda en contra de Pedro P. y su amasia Juana P. por el delito de rapto, Parral, 6 de mayo de 1918, AJ.

85. In one such case, a young woman states that the constant "disgustos" that she has with her father over a woman who isn't his wife motivated her to leave home; see Criminal contra Leonardo P. por estupro en la persona de María Francisca E., Año 1888, AJ. In another case, in response to a question from judicial authorities, one young woman, also experiencing difficult treatment at home because of her courting relationship, stated that she did not know whether or not she was free (libre); see Criminal por rapto cometido con la joven María Tomasa J. por German P. la noche del día 15 del corriente en la Municipalidad de Minas Nuevas, Año de 1884, AJ.

86. Upon being accused of rapto, one man used the terms "libre," "mujer libre," "libremente" repeatedly in his brief statement to judicial authorities to refer to the young woman, by which he meant to describe her as free from parental control (*libre por su estado*); see Criminal contra Miguel A., por estupro, 1890, Valle de Zaragosa, AJ.

87. Young women also described themselves as "mujeres libres," which to them not only seemed to indicate a claim to freedom from parental control but also signified the occurrence of sexual relations prior to their current relationship. One stated that she was not a virgin, having had sexual relations with one man previously, and the other that she had lost her virginity five years earlier (at the age of fifteen) and that she had been in "carnal acts" with several people. In the second case, the statement about the loss of virginity was offered as further evidence of parental neglect and inability to provide for the family; the young woman seemed to be making the case that parental knowledge of, acquiescence in, or failure to control her sexual activities freed her from the usual power parents could be expected to exercise, making her, in effect, a "free woman." See Criminal contra Antonio M. por rapto, Parral, 7 de marzo de 1886 and Criminal contra Gregorio V., por rapto, Año 1885, AJ.

88. Sumaria instruida contra José María y Julio B. por rapto, 1882, AJ.

89. Querella interpuesta por la señora Marcelina Arrieta Viuda de Q. en contra de Pedro P. y su amasia Juana P. por el delito de rapto, Parral, 6 de mayo de 1918, AJ.

90. Criminal contra Miguel A., por estupro, 1890, Valle de Zaragosa, AJ.

91. Criminal contra Gabino Ch. Por rapto de la joven Candelaria S., 1885, Juzgado Rural de San Antonio de Corralejo, AJ.

92. Criminal contra Rafael M. por rapto de la joven María Rosa B., Año de 1885, AJ. Also see the statements of a seventeen-year-old woman who, in the face of violence and the threat of violence from her family after she returned home after leaving with her suitor, found it necessary to leave with him once again, in Criminal contra José Urbina por el delito de rapto, Año de 1903, AJ.

93. Criminal contra Jesús B. por rapto, Villa Escobedo, 5 de febrero de 1912, AJ.

94. Querella interpuesta por el Sr. Encarnación O. contra el sub-teniente Lázaro M. por el delito de rapto, iniciación enero 3 de 1918. In this case, the threat of a medical examination precipitated the rapto, that is, the abandonment of the parental home by the young woman to live in a relationship of amasiato with a *sub-teniente* (second lieutenant) from Jalisco.

95. Jesús D. y Enrique G., por los delitos de rapto y estupro, Hidalgo del Parral, 18 de febrero de 1926. The men were freed on a legal technicality: the family members initiating the complaint did not legally document their relationship to the young women.

96. Rama, *Lettered City*, 58.

97. In this instance, the initial judgment against the man, resulting in a sentence of four years at public works and a 250 peso fine, was overturned for this reason alone; see Criminal contra Indalesio P. por rapto, Valle de Olivos, 6 de abril de 1894, AJ.

98. As stated in one judgment, "That the complainant not having proven her civil status as mother of the young woman; this defect will be sufficient to suspend the proceeding in agreement with Article 130 of the Code of Criminal Procedures." See Criminal contra Felipe B. R. por rapto y estupro, 19 de septiembre de 1905, Santa Bárbara, AJ.

99. "Deflowered" (*desflorada*) is the language used in medical reports. See Criminal en contra de José C. por el delito de violación, iniciación 3 March 1926, AJ; Ejecutoria contra Roque B. . . . por estupro . . . tercera sala . . . August 1901, AJ; and Criminal contra Felix M. por estupro, Año de 1890, Hidalgo del Parral, AJ.

100. Criminal contra Celestino G. por el delito de estupro, 1 Sept. 1894, Parral, AJ.

101. Criminal contra Marcos G. por el delito de rapto, San Antonio del Tule, 8 February 1908, AJ.

102. Criminal en contra de José C. por el delito de violación. Iniciación 3 March 1926, AJ. On injury as a sign of rape, see also Ejecutoria contra Federico Ch., por el delito de violación, 17 August 1898, AJ.

103. Overturned at the Segunda Sala del Supremo Tribunal de Justicia, Chihuahua; see Criminal contra Indalesio P. por rapto, Valle de Olivos, 6 abril 1894, AJ.

104. The term *"delito privado"* is used by one of the complainants making a statement of desisting; see Sumaria instruida contra José María y Julio B. por rapto, 1882, AJ.

105. The following statements of desisting mention an "arrangement" (*un arreglo/un arreglo privado*): Contra Joaquín H. por los delitos de estupro y violación perpetrados en la persona de la Señorita María S., Parral, 20 marzo 1923, AJ; Criminal contra Merced F. por el delito de rapto perpetrado en la joven Beatriz T., Villa Escobedo, 11 julio 1905, AJ (in which the arrangement is a dowry); and Criminal contra Zeferino A. por estupro, 1890. Parral, 17 de abril de 1890, AJ.

106. Criminal contra Cruz C. por estupro, año 1896, AJ.

107. Statement by Doña Cacimira A., complainant, in Criminal promovida por Doña Casimira A. contra D. Ysauro A. por delito de estupro, principió el 22 de octubre 1888, AJ. Here, ending the proceeding was seen to be in the best interest of the honor of her daughter.

108. Statement by Francisco M: "Por no serle conveniente ver envuelta en un proceso á su expresada hija." In Criminal contra Lucas T. y Andrés S. por rapto, año del 1882, AJ. See also the statement by Higinio M.: "Deasando que esto no se haga mas público se desiste." ("Desiring that this not be made more public he desists.") In Criminal contra Liberato M. por rapto y contra José J. por complicidad en dicho delito. Septiembre 26 de 1894. Huejotitlan, AJ.

109. Criminal contra Manuel H., por rapto, Parral, 17 de febrero de 1891, AJ.

110. Statements like these and others highlight the project of self-construction and self-presentation taking place in the venue of the court; such posturing in statements of desisting, as in those found in the original statements of complaint, could also be contested by daughters who, at times, stripped away parental pretensions to reveal the abdication of parental responsibilities. See the letter by Jovita A. to the Sr. Jues (sic) Letrada in Sumaria instruida contra José María y Julio B. por rapto, 1882, AJ.

111. Statement by Fernando A., in Sumaria instruida contra José María y Julio B. por rapto, 1882, AJ.

112. Criminal contra José R. R. acusado por delito de rapto, Minas Nuevas, 26 de octubre de 1897, AJ. Here the negotiating taking place was between two men probably of the same age, given that the abductor was forty-eight.

113. Criminal contra Joaquín P. por el delito de rapto, octubre de 1894, AJ. For a similar instance in which a parent, this time a mother, specifically states that it is the will (voluntad) of her daughter to marry her abductor, see the statement of desisting by Soledad F. in Averiguación criminal en contra de Jesús H., por rapto y estupro, Parral, 30 de octubre de 1912, AJ.

114. Criminal contra Francisco S., por rapto. Año 1896. The woman returns to the concept of "voluntad" or will a number of times in her statement and uses the term "estimación," translated here as "regard."

115. Contra Joaquín H. por los delitos de estupro y violación perpetrados en la persona de la Señorita María S., Parral, 20 marzo 1923, AJ.

116. Criminal contra Zeferino A. por estupro, 1890, Parral, 17 de abril de 1890, AJ.

117. On the dowry during the colonial period, see Seed, "Marriage Promises," 267–68.

118. Criminal contra Merced F. por el delito de rapto perpetrado en la joven Beatriz T., Villa Escobedo, 11 julio 1905, AJ. For another case in which one hundred pesos is mentioned as the size of the dowry, see Marcial Velez to jefe político, 1 March 1907, Archivo Municipal, caja 1907Ll and P. Alvidres, Juez Suplente de Zaragoza, to jefe político, 11 March 1907, Archivo Municipal, caja 1907Ll.

119. Contra Joaquín H. por los delitos de estupro y violación perpetrados en la persona de la Señorita María S., Parral, 20 March 1923, AJ.

120. One young woman specifically mentions the threat of having her face scarred should she not leave with her abductor; see Criminal contra Agripino H., por estupro, Parral, Año 1891, AJ.

2. THE LETTERED COUNTRYSIDE

1. Criminal contra Liberato M. por rapto y contra José J. por complicidad en dicho delito, 26 September 1894, Huejotitan, Chihuahua, AJ.

2. Before 1914, the ecclesiastical and secular forms of divorce that existed did not permit the dissolution of the marriage; see García Peña, *El fracaso del amor*. See p. 71 for a discussion of the changes to understandings of divorce over time.

3. Twinam, "Honor, Sexuality and Illegitimacy," 135.

4. See French, *Peaceful and Working People*.

5. See Rama, *Lettered City*, on the relationship between the city of letters and the newly independent states in Latin America, pp. 40–49.

6. Among other things, Carlos Monsiváis sees the lettered city in Mexico during the Porfiriato as small, focused on Paris, self-delusional, and serving to "spice up" the dictatorship as the price for its very existence; see Monsiváis, "Del saber compartido en la ciudad indiferente."

7. See the discussion of coplas at the end of this section.

8. Rama, *Lettered City*, 66–67.

9. Ong, *Orality and Literacy*, 78.

10. On the "event-centered" approach to literacy or "literacy events," see Besnier, *Literacy, Emotion and Authority*. See also Barton, Hamilton, and Ivanic (eds.), *Situated Literacies*.

11. Ahearn, *Invitations to Love*.

12. Ahearn spends considerable time setting out her understanding of the key concepts with which she works; for a discussion of "literacy," see pp. 46–48.

13. Criminal contra Ysmael M., acusado por delito de estupro, Parral, Año 1891, AJ.

14. Criminal contra José Ysidro C. por el delito de estupro, Parral, 11 de abril de 1903, AJ.

15. Averiguación por el delito de rapto en contra del Teofilo T., 27 de Julio de 1910, Santa Bárbara, AJ.

16. Payno, *Los bandidos de Río Frío*. The novel is now available in English; see Payno, *Bandits from Río Frío*.

17. My discussion of the novel first appeared in French, "'Cartas y cartas, compadre . . .'"

18. As are you—for a recent study of this institution, please see Arrom, *Containing the Poor*.

19. Payno, *Bandits from Río Frío*, 246.

20. On "foundational fictions," the work of Doris Sommer has been, well, foundational; see Sommer, *Foundational Fictions*.
21. Payno, *Bandits from Río Frío*, 240; the immediately preceding quotation is from pp. 148–49.
22. When I was discussing the literary genre of costumbrismo with him, Miguel Angel Avilés Galán, a student completing his doctorate in Mexican history at the University of British Columbia, remembered that his grandmother had read *Los bandidos* to him when he was a child of five or six years of age (conversation with author, 22 May 2009, Vancouver). In 1995, Carlos Monsiváis quoted long passages from the novel in his address to the Canadian Association of Latin American Studies, held in Vancouver, in order to make apparent the close links between the prose and the rhythms, cadences and expressions of the Spanish spoken at the time.
23. Payno, *Los bandidos de Río Frío*, 240–42.
24. Payno, *Los bandidos de Río Frío*, 242.
25. Payno, *Los bandidos de Río Frío*, 243. On middle-class discourse, see French, "Prostitutes and Guardian Angels."
26. *Los bandidos de Río Frío*, 244–45.
27. Collapsing the distinction between state and criminal organization, Juan Pablo Dabove argues that it is precisely "order and progress" and modern bureaucratic organization that the bandit state run by Relumbrón in *Los bandidos* bring to Porfirian Mexico. Dabove thus reads the novel as a critique of Porfirian modernity as well as of the presuppositions that underpinned the Mexican nation-state in the making. See his chapter entitled "Los bandidos de Río Frío: Banditry, the Criminal State, and the Critique of Porfirian Illusions" in Dabove, *Nightmares of the Lettered City*. Although readers will have to decide for themselves whether or not this is the case, it is not that much of a stretch to compare Relumbrón's manipulation of the technology of the written word to the ways that contemporary businesses nowadays hope to harness social networking sites to target their advertising in a highly specialized and directed manner.
28. For this and other reasons, Evelia Trejo and Alvaro Matute have referred to the novel as a "parahistoria." They are cited in Staples, "*Los Bandidos de Río Frío* como fuente primaria," 352n8.
29. "La tragedia del Hotel Palacio," *El Correo de Chihuahua*, 25 January 1906; "A última hora: Muerte de la señora Reig," *El Correo de Chihuahua*, 26 January 1906.
30. "La tragedia del Hotel Palacio," *El Correo de Chihuahua*, 31 January 1906; "El Hospital 'Porfirio Díaz,'" *El Correo de Chihuahua*, 24 March 1906.
31. "Horrible crimen en la Habana," one of the stories in the column México al Día, *El Correo de Chihuahua*, 23 July 1906; "Terrible drama en Puebla," in México al Día, *El Correo de Chihuahua*, 26 Nov. 1906; "Suicidio de Beatriz Franco," in México al Día, *El Correo de Chihuahua*, 25 June 1906; "Suicidio en un hotel," in México al

Día, *El Correo de Chihuahua*, 23 June 1906; "Suicidio de un joven," *El Correo de Chihuahua*, 18 Dec. 1906; and others.

32. Much of this discussion was prompted by the arguments put forward by Anderson in *Imagined Communities*; it is Anderson who stresses the centrality of print-capitalism to imagining the nation and his phrase that describes newspapers as "one-day best sellers"; see p. 35. Anderson's work, especially his arguments concerning the timing of the emergence of such national imaginings in Latin America, has been much debated; see especially Lomnitz, "Nationalism as a Practical System," and Unzueta, "Scenes of Reading."

33. "El Hospital 'Porfirio Díaz,'" *El Correo de Chihuahua*, 31 March 1906, 1:1 M F 9636 reel 1.

34. "Horrible crimen en C. Camargo," *El Correo de Chihuahua*, 16 May 1906.

35. "Horrible crimen en C. Camargo," *El Correo de Chihuahua*, 16 May 1906; and "El Crimen de C. Camargo," *El Correo de Chihuahua*, 18 May 1906.

36. "La tragedia de Chihuahua" in México al Día, *El Correo de Chihuahua*, 24 January 1906. The quotation reads: "Por todas partes no se oye otra conversación que del sangriento drama Algara-Reig." ("Everywhere no other conversation is heard other than the bloody Algara-Reig drama.")

37. "Tragedia horrible por celos," *El Correo de Chihuahua*, 16 February 1909.

38. "El crimen de Santa María," *El Correo de Chihuahua*, 18 February 1909.

39. "Mañana daremos detalles," the quote reads, in "A última hora: Muerte de la señora Reig," *El Correo de Chihuahua*, 26 Jan. 1906; "Seguiremos informando de todo lo nuevo que haya en este asunto" is the quotation from "La tragedia del Hotel Palacio," *El Correo de Chihuahua*, 31 Jan. 1906.

40. "El Sensacional Jurado de Enrique Villaseñor," *El Correo de Chihuahua*, 23 September 1909.

41. "¡Una ola más de sangre!" *El Correo de Chihuahua*, 26 February 1910, 1:3–4.

42. The entire letter is from "Sensación que causa. Una carta del suicida," *El Correo de Chihuahua*, 25 Sept. 1906, 4:1–2, and reads as follows:

A mi muy estimado amigo Sr. José Enríquez:
Estas líneas, querido amigo, te las dirijo para que cumplas con un deber que por derecho te corresponde por mostrarme durante el tiempo que nos conocimos, un afecto sincero.

A tí te dejo como dueño único de mis instrumentos, el clarinete y la viola, y el auto-harp es para tu Chiquita, para que si la Providencia te la conserva, tenga un recuerdo de un amigo tuyo que cuando vivía en el mundo se acordó de ella el último día de su vida y en recompensa de todo esto ó por un deber humanitario pásale á mi mamá un diario mientras vienen mis hermanos de los Estados Unidos.

Yo me voy para la otra vida y en mis brazos llevo á mi Ser Idolatrado. Hasme los honores de la sepultura y consuela á mi pobre mamá.

Sin más tu amigo que te desea felicidad durante el resto de tu vida. Pedro J. Grajeda.

43. "Se nos denuncia a un criminal," *El Correo de Chihuahua*, 19 March 1910.

44. "La Nota Roja: Los matadores de mujeres," *El Correo de Chihuahua*, 25 Sept. 1909. On moral reform discourse and vice, see French, *Peaceful and Working People*, chapter 3, "Moralizing the Masses," 63–86.

45. Alberto del Castillo Troncoso dates the emergence of the modern press in Mexico to the 1890s; see his "El surgimiento de la prensa moderna en México," in *República de las Letras*, 105–18.

46. For a pioneering work on the subject of the creation of a consumer culture in Porfirian Mexico, including the role of cigarette companies in the creation of modern advertising, see Bunker, *Creating Mexican Consumer Culture*.

47. "El Buen Tono, S.A." advertisement in *El Correo de Chihuahua*, 8 June 1906, 3.

48. "El Buen Tono, S.A." advertisement in *El Correo de Chihuahua*, 3 Jan 1909, 3.

49. "El Buen Tono, S.A." advertisement in *El Correo de Chihuahua*, 22 Aug. 1908, 3.

50. In *Authors of Their Lives*, Gerber warns those working with personal correspondence against joining the "cult of authenticity," that is, against assuming that letters "speak for themselves" and that they give us unmediated access to the "authentic consciousness" of those writing them; see his discussion on pp. 32–55.

51. Guadalupe's letter can be found in Criminal contra Felipe B.R. por rapto y estupro, 19 de septiembre de 1905, Santa Bárbara, AJ.

52. The end of the statement initiating the process reads, "Firmado por mi citada hija . . . por no saberlo hacer la subscrita" (signed by my above-mentioned daughter . . . as the undersigned does not know how to do so). In Criminal contra Felipe B. R. por rapto y estupro, 19 de septiembre de 1905, Santa Bárbara, AJ.

53. Criminal contra Marcos G. por el delito de rapto, San Antonio del Tule, 8 febrero 1908, AJ.

54. Breckenridge, "Reasons for Writing," 143.

55. Breckenridge, "Reasons for Writing," 151–52. See also Breckenridge, "Love Letters and Amanuenses."

56. I have discussed school attendance in Hidalgo District during the Porfiriato elsewhere; see French, *Peaceful and Working People*, 51–55, 91–97, 136–37. Between 1902 and 1906, for example, the jefe político Rodolfo Valles reported that the average number of students reported to be attending school in Parral grew from 526 to 1,480.

57. As quoted in the periodical *La Nueva Era*, 18 August 1901, as quoted in French, *Peaceful and Working People*, 136. For the quote on the substitution of education for unrest, see *El Correo de Chihuahua*, 1 March 1907, as quoted in French, *Peaceful and Working People*, 136.

58. Querella interpuesta por la señora Marcelina Arrieta Viuda de Quiñones en contra de Pedro P. y su amasia Juana P. por el delito de rapto, Parral, 6 de mayo de 1918,

AJ. Other cases in which young women serve as maids and kitchen helpers do not specify the wages obtained.

59. Criminal promovida por Doña Casimira A. contra D. Ysauro A. por delito de estupro, Principio el 22 de octubre, 1888, No. 16, fs. 22, AJ.

60. Criminal en contra de Joaquín H. por los delitos de violación y estupro, 3 de marzo de 1925, AJ.

61. See for example Criminal contra Estéban R. por estupro cometido en la joven Aurelia M., Año de 1885, AJ.

62. Criminal contra Celestino G. por el delito de estupro, septiembre 1 de 1894, Parral, AJ. This case was briefly discussed in section 1 as well. All quotations from letters and testimony regarding this case are contained in this expediente.

63. Many of the other heads of households in the cases discussed in this section describe themselves as widows or widowers.

64. All the testimony as well as the letters exchanged between Felipe and Guadalupe are located in Criminal contra Felipe B. R. por rapto y estupro, 19 Sept. 1905, Santa Bárbara, AJ.

65. All correspondence between Pedro and Enriqueta located in Averiguación: con motivo a la muerte trágica de Pedro V. y la joven Enriqueta B., 25 Feb. 1919, AJ.

66. Monsiváis, *El género epistolar*; see especially the section entitled "Puedo escribir los versos más tristes esta noche," pp. 31–41.

67. Monsiváis, *El género epistolar*, 40.

68. Monsiváis, *El género epistolar*, 26.

69. Criminal contra José María Z., por estupro, Parral, 30 de abril de 1893. The letter in Spanish reads: "Apreciable Señorita, Desde el momento mismo en que el cielo divino se digno darme licencia para conocer a Ud. se despertó en mi corazon ese sentimiento sublime e inexplicable que se llama amor y no siendo me posible presindir me tomo la libertad de aserle a Ud. esta declaración y solo espero que bondadosamente acetara mi solicitud por que la amo y sera muy grato para mí ser correspondido de Ud. y queda en espera de su contestación el que solo desea ser feliz a su lado, Quien Ud. Sabe."

70. *Compendio del manual de urbanidad y buenas maneras.*

71. The discussion of epistolary correspondence occurs in chapter 6 of part 2, "Urbanidad," in the manual. See *Compendio del manual de urbanidad y buenas maneras*, 84–87. A number of the subsections deal with "inferiors" addressing social "superiors"; the dangers of presuming links of *amistad* (friendship) where none might exist; and how the quality of writing paper should reflect the degree of consideration and respect that was owing to the person being addressed in the letter.

72. Monsiváis, *El género epistolar*, 34.

73. *Cartas amorosas y felicitaciones.* Other booklets I have subsequently purchased in Mexico City include *El consejero de los enamorados*; *Declaraciones amorosas*; and *Como enamorar a las mujeres.*
74. Speckman Guerra, *Temblando de felicidad me despido*, 69–73.
75. Letter is reproduced in Speckman Guerra, *Temblando*, 22. Quotation reads as follows: "Y sin embargo no está en mis fuerzas dominar la pasión que me consume y he resuelto decir a Ud. que la adoro ciegamente."
76. See "Primer Carta de Declaración de Amor" and the response in *Cartas amorosas, colección no. 1, Ultima edición.* Vanegas Arroyo material consulted in Mexican Chapbook Collection, Center for Southwest Research, University Libraries, University of New Mexico, Albuquerque, New Mexico (hereafter referred to as MCC).
77. *Cartas amorosas, colección no. 1*, MCC.
78. *Cartas amorosas, colección no. 1*, MCC.
79. *Cartas amorosas, colección no. 1*, MCC.
80. "Caprichos de la mujer" in *Cartas amorosas, colección no. 1*, MCC.
81. Quotes are from *Cartas amorosas*, collections no. 1 and 5, MCC.
82. Speckman Guerra makes the same observation; see *Temblando*, p. 10.
83. *Cartas amorosas, colección no. 1*, MCC.
84. *Cartas amorosas, colección no. 5*, MCC.
85. *Cartas amorosas, colección no. 5*, MCC.
86. *Cartas amorosas, colección no. 5*, MCC.
87. "Utiles consejos a las mujeres para hacerse amar," *Cartas amorosas, colección no. 5*, MCC.
88. Behar, "Sexual Witchcraft."
89. "Utiles Consejos a las Mujeres Para Hacerse Amar," *Cartas amorosas, colección no. 5*, MCC.
90. *Cartas amorosas, colección no. 5*, MCC.
91. Copla 3237 in Frenk (compiler), *Cancionero folklórico de México*, Tomo 2, 66.
92. I develop this discussion of coplas much more fully in French, "'I'm Going to Write You a Letter.'"
93. The five volumes were published between 1975 and 1985 and contain more than 10,000 coplas from all over Mexico; they are entitled as follows: Tomo 1, *Coplas del amor feliz*; Tomo 2, *Coplas del amor desdichado y otras coplas de amor*; Tomo 3, *Coplas que no son de amor*; Tomo 4, *Coplas varias y varias canciones*; Tomo 5, *Antología, glosario, y índices.*
94. Monsiváis, *El género epistolar*, 37.
95. Copla 1082, *Cancionero*, Tomo 1, 138.
96. Copla 3142a, *Cancionero*, Tomo 2, 52.
97. Copla 1005, *Cancionero*, Tomo 1, 129. Accompanying notes reveal that a version replaces the first line with the following line: "No te pongo la firma" (I'm not signing this).

98. Copla is from Frenk Alatorre, *Cancionero*, Tomo 1, copla 2277, 301.

3. THE BODY OF THE LETTER

1. See the discussion of the catechism of Padre Ripalda and other similar texts in Monsiváis, "La tradición de la memoria religiosa"; excerpt about writing is from p. 130.

2. A number of authors have remarked on the similar claims made by letters and gifts; see, for one recent example, Broomhall and Van Gent, "Corresponding Affections," 147. Other authors refer to the informal rules of reciprocity that characterized correspondence; see, for example, Lyons, "Love Letters and Writing Practices," 235. Still others have captured this sense of reciprocity by referring to the ways an exchange of correspondence forms an "epistolary pact"; see, for example, Foley, "'Your Letter is Divine, Irresistible, Infernally Seductive,'" 248, 263. A number of years ago Roger Chartier concluded that every letter has as its main topic the pact that binds correspondents; see Chartier, "Introduction," 19. Roland Barthes describes this pact or call formed by correspondence as follows: "Like desire, the love letter waits for an answer; it implicitly enjoins the other to reply" (Barthes, *A Lover's Discourse*, 158).

3. Carlos Monsiváis suggests that the poetic language of love letters enabled the couple to distance themselves from the everyday to become, in his term, the "classic couple"; see Monsiváis, *El género epistolar*, 34–35.

4. Zorrillo, *Don Juan Tenorio*.

5. Refugio's letters are located in AJ, Hidalgo del Parral, 1905.

6. The letter from Lino M. is located in Criminal instruida con motivo del delito de homicidio, San Francisco del Oro, 4 Oct. 1925, AJ.

7. The letters of Pedro and Enriqueta are found in Averiguación: con motivo a la muerte trágica de Pedro V. y la joven Enriqueta B., 25 Feb. 1919, AJ.

8. Letter found in Criminal contra José María Z., por estupro, Año 1893, Parral, 30 April 1893, AJ.

9. Given that the letter is not authorized with a formal signature but ends only with "you know whom," readers might object that it should not be considered a forgery at all, that it is more an exercise in creating confusion by the group of women who saw in its composition a means of avoiding the legal consequences of selling the sexual favors of a young woman.

10. Felipe and Guadalupe's letters are found in Criminal contra Felipe B. R. por rapto y estupro, 19 September 1905, Santa Bárbara, AJ; Lino's are in Criminal instruida con motivo del delito de homicidio, San Francisco del Oro, 4 October 1925, AJ, caja 1925L.

11. Averiguación: con motivo a la muerte trágica de Pedro V. y la joven Enriqueta B., 25 Feb. 1919, AJ.

12. Contemporary versions of the song do not seem to include the verses concerning passion; see, for example, that recorded by Pedro Vargas, "Pedro Vargas (Un Viejo

Amor)," YouTube video, 4:26, posted by "MemasMusic45," August 13, 2008, http://www.youtube.com/watch?v=6ZR3raOrpXQ .

13. Criminal contra Liberato M. por rapto y contra José J por complicidad en dicho delito, Sept. 26, 1894, Huejotitan, AJ.

14. Averiguación: con motivo a la muerte trágica de Pedro V y la joven Enriqueta B., 25 February 1919, AJ.

15. Altamirano, *El Zarco*. See the prologue by Carlos Monsiváis for details concerning the original publication date of the novel, p. 11.

16. Altamirano, *El Zarco*, 42.

17. Altamirano, *El Zarco*, 59.

18. Altamirano, *El Zarco*, 129.

19. Criminal contra Marcos G. por el delito de rapto, San Antonio del Tule, 8 February 1908, AJ.

20. Letters from Eleno to Tula located in Criminal contra Eleno G., por rapto, Parral, 23 March 1893, AJ.

21. Letters from Jesús to Maura located in Averiguación con motivo de querella presentada por Maximian M. por rapto y estupro en contra del acusado Jesús P., Parral, 28 May 1909, AJ.

22. Criminal contra Remedios V., por rapto, Year 1888, AJ.

23. Letters from Felipe to Guadalupe located in Criminal contra Felipe B.R. por rapto y estupro, 19 September 1905, Santa Bárbara, AJ.

24. Averiguación: con motivo a la muerte trágica de Pedro V. y la joven Enriqueta B., 25 February 1919, AJ.

25. Querella presentada por Feliciana E. en contra de Joaquín S, 12 April 1924, Parral, AJ.

26. Carta de Ysidro C a Maria A L M in Criminal contra José María Z., por estupro, Parral, 30 April 1893, AJ. (This, of course, is the forged love letter written by women.)

27. Criminal contra Ysmael M., acusado por delito de estupro, Parral, 1891, AJ.

28. Criminal contra Eleno G., por rapto, 23 March 1893, AJ.

29. Flores, *El hímen*, 28.

30. Flores, *El hímen*. See pp. 97–99 for his conclusions.

31. All Eleno's letters are located in Criminal contra Eleno G., por rapto, Parral, 23 March 1893, AJ. Just in case readers still remain unconvinced by the examples provided in the text, here is one more request from Eleno: "Once you've given me the proof of Love I've asked you for I can give you what you need within the time period that I've set so that we can be happy, the two of us."

32. Criminal contra Ysmael M., acusado por delito de estupro, Parral, Año 1891, AJ. Students in my classes who have been asked to read this message are unanimous in refusing to accept it as pertaining to the category of "love letter."

33. Criminal contra José Ysidro C. por el delito de estupro, Parral, 11 April 1903, AJ.

34. *Criminal instruida con motivo de las lesions que le fueron inferidas al señor Rodolfo L. por unos individuos desconocidos*, Parral, 18 Nov. 1925, AJ, caja 1925L. The back of the pink sheet reads, "In answer to your kind note I say to you that I accept your visit with much pleasure, asking you not to let it be known you can come at 7 in the afternoon to my house it's a time when my husband isn't at home."

35. *Querella presentada por Feliciana E. en contra de Joaquín S.*, 12 April 1924, Parral, AJ.

36. For an example set in the state of Chihuahua, see Heriberto Frías's novel/testimonio/fictionalized history *The Battle of Tomochic*. Here Frías narrates the events of the military campaign against Tomochic in 1892 partly through the lens of the relationship between two of the characters, Miguel Mercado, a member of the Mexican military who served in the expedition, and Julia, a young woman from Tomochic. Although hardly a typical courtship, the relationship enables a discussion of love, passion, literacy, duty, faith, honor, virginity, and family across a number of divides while presenting a fictionalized account of the exchange of the initiation of sexual relations for a promise of marriage as well as a critique of the Díaz regime. The novel was first published anonymously and in installments in the newspaper *El Demócrata* in 1893. For a reading of this novel through the lens of the "romance nacional," see Dabove, "'Tomochic' de Heriberto Frías," 351–73.

   Of course the most famous novel treating the theme of the consequences of women yielding to desire during the Porfiriato was Federico Gamboa's *Santa: A Novel of Mexico City*, first published in 1903 and recently translated into English by John Charles Chasteen; see chapter 2 especially. Interestingly, the dichotomy between "true" and "feigned" love in the novel echoes the way love is framed in many of the love letters.

37. See the earlier discussion of the "epistolary pact," in note 3 of this section.

38. Refugio's letters in AJ, Hidalgo del Parral, 1905.

39. The reference to El Paso stands out; at the time, a floating population moved along the rail lines between northern Mexico and the southern United States looking for work. Women must have been part of this stream. Her familial or other connections in El Paso are not specified in any of her correspondence.

40. Another *novia*, Enriqueta, discussed in greater detail in the next part of this section, also uses *voluntad* in precisely the same way: "Excuse your Enriqueta who must have driven you to despair without answering your dear letter but you should take into account that it is not for lack of will [*voluntad*] well you see now that all this time I have been sick and it has been impossible for me [to answer]."

41. The editors of a recent collection of articles on love in twentieth-century Africa, mostly after 1930, make a related point, stating (as one of the three main arguments that come out of the volume) that "although women in Africa have often embraced romantic love as a strategy for establishing more egalitarian gender relations, it is a

strategy that has met with uneven success." See Thomas and Cole, "Introduction," 13.

42. Criminal contra Remedios V., por rapto.1888, AJ.

43. Averiguación con motivo de querella presentada por Maximian M. por rapto y estupro en contra del Acusado Jesús P., Parral, 28 May 1909, AJ.

44. Criminal contra José E., acusado del delito de estupro, Santa Bárbara, 9 March 1912, AJ.

45. Criminal contra Marcos G. por el delito de rapto, San Antonio del Tule, 8 February 1908, AJ.

46. Averiguación con motivo de querella presentada por Maximian M. por rapto y estupro en contra del Acusado Jesús P., Parral, 28 May 1909, AJ.

47. Averiguación con motivo de querella presentada por Maximian M. por rapto y estupro en contra del Acusado Jesús P., Parral, 28 May 1909, AJ.

48. Criminal contra Eleno G., por rapto, Parral, 23 March 1893, AJ.

49. Averiguación con motivo de querella presentada por Maximian M. por rapto y estupro en contra del Acusado Jesús P., Parral, 28 May 1909, AJ.

50. Criminal contra Remedios V., por rapto, Año 1888, AJ.

51. Alan Knight proposed this term many years ago; the struggle over the imposition of such an ethic is explored in French, *Peaceful and Working People*.

52. The original letter reads thusly:

> P   Pasión veemente abraza el alma mía
> E   En este corazón vive enserrada
> D   Divinos ojos de mi prenda amada
> R   Retira de mi alma esta agonía
> O   Orgullosa de amarte enamorado
>
> V   Vibrar yo siento candenciosa voz
> I   Iluminando mi existir sombrio
> LL Llamame, tuya; unidos ya los dos
> A   Acabara en mi alma esta agonía

53. All the letters exchanged by Enriqueta and Pedro are found in Averiguación: con motivo a la muerte trágica de Pedro V. y la joven Enriqueta B., 25 February 1919, AJ.

54. Paper presented at the Facultad de Derecho y Ciencias Sociales, Universidad Autónoma 'Benito Juárez' de Oaxaca, Oaxaca, México, July 2010.

55. Monsiváis, *El género epistolar*, 32.

56. James Collins and Richard K. Blot juxtapose the "magic" of writing with the "reason" of writing, that is, the symbolic properties of writing and the written form with the meaning of the words on the page; see Collins and Blot, *Literacy and Literacies*,

21. Others have stressed the "materiality" of letters; see, for example, Schneider, *Culture of Epistolarity*, especially chapter 3, "Affecting Correspondences: Body, Behavior, and the Textualization of Emotion," p. 124. Susan Foley, cited above in note 2 of this section, among others, calls the letter a "fetish" ("'Your Letter is Divine,'" 253).

57. Criminal en contra de Joaquín H. por los delitos de violación y estupro, 3 March 1925, AJ.

58. Eleno's letters are found in Criminal contra Eleno G. por rapto, Parral, 23 March 1893, AJ.

59. Letters are located in Averiguación criminal en contra de Jesús H., por rapto y estupro, Parral, 30 October 1912, AJ.

60. Esther Gabara argues that the circulation of photographic images had much to do with the assumption that visuality—"seeing" is her term—was essential to knowing; as she puts it, "photographs captured the circulation of products, objects and people that contributed to the development of an epistemology that related seeing with knowing and represented the subjects of modernity marked by race and gender" (Gabara, *Errant Modernism*, 2).

61. I spent approximately one month in 2007 working in the Fototeca Romualdo García, part of the Museo Regional de Guanajuato, located (at that time) in the basement of the Alhóndiga in the city of Guanajuato. Thousands of glass plates containing images, mostly taken between 1905 and 1914 by Romualdo García, can be found there. All levels of society seem represented, including a large number of workers, all of whom shared the backdrops and props that characterized a portrait photography studio of the Porfiriato. Many of his photos have been published; see, for example, García, Poniatowska, and Canales, *Romualdo García*; they are also available online. Many thanks to Flaviano Chávez, director, for making it possible for me to consult the Romualdo García images there.

62. Averiguación por el delito de rapto en contra de Teofilo T., 27 July 1910, Santa Bárbara, AJ.

63. Criminal contra Liberato M. por rapto y contra José J. por complicidad en dicho delito. 26 September 1894. Huejotitan, AJ.

64. Gallardo, Luciano J. Diaries recollecting courtship of Carlota Gil: Guadalajara, San Luis Potosí, etc. 1864, 1869. Bancroft Library: BANC, MSS M-B 13, box 1; microfilm version consulted. Discussion of the "soul" of Carlota's mother runs through the first volume.

65. See chapter 17, "La agonía," or "Death Throes," in *El Zarco*, 130–33.

66. Criminal contra Ysmael M., acusado por delito de estupro, Parral, Año 1891, AJ.

67. Querella presentada por Feliciana E. en contra de Joaquín S., 12 April 1924, Parral, AJ. Eleno's letters to Tula are located in Criminal contra Eleno G., por rapto, Parral, 23 March 1893, AJ.

68. Jesús to Carlota in Averiguación criminal en contra de Jesús H., por rapto y estupro, Parral, 30 Oct. 1912, AJ; Liberato's letters are in Criminal contra Liberato M. por rapto y contra José J. por complicidad en dicho delito. 26 Sept. 1894. Huejotitan, AJ.

69. Felipe's letters in Criminal contra Felipe B. R. por rapto y estupro, Santa Bárbara, 19 Sept. 1905, AJ.

70. The other two faculties of the soul were memory and understanding; see the discussion of the catechism of Padre Ripalda, formally known as Catecismo y exposición breve de la doctrina Cristiana con un trato muy útil del orden en que el cristiano debe ocupar el tiempo y emplear el día, in Monsiváis, "La tradición de la memoria religiosa," 126. In addition to discussing some of the contents of the catechism, Monsiváis points to its emphasis on memorization over comprehension and to the centrality of images to informing understandings of spirituality.

71. This right to petition is also part of political discourse; see, for example, the letters written to Mexican presidents as gathered in Nava Nava, Los abajo firmantes. One of the letters, sent in 1921, is in the form of an acrostic to then-president Alvaro Obregón in which the soul (alma) figures prominently—see p. 49.

72. In his book on the ways in which the construction of death helped shape popular culture and the state in Mexico, Claudio Lomnitz cites a list of references for death compiled by Lope Blanch; among the many terms for death is "la novia fiel" (the faithful novia); see Lomnitz, Death and the Idea of Mexico, 26.

73. Criminal contra Marcos G. por el delito de rapto, San Antonio del Tule, 8 February 1908, AJ.

74. Jesús's letters to Maura are in Averiguación con motivo de querella presentada por Maximian M. por rapto y estupro en contra del Acusado Jesús P., Parral, 28 May 1909, AJ.

75. Description and letters are located in Averiguación con motivo de la muerte de Jesús José Z. y Josefa H., Parral, 16 February 1912, AJ.

76. One can only wonder at the horror this woman must have experienced being confronted not only with the death of her daughter but also with the murderer's explanation for it.

77. Here I offer a somewhat impressionistic conclusion based on reading a twenty-year run of the El Paso Morning Times. Although I was reading that newspaper for other reasons (to understand the activities of United States mining companies in Chihuahua), I could not help but be struck by what seemed to me as the constant front-page references to such events.

78. I've tried to heed David Gerber's warning to historians working with letters as I've used this material; he argues that personal letters need to be treated as every bit as complicated and in need of interpretation and analysis as any other source, as they are embedded in the complexities of the personal relations between people. This

point is developed in Gerber, *Authors of Their Lives*, 32–46. Gerber was chair of a session in which I presented an earlier version of some of these ideas, entitled "Love Letters and the Dynamics of Gender, Feeling and Agency," at the Social Science History Association Meeting in Chicago in November 2007, and he was kind enough to provide written comments making this, along with several other, points.

79. On a personal note, when renting a car in San Francisco recently, I expressed concern in casual conversation that I feared that I might leave my notebook behind in the car when returning it; this prompted a concerned response on the part of the employee who said every effort would be made to return it, especially since it was something so personal, representing something I had touched, in fact, an extension of myself because it had been written by my hand. Additionally, some eschew Facebook and other social media sites as somehow not having this capacity, partly because they are mediated through a keyboard and digitally rather than representing a direct touch.

POSTSCRIPT

1. See "Kutlug Ataman: Paradise and Küba," Vancouver Art Gallery website, consulted 24 May 2013, http://www.vanartgallery.bc.ca/the_exhibitions/exhibit_kutlug_ataman.html.
2. Jonathan Jones, "Full of eastern promise," *The Guardian*, 18 Jan. 2005, consulted 24 May 2013, http://arts.guardian.co.uk/features/story/0,11710,1392855,00.html.
3. Ataman quoted in Adrian Searle, "Talking Heads," *The Guardian*, 29 March 2005, consulted 24 May 2013, http://www.guardian.co.uk/culture/2005/mar/29/1; see the discussion of Kuba on the artist's own website at http://www.saatleriayarlamaenstitusu.com/site/artworks/work/10/ (consulted 24 May 2013); see also "Q&A Kutlug Ataman," *National Post*, 29 Feb. 2008, consulted 24 May 2013, http://neditpasmoncoeur.blogspot.ca/2008/04/interview-kutlug-ataman.html.
4. Gamboa's *Santa* was published in 1903 and subsequently adapted into film, first silent and then as Mexico's first sound feature film, or talkie; the quotation is from p. 46.
5. Vargas, "Epistolary Communication," 133.
6. Salomon and Niño-Murcia, *Lettered Mountain*, 9. This recently published book came to my attention after the middle section of my own book, "The Lettered Countryside," had been completed. Their own engagement with Rama, which they describe as from the perspective of "loyal opposition," is signaled by their title as well as their interest in the heretofore overlooked literacy of Andean peoples. The goal of their book, as they state it, is to "explore how one peasant village has made the alphabet its own and developed an internal graphic community" (p. 2).
7. Averiguación criminal en contra de Jesús H., por rapto y estupro, Parral, 30 October 1912. See also the case of José E., who, rather than face charges, had left Santa

Bárbara for the Sierra Mojada to join the Cuerpo de Voluntarios: Criminal contra José E., acusado del delito de estupro, Santa Bárbara, 9 March 1912, AJ.

8. Jesús D. y Enrique G., por los delitos de rapto y estupro, Hidalgo del Parral, 18 Feb. 1926, AJ.

9. Hirsch, *Courtship after Marriage*, especially chapter 3, "From Respeto (Respect) to Confianza ('Trust')," 81–111. Hirsch is careful to limit her conclusions concerning the timing of the shift to companionate marriage in the two small communities she studied, those of Degollado and El Fuerte; see 300n1.

10. Angel Rama, *The Lettered City*, 37.

BIBLIOGRAPHY

ARCHIVAL SOURCES

Archivo Judicial, Hidalgo del Parral, Chihuahua, México.

Archivo del Distrito, Hidalgo del Parral, Chihuahua, México.

Mexican Chapbook Collection, Center for Southwest Research, University Libraries, University of New Mexico, Albuquerque, New Mexico.

Fototeca Romualdo García, Museo Regional de Guanajuato, Guanajuato, México.

Gallardo, Luciano J. Diaries recollecting the courtship of Carlota Gil: Guadalajara, San Luis Potosí, etc. 1864, 1869. Bancroft Library: BANC, MSS M-B 13, box 1; microfilm version consulted.

PUBLISHED SOURCES

Ahearn, Laura M. *Invitations to Love: Literacy, Love Letters, and Social Change in Nepal.* Ann Arbor: University of Michigan Press, 2001.

Alonso, Ana M. "Love, Sex and Gossip in Legal Cases from Namiquipa, Chihuahua." In *Decoding Gender: Law and Practice in Contemporary Mexico,* edited by Helga Baitenmann, Victoria Chenaut, and Ann Varley. New Brunswick NJ: Rutgers University Press, 2007.

———. *Thread of Blood: Colonialism, Revolution, and Gender on Mexico's Northern Frontier.* Tucson: University of Arizona Press, 1995.

Altamirano, Ignacio Manuel. *El Zarco.* México: Editorial Occano de México, 1999.

Anderson, Benedict. *Imagined Communities,* revised edition. London: Verso, 2006.

Arrom, Silvia M. "Changes in Mexican Family Law in the Nineteenth Century: The Civil Codes of 1870 and 1884." *Journal of Family History* (Fall 1985).

———. *The Women of Mexico City, 1790–1857.* Stanford: Stanford University Press, 1985.

Barber, Karin, ed., *Africa's Hidden Histories: Everyday Literacy and Making the Self.* Bloomington: Indiana University Press, 2006.

Barthes, Roland. *A Lover's Discourse: Fragments.* Translated by Richard Howard. New York: Hill and Wang, 2010.

Barton, David, Mary Hamilton, and Roz Ivanic, eds., *Situated Literacies: Reading and Writing in Context*. New York: Routledge, 2000.

Behar, Ruth. "Sexual Witchcraft, Colonialism and Women's Powers." In *Sexuality and Marriage in Colonial Latin America*, edited by Asunción Lavrin. Lincoln: University of Nebraska Press, 1989.

Benítez Barba, Laura. "El rapto: Un repaso histórico-legal del robo femenino." *Estudios Sociales* 1 (July 2007): 103–32.

———. "Raptadas tapatías: Mujeres fuera del estereotipo (1885–1933)." In *Mujeres jalisciences del siglo XIX: cultura, religión y vida privada*, edited by Lourdes Celina Vázquez and Darío Armando Flores Soria. Guadalajara: Editorial Universitaria, Universidad de Guadalajara, 2008.

Besnier, Niko. *Literacy, Emotion and Authority: Reading and Writing on a Polynesian Atoll*. Cambridge: Cambridge University Press, 1995.

Blanco, José Joaquín. *Cuidado con el corazon: los usos amorosos en el México moderno*. México: Instituto Nacional de Antropología e Historia, 1995.

Breckenridge, Keith. "Love Letters and Amanuenses: Beginning the Cultural History of the Working Class Private Sphere in Southern Africa, 1900–1933." *Journal of Southern Africa Studies* 26, no. 2 (June 2000): 337–48.

———. "Reasons for Writing: African Working-Class Letter-Writing in Early Twentieth-Century South Africa." In *Africa's Hidden Histories: Everyday Literacy and Making the Self*, edited by Karin Barber. Bloomington: Indiana University Press, 2006.

Broomhall, Susan, and Jacqueline Van Gent, "Corresponding Affections: Emotional Exchange among Siblings in the Nassau Family." *Journal of Family History* 34, no. 2 (April 2009).

Bunker, Steven B. *Creating Mexican Consumer Culture in the Age of Porfirio Díaz*. Albuquerque: University of New Mexico Press, 2012.

Cartas amorosas y felicitaciones. México, DF: El Libro Español, n.d.

Castañeda García, Carmen. *Violación, estupro y sexualidad. Nueva Galicia, 1700–1821*. Guadalajara: Hexágono, 1989.

Castro-Klarén, Sara, and John Charles Chasteen, eds., *Beyond Imagined Communities: Reading and Writing the Nation in Nineteenth-Century Latin America*. Washington and Baltimore: Woodrow Wilson Center Press/Johns Hopkins University, 2003.

Caulfield, Sueann. *In Defense of Honor: Sexual Morality, Modernity, and Nation in Early-Twentieth-Century Brazil*. Durham: Duke University Press, 2000.

Chartier, Roger. "Introduction: An Ordinary Kind of Writing: Model Letters and Letter-Writing in Ancien Regime France." In *Correspondence: Models of Letter-Writing from the Middle Ages to the Nineteenth Century*, edited by Roger Chartier, Alain Boureau, and Cecile Dauphin. Translated by Christopher Woodall. Cambridge: Polity Press, 1997.

Clagett, Helen L., and David M. Valderrama. *A Revised Guide to the Law and Legal Literature of Mexico.* Washington: Library of Congress, 1973.

Código civil del distrito federal y territorio de la Baja California, 1884. In *Legislación Mexicana ó Colección completa de las disposiciones legislativas expedidas desde la independencia de la República,* Tomo XV, edited by Manuel Dublan and José María Lozano. México: 1886.

Código de procedimientos penales del estado libre y soberano de Chihuahua. Chihuahua: Edición Oficial, Imprenta del Gobierno a cargo de Gilberto A. de la Garza, 1906.

Código penal del estado libre y soberano de Chihuahua. Chihuahua: Edición Oficial, Imprenta del Gobierno á cargo de Gilberto A. de la Garza, 1905.

Código penal para el Distrito Federal y territorio de la Baja California sobre delitos del fuero común y para toda la República sobre delitos contra la federación. México: Tip. De Flores y Monsalve, 1874.

Código penal para el distrito y territorios federales de 13 de agosto de 1931. México: Información Aduanera de México, 1943.

Collins, James, and Richard K. Blot. *Literacy and Literacies: Texts, Power, and Identity.* Cambridge: Cambridge University Press, 2003.

Como enamorar a las mujeres, second edition. México, DF: El Libro Español, n.d.

Compendio del manual de urbanidad y buenas maneras de Manuel Antonio Carreño. México: Editora Clásica, 1963.

Dabove, Juan Pablo. *Nightmares of the Lettered City: Banditry and Literature in Latin America 1816–1929.* Pittsburgh: University of Pittsburgh Press, 2007.

———. "'Tomochic' de Heriberto Frías: Violencia campesina, melancolía y genealogía fratricida de las naciones." *Revista de Crítica Literaria Latinoamericana* 30, no. 60 (2004), 351–73.

Davis, Natalie Zemon. *Fiction in the Archives: Pardon Tales and Their Tellers in Sixteenth-Century France.* Stanford: Stanford University Press, 1987.

de la Peza Casares, María del Carmen, and Zeyda Rodríguez Morales, eds., *Culturas amorosas: Prácticas y discursos.* Guadalajara: Editorial Pandora, 2004.

Declaraciones amorosas. México: Gómez Gómez Hnos. Editores, n.d.

del Castillo Troncoso, Alberto. "El surgimiento de la prensa moderna en México." In *La República de las letras: Asomos a la cultura escrita del México decimonónico,* edited by Belem Clark de Lara and Elisa Speckman Guerra. Vol. 2, *Publicaciones periódicas y otros impresos.* México: Universidad Nacional Autónoma de México, 2005.

Dyer, Abigail. "Seduction by Promise of Marriage: Law, Sex and Culture in Seventeenth-Century Spain." *Sixteenth Century Journal* 34, no. 2 (2003).

El consejero de los enamorados: Cartas amorosas. México: Gómez Gómez Hnos. Editores, n.d.

Flores, Francisco A. *El hímen en México: Estudio hecho con unas observaciones en la cátedra de medicina legal en la Escuela de Medicina el año de 1882.* México: Oficina Tip. de la Secretaría de Fomento, 1885.

Foley, Susan. "'Your Letter is Divine, Irresistible, Infernally Seductive': Léon Gambetta, Léonie Léon, and Nineteenth-Century Epistolary Culture." *French Historical Studies* 30, no. 2 (Spring 2007).

French, William E. *A Peaceful and Working People: Manners, Morals, and Class Formation in Northern Mexico.* Albuquerque: University of New Mexico Press, 1996.

———. "'Cartas y cartas, compadre . . .': Love and Other Letters from Río Frío." In *Latin American Popular Culture since Independence: An Introduction,* 2nd edition, edited by William H. Beezley and Linda A. Curcio-Nagy. Lanham: Rowman and Littlefield, 2012.

———. "I'm Going to Write You a Letter": Coplas, Love Letters and Courtship Literacy." In *Mexico in Verse: A History of Music, Rhyme, and Power,* edited by Michael Matthews and Stephen Neufeld. Tucson: University of Arizona Press, 2015.

———. "Prostitutes and Guardian Angels: Women, Work and the Family in Porfirian Mexico." *Hispanic American Historical Review* 72, no. 4 (1992).

Frenk, Margit, comp., *Cancionero folklórico de México.* Tomo 2, *Coplas del amor desdichado y otras coplas de amor.* México: El Colegio de México, 1998, first published in 1975.

Frenk Alatorre, Margit, comp., *Cancionero folklórico de México.* Tomo 1, *Coplas del amor feliz.* México: El Colegio de México, 1975.

Frías, Heriberto. *The Battle of Tomochic,* translated by Barbara Jamison. Oxford University Press, 2006.

Gabara, Esther. *Errant Modernism: The Ethos of Photography in Mexico and Brazil.* Durham: Duke University Press, 2008.

Gamboa, Federico. *Santa: A Novel of Mexico City,* translated by John Charles Chasteen. Chapel Hill: University of North Carolina Press, 2010.

García, Romualdo, Elena Poniatowska, and Claudia Canales. *Romualdo García: Retratos.* México: Educación Gráfica, 1990.

García Peña, Ana Lidia. *El fracaso del amor: Género e individualismo en el siglo XIX mexicano.* México: El Colegio de México/Universidad Autónoma del Estado de México, 2006.

Gerber, David A. *Authors of Their Lives: The Personal Correspondence of British Immigrants to North America in the Nineteenth Century.* Ithaca: New York University Press, 2008.

Giddens, Anthony. *The Transformation of Intimacy: Sexuality, Love and Eroticism in Modern Societies.* Stanford: Stanford University Press, 1992.

Hirsch, Jennifer S. *A Courtship after Marriage: Sexuality and Love in Mexican Transnational Families.* Los Angeles: University of California Press, 2003.

———. "'Love Makes a Family': Globalization, Companionate Marriage, and the Modernization of Gender Inequality." In *Love and Globalization: Transformations of Intimacy in the Contemporary World,* edited by Mark B. Padilla, Jennifer S.

Hirsch, Miguel Muñoz-Laboy, Robert E. Sember, and Richard G. Parker. Nashville: Vanderbilt University Press, 2007.

Kalman, Judy. *Discovering Literacy: Access Routes to Written Culture for a Group of Women in Mexico*. Hamburg: UNESCO Institute for Education, 2005.

Lomnitz, Claudio. *Death and the Idea of Mexico*. New York: Zone Books, 2005.

———. "Nationalism as a Practical System: Benedict Anderson's Theory of Nationalism from the Vantage Point of Spanish America." In *Deep Mexico, Silent Mexico: An Anthropology of Nationalism*. Minneapolis: University of Minnesota Press, 2001.

Lopez de Garay, Cesar, "El delito de estupro: Análisis dogmático," thesis, Facultad Nacional de Jurisprudencia, Universidad Nacional Autónoma de México, n.d.

Lyons, Martyn. "Love Letters and Writing Practices: On Ecritures Intimes in the 19th Century." *Journal of Family History* 2, no. 24 (1999).

———. *The Writing Culture of Ordinary People in Europe, c. 1860–1920*. Cambridge: Cambridge University Press, 2013.

Martínez-Alier, Verena. "Elopement and Seduction in Nineteenth-Century Cuba." *Past and Present* 55 (May 1972).

Martínez de Castro, Antonio. *Exposición de motivos del Código Penal vigente en el Distrito Federal y territorio de la Baja California*. México: Imprenta de Francisco Díaz de León, 1876.

Martínez Roaro, Marcela. *Delitos sexuales incluye delitos contra la correcta formación del menor, la libertad sexual y la moral social en lo sexual*. México: Editorial Porrúa, 1975.

McCaa, Robert. "Marriageways in Mexico and Spain, 1500–1900." *Continuity and Change* 9, no. 1 (1994).

Monsiváis, Carlos. "Del saber compartido en la ciudad indiferente. De grupos y ateneos en el siglo XIX." In *La República de las letras: Asomos a la cultura escrita del México decimonónico*. Vol. 1, *Ambientes, asociaciones y grupos movimientos, temas y géneros literarios*, edited by Belem Clark de Lara and Elisa Speckman Guerra. México: Universidad Nacional Autónoma de México, 2005.

———. *El género epistolar: Un homenaje a manera de carta abierta*. México: Miguel Ángel Porrúa, 1991.

———. "La tradición de la memoria religiosa: El catecismo del Padre Ripalda." In *Imágenes de la tradición viva*, 2nd edition. México: Universidad Nacional Autónoma de México y Fondo de Cultura Económica, 2006.

Nava Nava, María del Carmen. *Los abajo firmantes: Cartas a los presidentes 1920–1928*. México: Secretaría de Educación Pública y Unidad de Publicaciones Educativas, 1994.

Ong, Walter J. *Orality and Literacy: The Technologizing of the Word*. London: Metheun, 1982.

Padilla, Mark B., and Jennifer S. Hirsch, Miguel Muñoz-Laboy, Robert E. Sember, and Richard G. Parker, eds., *Love and Globalization: Transformations of Intimacy in the Contemporary World*. Nashville: Vanderbilt University Press, 2007.

Payno, Manuel. *Los bandidos de Río Frío*, 2 vols. México: Promexa Editores, 1979.

———. *The Bandits from Río Frío: A Naturalistic and Humorous Novel of Customs, Crimes and Horrors*, Part 1, translated by Alan Fluckey. San Francisco: Heliographica, 2005. Part 2, Tucson: Wheatmark, 2007.

Pérez Duarte y N., Alicia Elena. "Esponsales." In *Diccionario Jurídico Mexicano*, Tomo IV, E-H. México: Editorial Porrúa, 1985.

Rama, Angel. *The Lettered City*, translated by John Charles Chasteen. Durham: Duke University Press, 1996.

Rappaport, Joanne, and Tom Cummins. *Beyond the Lettered City: Indigenous Literacies in the Andes*. Durham: Duke University Press, 2012.

Ruiz, Eduardo. *Bosquejo biográfico del ciudadano Melchor Ocampo*. Morelia: Imprenta del Gobierno en Palacio, 1875.

Salomon, Frank, and Mercedes Niño-Murcia. *The Lettered Mountain: A Peruvian Village's Way with Writing*. Durham: Duke University Press, 2011.

Schneider, Gary. *The Culture of Epistolarity: Vernacular Letters and Letter Writing in Early Modern England, 1500–1700*. Newark: University of Delaware Press, 2005.

Socolow, Susan M. "Acceptable Partners: Marriage Choice in Colonial Argentina, 1778–1810." In *Sexuality and Marriage in Colonial Latin America*, edited by Asunción Lavrin. Lincoln: University of Nebraska Press, 1989.

Sommer, Doris. *Foundational Fictions: The National Romances of Latin America*. Berkeley: University of California Press, 1991.

Speckman Guerra, Elisa. *Crimen y castigo: Legislación penal, interpretaciones de la criminalidad y administración de justicia, Ciudad de México, 1872–1910*. México: El Colegio de México/Universidad Nacional Autónoma de México, 2002.

———. *Temblando de felicidad me despido*, illustrated by Margarita Sada. México: Ediciones Castillo, 2006.

Staples, Anne. "*Los Bandidos de Río Frío* como fuente primaria para la historia de México." In *Literatura mexicana de otro fin de siglo*, edited by Rafael Oleo Franco. México: El Colegio de México, 2001.

Thomas, Lynn M. "Schoolgirl Pregnancies, Letter-Writing, and 'Modern' Persons in Late Colonial East Africa." In *Africa's Hidden Histories: Everyday Literacy and Making the Self*, edited by Karin Barber. Bloomington: Indiana University Press, 2006.

Thomas, Lynn M., and Jennifer Cole, "Introduction: Thinking Through Love in Africa." In *Love in Africa*, edited by Jennifer Cole and Lynn M. Thomas. Chicago: University of Chicago Press, 2009.

Tuck, Jim. "Melchor Ocampo (1814–1861)." Mexconnect website. Last updated 9 October 2008. Consulted 4 October 2014. http://www.mexconnect.com/articles/287-melchor-ocampo-1814%E2%80%931861.

Twinam, Ann. "Honor, Sexuality and Illegitimacy in Colonial Spanish America." In

Sexuality and Marriage in Colonial Latin America, edited by Asunción Lavrin. Lincoln: University of Nebraska Press, 1989.

Unzueta, Fernando. "Scenes of Reading: Imagining Nations/Romancing History in Spanish America." In *Beyond Imagined Communities: Reading and Writing the Nation in Nineteenth-Century Latin America*, edited by Sara Castro-Klarén and John Charles Chasteen. Washington and Baltimore: Woodrow Wilson Center Press/Johns Hopkins University, 2003.

Vargas, Miguel Angel. "Epistolary Communication between Migrant Workers and Their Families." In *Letters across Borders: The Epistolary Practices of International Migrants*, edited by Bruce S. Elliott, David A. Gerber, and Suzanne M. Sinke. New York: Palgrave Macmillan, 2006.

Vaughan, Mary Kay. "Modernizing Patriarchy: State Policies, Rural Households, and Women in Mexico, 1930–1940." In *Hidden Histories of Gender and the State in Latin America*, edited by Elizabeth Dore and Maxine Molyneux. Durham: Duke University Press, 2000.

Zorrillo, José. *Don Juan Tenorio*. Translated by N. K. Mayberry and A. S. Kline. Project Gutenberg. Last updated 14 January 2011. Consulted 4 October 2014. http://www.gutenberg.org/files/5201/5201-h/5201-h.htm.

INDEX

The Inevitable Bandstand: The State Band of Oaxaca and the Politics of Sound
Charles V. Heath

Gender and the Negotiation of Daily Life in Mexico, 1750–1856
Sonya Lipsett-Rivera

Mexico's Crucial Century, 1810–1910: An Introduction
Colin M. MacLachlan and William H. Beezley

The Civilizing Machine: A Cultural History of Mexican Railroads, 1876–1910
Michael Matthews

The Lawyer of the Church: Bishop Clemente de Jesús Munguía and the Clerical Response to the Liberal Revolution in Mexico
Pablo Mijangos y González

¡México, la patria! Propaganda and Production during World War II
Monica A. Rankin

Murder and Counterrevolution in Mexico: The Eyewitness Account of German Ambassador Paul von Hintze, 1912–1914
Edited and with an introduction by Friedrich E. Schuler

Pistoleros and Popular Movements: The Politics of State Formation in Postrevolutionary Oaxaca
Benjamin T. Smith

Alcohol and Nationhood in Nineteenth-Century Mexico
Deborah Toner

To order or obtain more information on these or other University of Nebraska Press titles, visit nebraskapress.unl.edu.

CPSIA information can be obtained at www.ICGtesting.com
Printed in the USA
LVOW10*0416120515

438108LV00001B/5/P